# THE CECILS

*Privilege and Power*

*Behind the Throne*

DAVID LOADES

# THE CECILS

*Privilege and Power Behind the Throne*

the national archives

First published in 2007 by The National Archives, Kew, Richmond Surrey, TW9 4DU, UK
www.nationalarchives.gov.uk
The National Archives brings together the Public Record Office, Historical Manuscripts
Commission, Office of Public Sector Information and Her Majesty's Stationery Office.

A catalogue card for this book is available from the British Library

ISBN 978 1 905615 20 9

Jacket, page design and typesetting by Ken Wilson | point 918
Printed in Great Britain by Biddles Ltd, King's Lynn

*Jacket image*: LEFT: 16th-century English portrait of William Cecil, Lord Burghley (1520–98),
image from Burghley House Collection / Bridgeman Art Library; RIGHT: Portrait of Robert Cecil
(1563–1612), Viscount Cranborne and 1st Earl of Salisbury, by John de Critz (*c.*1555–*c.*1641),
photo © Bonhams / Bridgeman Art Library; BACKGROUND: the barrel-vaulted ceiling of the
'Roman' staircase, Burghley House, Lincolnshire, image from Burghley House Collection /
Bridgeman Art Library.

# Contents

# Introduction

THE CECILS WERE, and are, one of the most remarkable families to have graced British history. Presently represented by the 7th Marquis of Salisbury and the 8th Marquis of Exeter, they rate no fewer than 16 entries in the *Oxford Dictionary of National Biography*, not counting Cecils who had no traceable connection to the main lines. Their present titles date from the 18th century, but in 1605 the half-brothers Thomas and Robert, the first and second sons of Lord Burghley, were ennobled as earls by James I. The family has produced statesmen, ambassadors, soldiers, and athletes of distinction, one Victorian prime minister and a 20th-century peace campaigner.

It is not my intention here to encompass their entire history, but rather to trace them from their origins as a minor gentry family in a Welsh-speaking corner of Herefordshire to high office in the Tudor state, and eventually to the upper reaches of the Jacobean aristocracy. The focus is particularly upon William, Queen Elizabeth I's secretary, who became Lord Burghley and lord treasurer in 1572, and upon his younger son, Robert, who became secretary in 1596, lord privy seal in 1601 and lord treasurer in his turn in 1608. The aim is partly biographical, but more importantly to place these men in their context as royal servants and to assess their contribution to the history of England between 1550 and 1612.

Up to a point each of them is transparent, both as an official and as a person. Both left copious records behind—correspondence, treatises and memoranda. We have a pretty good idea of how their estates were assembled, what they were worth and the scale of their debts. We can trace in some detail their relationships with their colleagues and their rivalries with the likes of the earls of Leicester and Essex. Each had a network of clients, some of whom were handed on from William to

Robert, and some of whom were more responsive and grateful than others. William Cecil had a kind of avuncular relationship with Elizabeth and disagreed with her frequently, and sometimes vehemently. Occasionally, especially in the earlier days of their working together, she drove him close to despair and sometimes abused his loyalty quite disgracefully. Nevertheless, as they both grew older and understood each other's minds better, they became a unique partnership. Robert inherited his father's power, but not this special relationship. Elizabeth appreciated him for what he was — a diligent and talented civil servant, but never a unique councillor as William had been. Nor did he enjoy a special personal relationship with James. In spite of the effusiveness of some of the latter's letters and the rewards that he showered on Robert, there is no sign of any affection between them. James, notoriously, preferred fine upstanding young men; but even at the end of Robert's life, when he was seriously out of favour, the king never considered replacing him before the course of nature so dictated. Each had enemies, both within the court and outside it, and from about 1590 onwards the Cecil ascendancy was much resented, especially by those who considered themselves to have been disenfranchised by it. Robert, in particular, suffered a great deal of abuse, both literary and popular. The pejorative term *regnum Cecilianum* was coined to suggest this monopolization of power. Only in recent years have historians disclosed the extent of that misrepresentation.

Of William and Robert's 'private lives' there is much less to go on, compared to the wealth of evidence as to their public lives. Perhaps this in itself suggests the submerging of the former by the latter, as both men were tireless workhorses. Although he liked to play the stoic over his health (his gout was frequently troublesome), William was not particularly reticent about his feelings. He loved his wife, the not very loveable Mildred, deeply, and was greatly saddened by her death. He loved both his sons to the extent of fidgeting endlessly about their behaviour and prospects, although his harsh treatment of Thomas does not demonstrate much affection to modern eyes. However, the desire to correct was seen as a form of parental love at the time, and of that there was plenty. His daughters, Anne and Elizabeth, both taxed his love in different ways, and what we know about them derives rather from what they (and William) did, rather than from what was said. Robert was the apple of his father's eye, but of his own emotional responses there is much less trace. His love for his wife, Elizabeth, can only be assumed, not demonstrated. He never remarried, but whether that was because of cherished memories, we do not know. He loved his daughter Frances sufficiently to spend a lot of money on what we would now call physiotherapy—but in what spirit this was done, again we do not know. His relationship with his son can best be described as 'chilly', and the general impression that we get is of a man who found emotional expression difficult, if not distasteful. He seems to have been the kind of man more familiar in the 21st century than in the 17th, who lived his life for his office, its functions and rewards.

Some new research has gone into this book, but it is also based on the writings of earlier historians who, over the last century, have addressed these themes. Sometimes I agree with them, sometimes I do not, but it is now almost half a century since Conyers Read, B.W. Beckinsale and P.M. Handover published their findings and the time has come for a fresh look. So *The Cecils* looks closely at William and Robert, the personalities of father and son and the way in which they exercised their responsibilities. In particular, it explores their complex relationships with two remarkable and very different rulers, and the ways in which they helped to change the concept of noble service forever.

# CHAPTER I

# From David Sitsylt
# to William Cecil

IN ORDER TO understand the Cecils' origins, we need to explore those of the Tudors themselves. The Tudor dynasty, and the Cecil lineage, was Welsh—up to a point. Henry VII's paternal grandfather, Owain of Penmynydd, had been entirely Welsh, his correct name being Owain ap Meredudd ap Tudor. He could trace his ancestry back to Lord Rhys, the last independent ruler of the Welsh kingdom of Deheubarth, who had died in 1197.[1] However, Owain's wife and the mother of his son had been Catherine de Valois of the royal house of France, and his son Edmund had married Margaret Beaufort, whose ancestors had been a mixture of English and French. In spite of his name, therefore, even on the most optimistic count Henry was no more than 25 per cent Welsh, and it is unlikely that he spoke a word of that highly distinctive language.

Henry was born in Pembroke Castle on 28 January 1457. His father Edmund had died on campaign at Carmarthen the previous November, and responsibility for caring for the child and his mother devolved on Edmund's brother Jasper, Earl of Pembroke, at that time the royal lieutenant in Wales.[2] The young Earl of Richmond, Henry's title from his birth, was thus initially brought up in the principality, and the servants by whom he was surrounded during the earliest years of his life would certainly have been Welsh speaking. However, the Herbert household to which he was transferred in 1462 was English speaking, and in the course of his education Henry would have learned both Latin and French; so it is likely that the servants' language of his infancy faded rapidly from his memory.

When, on the other hand, his chance came in 1485 to topple Richard III and claim the English throne, it soon transpired that Henry had not forgotten the land of his upbringing—nor had it forgotten him. The bards of Wales, ever addicted to forlorn hopes, had several years earlier identified him as the *mab darogan*, or son of prophecy, that messiah-like figure who would one day restore sovereignty of the Britons over what had long ago become England.[3] The original prophecy was ascribed to Merlin and had lurked in the bardic consciousness for generations before it surfaced in this guise. Consequently it was not chance, or the random nature of the winds, that caused him to land in Milford Haven on 7 August. John Morgan of Tredegar had sent him word that he could count upon the support of Sir John Savage and, more importantly, of Rhys ap Thomas. Rhys was a powerful man in South Wales, particularly in Pembrokeshire. Rhys proved to be as good as his word, and joined Henry at Welshpool on 14 August, with a substantial force.[4] In his company was David Philips, a servant of Lady Margaret Beaufort, mother of Henry Tudor. Philips had a following in Herefordshire and the southern Welsh marches, because he had also been steward of two lordships belonging to the earldom of March, which rallied to him in support of Rhys on this occasion. And among those followers was his relative by marriage, one David Sitsylt of Alltyrynys.

David Sitsylt was the third son of Philip (also known as Richard) Sitsylt, a well-established minor gentleman in the southwestern corner of Herefordshire. Alltyrynys was in the parish of Walterstone, close to Ewas Lacey, and the area was at that time Welsh speaking, so although there is no conclusive evidence it may be presumed that David was bilingual. It appears that he fought at the Battle of Bosworth, which handed the crown to Henry, because he was rewarded with a position among the new king's yeomen of the guard, an elite group of soldiers formed for Henry's personal protection. David, who seems to have anglicized his surname to 'Cecil' in the 1490s, was by no means the only Welsh gentleman to have followed Henry's fortunes or to have taken swift advantage of his success. The king encouraged minor servants such as David to reward themselves by their own efforts in whatever circumstances they found themselves, with the assistance of a little judicious patronage.

David Cecil's public career—insofar as he had one—began at Stamford in Lincolnshire in 1494, when he was granted the freedom of the borough. He was about 35 years old, and his father had been variously styled gentleman or yeoman. As a follower of David Philips, he was later close enough to his patron to be an executor of his will. He was literate in English, which suggests some schooling, but there was no established school within easy reach of Alltyrynys, so he was probably tutored by the parish priest. His father Philip was not prosperous enough to have paid a full-time tutor for his sons. As a yeoman of the crown, David would have been expected to undertake regular turns of duty at court and to have been available when called upon for ceremonial occasions, or crises. For that reason he may well have fought for the king at the Battle of Stoke, against the rebellious Yorkists, in 1487, although there is no record of it.

How David ended up in Stamford is a matter for conjecture, but the connection with David Philips is suggestive. Philips's service to Lady Margaret included the role of constable of her castle of Maxey and she was alleged to keep a house in Stamford to accommodate some of her numerous wards—a sort of overspill. Philips was probably a member of her council and also the steward of several of her manors, including Collyweston in Northamptonshire, one of her favourite residences.[5] Margaret had not only been restored by her son, but also extremely well endowed, particularly in Northamptonshire, Lincoln and Rutland. The merchants of Spalding regularly supplied her household, and she was powerful in Stamford, which was a prosperous and welcoming town in the late 15th century. So it is entirely likely that David Cecil owed his establishment in Stamford to his patron's influence and his known connections with the court. In spite of wide-ranging commitments, including vice-chamberlain to Arthur, Prince of Wales,[6] serving on numerous commissions and acting as captain of Jersey 'for services beyond the seas and within the realm'[7] (an indication of Henry VII's esteem), towards the end of his life David Philips seems to have lived in Stamford. He died there in 1506, being buried in St Mary's Church. At the time of his death he was sheriff of Northampton, Bedford and Buckingham, positions for which David Cecil as his executor sought pardon and release on 10 November.[8]

How, or just when, David Cecil acquired his first property in the town is not known, but he seems to have been accepted as a gentleman from the start and is not known to have practised any of the trades or crafts that were then flourishing. He did not receive any grant, so it must be presumed that his service both to the king and to Philips was sufficiently well rewarded in other ways to enable him to buy his way into that fairly modest urban elite. His freedom seems to have come as a consequence of marriage, because in 1494 he was newly wedded to Alice, the daughter of John Dycons, a prominent townsman who had already been alderman (mayor) three times, and seems to have been a kinsman of David Philip's wife.[9] Dycons was a prosperous merchant who clearly considered a yeoman of the crown, and a client of Philips, to be a good match for his daughter. David and Alice's eldest son, Richard, was born at some time in 1495.

David Cecil's undoubted wealth is something of a mystery. He was one of 'the twelve'—the inner ring of the Stamford oligarchy—from at least 1495, was elected alderman three times (in 1504, 1515 and 1526) and represented the borough five times in parliament, between 1504 and 1523.[10] Yet he seems to have secured only modest promotion at court, being a yeoman of the chamber from 1506 until his death and sergeant at arms from 1513. After 1500 the situation becomes a little clearer. In 1503, and again in 1505, he was a commissioner for sewers, which was a clear recognition of his status as gentleman, and in 1506 was granted (jointly with Sir David Philips) the position of keeper of Kings Cliffe Park in nearby Rockingham Forest, a favour that he probably owed to the king's mother. When Philips died later that year, Cecil became sole keeper. When his father-in-law also died, he acquired the Tabard Inn in Stamford in trust. It is highly unlikely that he ever managed the place, or had much to do with it, but his involvement provided the grounds, many years later, for William Cecil's enemies to accuse him of being the grandson of an inn keeper.[11] In 1506 also, described as 'the king's servant', he was created bailiff and swankeeper of Whittlesea Mere in Cambridgeshire, with a fee of £8 a year, and in the same year was licensed to found a chantry in St Mary's Church, Stamford, to pray for the king, the late queen, his parents, himself and his wife Alice.[12] However, as late as 1523 he was assessed at only a modest £6 13s 4d for the 'subsidy', that relatively recent form of direct taxation assessed by county.

In 1509, David became bailiff of Preston, Uppingham and Essendine in neighbouring Rutland, a position that presumably qualified him to serve on the commission of the peace to maintain law and order in that county. In spite of the fact that he cannot have been spending much time at court, when he became a sergeant at arms in 1513 he received the enhanced fee of 12d a day. This was about the same wage as a master carpenter, and would not have been very significant as income, but it was a further enhancement of his status, or 'honour', and meant increased opportunities for access to the king. More significantly, he was by this time receiving leases of crown properties in Lincoln, Northampton and Rutland and, by shrewd management, was building himself a substantial estate. David Cecil succeeded his erstwhile patron as steward of Collyweston in 1523, by which time Margaret Beaufort was long dead and the manor was in the hands of the crown, and had received the same office in respect of Nastington, Upton and Yarwell, also in Northamptonshire, by 1534. He served as 'escheator' for Northamptonshire and Rutland from 1514 to 1515 and for Lincolnshire from 1529 to 1530, collecting crown revenues for land that had reverted to the king.[13] In 1526, he was given the honour of entertaining the young Duke of Richmond when the latter visited Kings Cliffe on his way to Middleham to take up his (notional) duties as the king's lieutenant in the north, and was sheriff of Northamptonshire in 1532–3.

Alice bore him a second son, David (named for Philips, who stood as godfather), but at some unknown date, probably about 1520, she died. The elder David then remarried, his second wife being Jane Roos, the daughter of Thomas Roos of Dawsby, Lincolnshire, and widow of Edward Villers of Flore, Northamptonshire. Not very much is known about her, but she was reputedly an heiress and was probably considerably younger than her husband, who must have been approaching 60. She bore him one child, a daughter named Joan, but it is not known whether they had other children. She appears to have outlived him, but not by many years.

David lived until 1540 and died a wealthy man. In his will, which is dated 25 January 1535, he described himself as esquire, and requested burial in St George's Church in Stamford. In addition to providing for his wife and children, he requested that an additional £5 be paid to the incumbent of St George's to pray for his soul. His executor was his eldest son, Richard, and the will was proved on 16 March 1541.[14]

The career of his eldest son is sufficient testament to the fact that David had successfully raised himself not merely from the yeomanry into the gentry, but into the ranks of the major gentry. That he served in parliament merely indicated the value of his court connections and the fact that someone must have taken over as his patron after the death of Philips and Margaret Beaufort, but that he was also a member of the commission of the peace and sheriff shows that he had standing in his own community. That community extended well beyond the boundaries of Stamford.

Richard seems to have started his career through his father's enterprise and initiative. Little is known about his upbringing, which presumably took place in Stamford. There was a school in the town, which was later famous, but nothing is known about its condition at this time and it is unlikely that Richard attended it. He was probably taught at home by a tutor, or by a local priest offering similar services, and was literate, at least in English. He later seems to have inclined to the new religious views, although how much that owed to his schoolmaster and how much to subsequent experience is not known. He was also sufficiently presentable to be introduced at court, where he was a page of the chamber by 1517. As he was 22 years old by that time, which was a mature age for a page, he may well have been appointed several years earlier. In 1520 he accompanied the court at the Anglo-French diplomacy and festivities of the 'Field of the Cloth of Gold', probably as a yeoman of the chamber, although that is not clear.

Like his father's career, Richard's court advancement developed only slowly and did not ascend to any great height. He was a groom of the robes by 1528 and yeoman by 1539, in which position he continued to serve until Henry's death. A household and chamber list of 1540 shows his name last among 32 'gentlemen of the privy chamber', but he is never otherwise referred to as holding such a position. These gentlemen were appointed personally by the monarch, had guaranteed access to his person and were used on confidential missions. They were also expected to be in regular attendance and were frequent mediators to the king for petitioners, who often paid handsomely for their intercession. They numbered between 20 and 30 and were recognized as the elite of the court—although they could also be very exposed if the king's anger was aroused. How much Richard actually appeared at court we do not know[15]—although, as yeoman of the robes, he would have been expected to attend regularly, if not frequently. He was in charge of that department by 1543, and accounting for expenditure there. In 1543, he even distributed the traditional royal Maundy money.

Richard's position, however, depended upon the court, and if he had any other patron then it has escaped the record. He was certainly not much of a burgess. He was never a member of the 'twelve', let alone an alderman, and he sat only once for the borough in parliament. That was in 1539, and is thought to have been due to the favour of Henry VIII's secretary, Thomas Cromwell, rather than to any local influence. Even that favour is a little speculative. Nevertheless, Richard was a man of substance in his country, which continued to be the area around Stamford. He was joined with his father in the keepership of Kings Cliffe Park as early as 1517, became bailiff of Bourne (beside Stamford) in 1525, and porter of Warwick Castle in 1528. More significantly, he purchased the manor of Little Burghley from Sir William Compton in 1527.[16] Whether he knew Compton through the court, and cut a favourable deal by that means, we do not know, but the acquisition was to be an important one for him. By 1528 Burghley had become his principal residence and remained so thereafter.

In 1532 Richard was promoted to the keepership of Warwick Castle, and so to a position of considerable trust. The earldom of Warwick had been in abeyance since the execution of Edward Plantagenet in 1499 for involvement with the pretender Warbeck, and the castle was an important royal stronghold. It is a little early for any connection with Cromwell to have been influential in the appointment, so Richard must have been known as a 'safe pair of hands' by those who were most about the king at that point. How well Henry himself knew this relatively obscure yeoman of his chamber is uncertain, although there are some positive suggestions in the surviving documents. Richard succeeded his father as keeper of Whittlesea Mere in 1536, became a justice of the peace for Northamptonshire in 1539 and was actually sheriff of Rutland at the time of his father's death.[17] Except within the borough of Stamford, he was very much David's heir.

Richard had married in about 1519, his bride being Jane (plate 1), the daughter of William Heckington of Bourne. Their son William was born in 1520 (or possibly 1521—William himself was unsure). Jane was probably somewhat younger than her husband, and was to outlive him by more than 30 years, dying at a very advanced age in 1584. William appears to have been born at his mother's family home, but we do not know whether that was their normal residence, or whether she was there as a matter of convenience for her confinement. She later presented her husband with three daughters, Elizabeth, Margaret and Ann, all of whom turned out to be as durable and as fruitful as herself. In later life, William was extremely fond of his mother, and she was apparently both amiable and strong minded, but little is known about her. She seems never to have accompanied Richard when he was on duty at the court, and presumably occupied herself with those housewifely and charitable duties that became a substantial gentle-woman at that time. The few letters that survive from her among William's papers confirm that impression. Her long widowhood was focused mainly upon the career of her son.[18]

Apart from occasional service as a muster commissioner, raising troops, there is no trace of military activity in Richard's career. His appearance as a member of the chamber in Henry VIII's siege of Boulogne in 1544 is unlikely to have involved fighting, although he was expected to provide six archers and six billmen (a bill being a type of battle axe), quite a large contingent. He was also approaching the age of 50 by that time, so he is likely to have served in a supporting role.

David Cecil, no doubt judging his son to be a man of independent means, had left the bulk of his property to his widow in the first instance, and it is not certain how long Richard had to wait for his step-mother's death in order to inherit. It is possible that her passing was marked by a transaction in 1547, when Richard bought the manor of Tinwell in Rutland for £1160 10s 3d. Such a large expenditure argues an acquisition of funds from somewhere, and that is the most likely source. Like many of his contemporaries, Richard profited significantly from the dissolution of the monasteries. In 1544 he purchased (no doubt at a concessionary price) the premises and most of the land of the nun-nery, priory and friary that had stood in Stamford. These properties he may have disposed of to the citizens fairly quickly, because he is not known to have increased his involvement in the town's affairs, and if he had retained these houses he would have raised his stake considerably. In the same year he also purchased the manor of Essendine in Rutland, of which his father had been steward, for £373 9s 4d. In 1548 he served as a chantry commissioner in Northamptonshire, Rutland, Oxfordshire and Oxford City—the fact that this was outside his usual territory per-haps indicating that he was regarded as a supporter of the 'king's pro-ceedings', as the dissolution of the monasteries and rejection of papal authority were termed.[19] Richard was also a commissioner for the poor relief in Lincolnshire, Northamptonshire and Rutland in 1550, and for church goods in Lincolnshire and Northamptonshire in 1553—the year of his death. If, as his son's development would seem to suggest, Richard was sympathetic to Protestantism, then his departure from the world may, as Mary became queen, have been timely.

At some unknown date, but probably while he was a member of the House of Commons, Richard found it convenient to establish a base in the capital, and purchased a house in Cannon Row, Westminster. It was there that he died, having apparently made no will, and was buried in St Margaret's Church, beside the old palace. His wealth at the time of his death is thus as indeterminate as it was during his life, although according to one account William inherited lands to the value of £200 a year. In spite of the status that his son later acquired and the early attentions of adulatory biographers, we know remarkably little about Richard Cecil. There is not even a portrait of him.

Something can be deduced, however, from the manner in which Richard brought up his son. William Cecil was born, as we have seen, in 1520 or 1521, on 18 September, and was baptized in the parish church at Bourne. This lay in the fen country about ten miles from Stamford, and it was there that he passed the first six or seven years of his life 'among the women', as the custom of the time was. When he was about seven, as we have seen, the family moved to Little Burghley, or Stamford Baron as it was also known, which was adjacent to the town on the other side of the Welland. There is a tradition that he attended school in both Stamford and Grantham, but that is based upon the assumption that he went to Grantham before the family moved, which seems unlikely. He would have been too young either to have boarded or to have made the 15-mile journey across the marshy countryside. Jane is also supposed to have been protective of her first born, so it seems reasonable to deduce that his first and only schooling was in Stamford, and that Richard's decision to move his base to Stamford Baron may have been connected with that fact.[20] It is very likely that William learned his first letters at home, either from the parish priest or from a tutor appointed for that purpose. He never later acknowledged any such start, so it is likely to have been fairly basic teaching. Stamford was a chantry-based grammar school, where the rudiments of reading and writing were taken for granted, and the curriculum was based upon the acquisition of Latin. The syllabus may well have been similar to that which Wolsey laid down in 1528 for his foundation in Ipswich. The basis would have been provided by something like John Stanbridge's revision of the *Lac Puerorum,* which was published in 1520, and the pupils would then have proceeded by way of Aesop and Terence to Vergil, Cicero and Sallust, before finishing with Horace's *Epistles* at the age of about 14 or 15.[21] It is also likely that a little Greek was also taught because, although Greek was a rare accomplishment, Stamford had in Libeus Bayard an exceptionally gifted teacher at that time. William benefited greatly from his school-ing and always remained grateful for it. He seems to have been a book-ish boy, not much given to the rough-and-tumble games of his schoolfellows, any more than he was to be a sportsman in later life. If he had not been the eldest son and the times were not 'a-changing', he might well have been destined for a career in the church. As it was, his father was sufficiently enlightened to see in what direction his talents lay, and in 1535 entered him at St John's College, Cambridge, with an eye on not the priesthood but on a career in the royal service.

William's biographer, Conyers Read, commented that the choice of St John's was eccentric, given that its co-founder and great benefactor, Bishop John Fisher, was in the Tower at the time on charges of treason, publicly opposing Henry VIII's divorce from Catherine of Aragon.[22] The college had shown solidarity with its patron and must have been under a cloud of royal displeasure. However, there is no clear evidence of that, and there were countervailing factors. The other founder of St John's had been Lady Margaret Beaufort, with whom the Cecils had, of course, been connected through David Philips, and links of that kind would have been remembered on both sides. It was also very much a foundation of the so-called New Learning—not heresy, but evangelically inclined humanism—and Richard would have been close enough to events to have realized that such learning was in the ascen-dancy at court, whatever Bishop Fisher's troubles.

At the time William entered the college, it was made up of 28 fel-lows, 22 scholars and an indeterminate number of 'commoners'. The fellows and scholars were financially supported by the foundation, but the commoners were expected to pay their own way, and it is very likely that William was one of the latter.[23] As the son of a substantial gentleman he would have been better off than most, but the evidence of his status is unclear.

In 1535 the Master of St John's was Nicholas Metcalf, an indifferent scholar himself but very good at attracting talent, including the reformer Roger Ascham. Later to become tutor to Prince (later King) Edward and to Princess (later Queen) Elizabeth, Ascham was a fellow of the college from 1534 to 1540. Five years older than Cecil, Ascham had entered St John's in 1530 and was in residence during almost the whole stay of the younger man, whom he must have known well. This friendship was later to be of great benefit to both of them.

The regime at St John's was severe in every sense of the word. The undergraduates, who varied in age from 14 to 20, were treated like schoolboys and were subjected to public beatings if their delinquencies seemed to merit it. They lived in college, taking all their meals in common, and were not allowed outside the bounds unaccompanied. In theory, they were protected from the contaminating world, and particularly from the distracting company of females; in practice, this was not altogether so, as we shall see, and news of what was going on outside did actually reach them—usually through clandestine channels. Rumours abounded, and tutors were occasionally constrained to give authentic information in order to correct them.

The working day was also highly disciplined. The first session started at six or seven o'clock (depending on the season) and lasted until eleven, when the main meal of the day was taken. A second session commenced at one and lasted until three or four, after which the students proceeded to supper. Bedtime varied with the time of year, but would never have been later than nine.[24] Chapel attendance was frequent and compulsory. Of organized or authorized recreation there was no sign, although presumably boys of that age would have found ways to amuse themselves during the few hours when that was permitted. There is some evidence that Greek plays were performed in the college hall while William was in residence, although whether these were supposed to count as work or play is not recorded.[25] A high level of proficiency in Latin was taken for granted, and that was the normal medium of instruction. It would also have been the language of daily discourse if the authorities had had their way—but instructions to that effect were almost certainly disregarded. The teaching syllabus started with Greek grammar, rhetoric and mathematics in the first year, and proceeded via dialectics, logic and philosophy until the whole 'trivium' (grammar, rhetoric and logic) and 'quadrivium' (arithmetic, geometry, astronomy and music) were completed in about four years. At that point it would have been normal for the student to have graduated as a

Bachelor of Arts before proceeding (if he stayed in residence) to a Master of Arts, or to a course in one of the higher disciplines, such as theology or medicine. There is no evidence that the young Cecil did any of these things, although he remained in residence for a total of six years.

To the modern eye, the value of such studies seems strictly limited. Everything was based upon classical literature, either in Latin or Greek, and lectures were often no more than the recitation of set texts. No modern subject intruded (unless one counts mathematics as such)—no modern languages, no history after the fall of the Roman Empire and no topography. Such subjects were studied, but not at the universities, and of disciplines such as science, geography or economics there was no sign. It is not surprising that in later life William Cecil spoke no Spanish or Italian, and that his French was seriously deficient; diplomacy could usually be conducted in Latin. As a training of the mind, however, the classical syllabus had much to commend it. The *exempla* may have been ancient, but moral discipline was taken very seriously and both logic and rhetoric were highly relevant to a career in public life.

As we have seen, William was scholarly inclined, and it is not surprising that he found Cambridge congenial. He also rubbed shoulders with many kindred spirits who were later to feature prominently in public affairs—John Redman, George Day, John Christopherson, Robert Horn, James Pilkington, Thomas Watson and John Cheke, as well as Ascham. Day, Christopherson and Watson were later to emerge as strong Catholics, Horn, Pilkington and Ascham as Protestants, but while at St John's they kept their disagreements within the civilized limits of academic discourse. William Cecil seems to have had an equally warm regard for them all.[26]

The man he was closest to, however, was John Cheke, who was for a time his tutor. Cheke was acknowledged to be the finest Greek scholar of his generation, and was subsequently Regius Professor. His father, Peter, was the university beadle and his mother kept a pub in the town, so John, who eventually became a knight and secretary of state, was a fine example of the career built on talent. Such was the main function of the universities at that time. For generations the sons of poor but (reputedly) honest men had climbed the social ladder by way of degrees and ordination. Now neither a degree nor ordination was necessary; rather, by exposing themselves to the teaching and networking of the universities the sons of the relatively humble could launch themselves into profitable careers.

In one respect, however, William's close connection with Cheke proved unfortunate, certainly in his father's eyes. John had a sister, Mary—not as bright as her brother, but definitely attractive. Cecil developed the habit of escaping from the rigours of college life, and resorting to Mrs Cheke's inn. His courtship of Mary was impulsive— perhaps the only time in his life when he was to act on impulse—and probably ill considered, but it was honest in every sense. His father was, allegedly, seriously displeased by this development and may only have agreed to continue his financial support on the condition that he left Cambridge.[27] This is not certain, because other considerations could have prompted the move. William was 21 years of age and was not seriously intending an academic career, so there would have been good reason for moving to London, even without the complication of Mary Cheke. Apparently his friends advised him in the same sense. In May 1541 William left Cambridge and enrolled at Gray's Inn to study law. In August of the same year (perhaps realizing that he had gone too far to retreat) he married Mary. Shortly afterwards Mary became pregnant, and gave birth to their son Thomas in December 1542. Thomas was born in Cambridge, probably at the family home, and it is not even certain that Mary ever joined her husband in London. In 1543 Mary died, perhaps the victim of a second pregnancy, although that is not known.[28] William certainly loved her, and, uncharacteristic of his cautious personality though the shotgun wedding was, it may be assumed that he was much moved by her death.

## WILLIAM CECIL AT GRAY'S INN, EARLY 1540s

B*UT AS HIS YEARS and company required, he would many times be merry among young gentlemen, who were most desirous of his company for his witty mirth and merry temper. Among the rest, I heard him tell this merriment of himself. That a mad companion of his, while he was thus at Gray's Inn, enticed him to play. Whereupon in a short time he lost all his money, bedding & books to his companion; having never used play before. And being afterwards among his other company, he told them how such a one had misled him; saying he would presently have a device to be even with him. And he was as good as his word. For* *with a long trunk he made a hole in the wall, near his play fellow's bed head & in a fearful voice spake thus, through the trunk.*

O mortal man repent! Repent of thy horrible time consumed in play, cozenage & such lewdness as thou hast committed, or else thou art damned and cannot be saved!

*Which being spoken at midnight, when he was all alone, so amazed him as drove him into a sweat for fear. Most penitent and heavy, the next day, in presence of the youths, he told with trembling, what a fearful voice spake to him at midnight, vowing never to play again. And calling for Mr. Cecil, asked him forgiveness on his knees, & restored all his money, bedding & books. So two gamesters were both reclaimed with this merry device, and never played more. Many other, the like merry jests, I have heard him tell, too long to be here noted.*

[Francis Peck, *Desiderata Curiosa*, 1779 edition, p. 5]

William had no more intention of being a professional lawyer than he had of becoming an academic, and the two or three years that he spent at Gray's Inn would not have so qualified him. He went, partly because some knowledge of the law was necessary to a young gentleman who was likely to have an estate to manage, and partly because he had every prospect of serving on the commission of the peace. How seriously he applied himself to his new studies we do not know, but it is unlikely that his engrained habits of hard work would have been completely abandoned. He was also a married man with no taste for robust sports. The early biographer Francis Peck (1732) recalled that, 'as his years and company required, he would many time be merry among young gentlemen', and it may well be that he took advantage of the fact that he was living unsupervised in London after the strictness of the regime at St John's. The same writer recalls as a 'merry jest' how he got fleeced at cards 'having never used play before', and how he spooked his gaming companion into returning his money and property with a terrified plea of penitence.[29] However, the writer's objective was clearly to portray the rather oppressively sober Lord Burghley of later years as a gay young dog, and the story should only tell us that his relative innocence was occasionally taken advantage of.

There is little reliable information about William's life in the latter part of Henry VIII's reign. It is possible that he sat for Stamford in the parliament that convened in 1542. His own notes confirm that he sat, but not for which constituency.[30] As we have seen, Richard had represented the borough in 1539, so the advancement of his son would have been logical. Whether or not he occupied his father's house in Cannon Row we do not know, but the indications are that he remained financially dependent on his father until about 1548.

This was important because in December 1545 William married again, his second wife being Mildred (plate 10), eldest daughter of Sir Anthony Cooke. She was in every way a more suitable match for William than Mary had been. She was not beautiful, but she was strong minded, intelligent and formidably learned. Their life together was in many ways to be long and happy, but of the five children she bore him, only one son and one daughter survived infancy. Mildred seems to have laid Mary's ghost to rest in other ways, because by the end of 1545 William's relations with his father were altogether restored. Richard is alleged to have made a will virtually disinheriting his son after his first marriage, but the dates of the story are confused and, as we have seen, and as far as anyone knows, he died intestate.[31] Perhaps he simply destroyed the will when William recovered his favour and never got around to making another. Whatever the true story, Mildred was always *persona grata*.

## THE MYSTERY OF RICHARD CECIL'S WILL, 1553

SHE [JANE CECIL] *stated that Cecil's father made a will touching his goods when he went to Boulogne, which not being forthcoming she said might be with Mr Digby. [Roger] Alford, thinking that this might have been about the time he conceived displeasure against Cecil for his first marriage, rode over to Mr Digby himself, especially as he had been required by Cecil's mother to arrange a lease of Tinwell. On broaching the matter of the will, Mr Digby at first denied that he had any, but after explaining that Cecil and his mother were now well accorded that nothing should remain contrary to the testator's meaning, said he thought he had one, but whether it was touching his good or land he could not say. Being further questioned said that about Michaelmas last Cecil's father showed him about 15 or 16 lines written on a great skin*

*of parchment with his own hand, which he told him was his will of his*
*goods, but was not made privy thereto, for he said that no man should*
*know his mind before his death …*

BURLEIGH, *9 April 1553.*

[From a letter of Roger Alford to Sir William Cecil. The inquisition post
mortem is dated 13 April 7 Edward VI. It states that Richard Cecil died on 19
March last past, and that Sir William Cecil is his son and heir, aged 30 years and
more. Delivered to the court 25 April 1553 by the hands of Roger Alford, gent.]

At some point before he became established in life—perhaps in connection with his marriage or while he was in disfavour with his
father—William appears to have written to a Mrs Pen, begging for the
loan of £50. This was a considerable sum, and the recipient was probably intended to be Sybil Penne, who had been Prince Edward's nurse.
The remarkable thing is that the draft of this letter survives in the
Burghley archive. It may never have been sent, or he may have kept it
as some sort of a souvenir of his misspent youth. If the money had
really been intended to equip him for his wedding, it may have been a
memento of a more romantic kind. Perhaps the loan was made and
never repaid.[32]

Whatever the circumstances, the idea of writing such a letter suggests that William knew his way around the court, and that knowledge
he must have owed to his father, either before or after the latter's fit of
indignation. William was apparently in the habit of visiting his father
when the latter was in attendance, and he may well have begun to do
that while he was still at Cambridge. Only one story survives of such a
visit, attributed simply to 'the latter days of Henry VIII'. It tells that
William met two Irish priests in the presence chamber and fell in talk
with them, disputing eventually in Latin. The priests were utterly
routed by this 'beardless youth', and the bystanders found this so amus-
ing that they told the king. Henry immediately sent for William and,
'after long talk', was so pleased with his answers that he invited
Richard to make out a suit on his behalf, the result being that Henry
granted William the office of 'custos brevium', worth £240 per year,
and which came into effect in May 1548.

The story cannot be verified, and the office may have been secured
in other ways, but it does seem to confirm that William was attracting
some favourable attention to himself where it mattered most. When

Henry died in January 1547, William was on the fringes of royal service. His chances of advancement were enhanced by the regime change because his old friends from St John's days, John Cheke and Roger Ascham, were the boy king Edward's tutors, and high in favour. Sir Thomas Smith, another Cambridge friend, was in the service of the new 'lord protector' at the head of the government, the Duke of Somerset, and was clerk to the privy council. In February 1547 William Cecil was named on the commission of the peace for Lincolnshire, and in May he entered Somerset's household.

# CHAPTER 2

# Opportunity and Danger

JUST HOW WILLIAM entered the service of the new Duke of Somerset (plate 5) is not known, but it is reasonable to suppose that his friendship with Sir Thomas Smith had something to do with it. Smith had entered Somerset's household almost as soon as he became protector to the adolescent Edward VI (plate 6). He was also a clerk of the privy council. Somerset was building a position at this time, and naturally wanted to attract an additional clientage of promising young gentlemen, so it is very likely that Smith introduced Cecil. During these early months it is not certain just what function William performed, but it is probable that he was a 'gentleman of business', an extra pair of hands for the administrative work that was beginning to pile up, because the protector quickly began to display a tendency to use his own servants and advisers for public tasks in which he should theoretically have used the king's.[1] William's first recorded task confirms that assumption, because when the protector launched his planned attack on Scotland in September 1547, in order to enforce Henry VIII's 1543 Treaty of Greenwich which the Scottish parliament had repudiated, the two judges of his provost marshall's court (who should have been royal lawyers) were his own servants, William Patten and William Cecil.

In 1548 Patten published what he described as a 'diary', *The Expedition into Scotland of the most worthily fortunate Prince Edward, Duke of Somerset* ... (London, 1548), full of contemporary political correctness. It praised the English excessively both for their objectives and achievements, and was extremely adulatory of the duke.[2] According to Patten, he was appointed by 'my very good Lord the earl of Warwick' to be a judge assistant to the high marshall, Lord Grey, 'as Master William Cecil was the other'. The pair of them, 'not being bound so straightly ... to the order of march', rode around when they were not in court, taking note of circumstances and developments, rather like a pair of modern journalists.[3] Apparently, Cecil's 'gentleness being such as to communicate his notes to me, I have, I confess, been thereby both much confirmed in many things I doubted, and somewhat reminded of that which else I might hap to have forgotten'.

Cecil's notes have not survived, and it may be that Patten never returned them. They were not fighting men, and how close either of them actually got to the action is not known. Many years later, Cecil's anonymous biographer recorded that his life had been saved by a colleague who, in pushing him out of the way of a cannon shot, lost his own arm. There is no contemporary allusion to such an event, but years later one George Calverley was granted the room of an alms-knight at St George's, Windsor, 'for his great hurt in the wars, specially at Leith in Scotland, where his arm was struck off with a great shot'. This was certified by Lord Burghley (as he then was), 'who was so near the shot himself as to be in great danger'.

Somerset left Scotland on 29 September, but the evacuation of the English army took rather longer, so it was probably well into October before Patten and Cecil returned to their normal duties. The protector seems to have been pleased with his (relatively) new servant, because at some time between his return and the end of the following January William was appointed the duke's master of requests.[4] This was not a post in the royal service, and in theory should not have been necessary, but seems to have arisen from another example of the protector engrossing business. One of the complaints made against him at the time of his fall in October 1549 was that he had established a court of requests in his own house, and Cecil seems to have been the officer who ran it.

At about the time of his return from Scotland, and possibly to while away the tedium of campaigning, Cecil also wrote an introduction to Catherine Parr's *The Lamentations of a Sinner*.[5] She was by this time, following her widowhood by Henry VIII, the wife of Lord Seymour of Sudeley, the protector's brother, and it is not obvious that she played any part in the publication apart, presumably, from giving her consent. The work is described as having been issued at the instance of Catherine, Duchess of Suffolk (a close friend of the queen dowager), and her brother William, Marquis of Northampton, so the initiative presumably came from them. That Cecil should have been chosen to write the introduction is another example of his successful networking, because he was by no means the most obvious person to do so. For those who could read between the lines of it, it was a clear statement that the present government endorsed the evangelical programme, which had cost several people their lives as late as 1546. By writing the introduction and arranging the printing, Cecil announced that he was of the same persuasion, although, quite typically, what he actually wrote was bland to the point of inconsequence.[6] Cecil was to write a great deal in the course of his long life, and this is the first sample to have survived. (Unfortunately, his literary style did not improve.)

It is not clear what William actually did as the protector's master of requests, but it may be deduced that his principal task was to sift through the vast number of petitions of all kinds that were addressed to the duke and decide which ones his lordship should respond to, which he should ignore and which he should refer to the king's Court of Requests. This was responsible work and could only have been entrusted to a man of proven integrity. Cecil clearly performed well, because in September 1548 he replaced Thomas Fisher as Somerset's private secretary. He was now almost on a par with Sir John Thynne, the steward of the protector's household, and a man of recognized influence in high places.[7] As secretary, he would have managed the duke's office and, given the structure of the minority government, was probably on a par with the king's secretaries, Sir William Petre and Sir Thomas Smith, except that he did not service the privy council. However, as the privy council became more formal and the protector paid less and less attention to its advice, it may well be that Cecil was closer to the actual decision-making processes than were the secretaries of state.

Beyond his duties with Somerset, which must have been fairly time consuming, William also sat in the first parliament of the reign as a member for Stamford borough. The parliament was an important one, repealing, among other things, the Act of Six Articles that had prescribed Henrician orthodoxy in religion, but of Cecil's role in it there is no record. We do not even know how frequently he attended, although the fact that he sat for Lincolnshire rather than the borough in March 1553 should be seen as a mark of his increasing status rather than of civic dissatisfaction.[8]

In May 1548 Cecil's exchequer office was also realized following the death of its incumbent, which made him for the first time an officer of the crown and considerably boosted his income, but he seems to have discharged the actual work entirely by deputy. His main political function between September 1548 and October 1549 was as a principal means of access to the protector. The only records of this activity that survive are some letters from hopeful petitioners, a few offering inducements. This was customary, and we cannot be sure that Cecil accepted nothing, but he was clearly not bribeable in the ordinary sense; so his reputation for integrity grew at the expense of his pocket, which, if it was calculated, was shrewdly done. From a rebuke directed to him years later by the Duchess of Suffolk, it would appear that he did not take the opportunities that his confidential relationship with the protector permitted to urge the latter in the direction of more zealous Protestant reform. This may well have been true—not from any lack of such convictions, but because he found the duke's moderate and measured approach very much in line with his own preferences and had no incentive to encourage a more confrontational approach.[9]

It was perhaps for that reason that Somerset had used him earlier in 1548, before he had become his secretary, as a principal intermediary with the troublesome Stephen Gardiner, Bishop of Winchester. Since the early 1530s Gardiner had been intermittently high in Henry's confidence, but he had been dropped from the list of executors of the king's will, ostensibly on the grounds that he was 'ungovernable' by anybody except Henry himself, but really (it would appear) because of his strong religious conservatism.[10] It was not long before he was protesting vigorously against the protector's somewhat tentative reforms. He objected vociferously to Cranmer's 'royal visitation' of churches, to ensure adherence to the royal injunctions issued the previous month, in the summer of 1547, and spent several months in the Fleet Prison in London, before being released under a general pardon in January 1548. It was Cecil who persuaded Somerset to allow the bishop, who was quickly re-imprisoned, to preach a 'test sermon', and who outlined to Gardiner the matters that he was expected to deal with. The sermon was duly preached at the end of June, but it was not satisfactory, as William (who was deputed to hear it) informed his master. Gardiner was committed to the Tower and Cecil's involvement in religious affairs seems to have come to a temporary end.

By the beginning of 1549, Cecil's surviving correspondence has become a little more revealing. Sir Thomas Chaloner, in conference with the French and Venetian ambassadors, writes to him for information, 'If you have any further news which I may publish to the ambassadors here, pray write to me ... If I need to return before Sunday, send me word.'[11] Chaloner was well informed himself, but clearly felt that the protector's secretary had his ear closer to the ground.

Equally interesting is his developing correspondence with John Dudley, Earl of Warwick. Warwick was himself close to Somerset, and was thought by many to be his most powerful supporter, but he was clearly going out of his way to cultivate Cecil's good will. Most of the letters have to do with petitions of one sort or another that Warwick was presenting or promoting, but the affable tone is more interesting than the content: 'Gentle Mr Cecil, this shall be to render unto the same my semblable thanks for your friendly remembrance of my suits to my Lord's Grace, and also for your advertisements.' What form these 'advertisements' took we do not know, but it looks as though Warwick had discovered a method of wheedling information out of the secretary that appeared to him to be useful.

In view of what happened later it would be easy to put a sinister construction on these exchanges, but they may well have been innocuous enough. For all Cecil knew, the two were close friends—and indeed, other evidence suggests that it was not until the disorders of the summer of 1549 (the rebellion against the new Book of Common Prayer in the southwest, and the unrelated, so-called Kett's Rebellion of agrarian discontent in East Anglia) that Warwick began to have serious doubts about the wisdom of Somerset's proceedings.[12] There is no evidence at all to support statements that were later made to the effect that Warwick had been scheming against the protector for years, and there is no reason to deduce that Cecil was intriguing with his master's prime enemy with a view to betraying him.

The crisis that overtook Somerset in October 1549 was entirely of his own making. He was pursuing policies of 'social responsibility' that were in line with Tudor precedent and an honest attempt to protect the rights of commoners and tenants against 'improving' initiatives by gentry landlords. However, the effectiveness of government depended heavily upon the cooperation of those same gentlemen and, in the absence of a strong king, this was no time to upset the commissioners of the peace. Moreover, Somerset had become deaf to good advice, both in respect of his social policy and in respect of his increasingly unsuccessful attempts to control the situation in Scotland. William Paget, who had been his closest ally in the early months of 1547, bombarded him with letters of mounting desperation, urging him to pay heed to what his colleagues were telling him.[13] Somerset appeared to have forgotten that he was not the king, and had even neglected to keep his fences at court in good repair, leaving the management of Edward to his brother-in-law, Sir Michael Stanhope, between whom and the boy king there was little affection.

By September there were plottings within the increasingly alienated council. Religious conservatives, such as the earls of Arundel and Southampton, were in touch with the Princess Mary, the king's heir and a notorious thorn in the government's side, discussing the possibility of a regency. The Earl of Warwick, while ostensibly making common cause with them, was ploughing his own furrow of opposition and carefully maintaining the armed force with which he had suppressed the 'camping movement', as the East Anglian revolt was called at the time.[14] Somerset seems to have been unaware of these developments until 4 or 5 October and had not even noticed that the council actually attendant at Hampton Court had shrunk to no more than four or five, while the rest gathered in London intent on pursuing their own agenda.[15] As Somerset's secretary, Cecil's place and his duty were clear and, once Sir William Petre had defected to the so-called 'London Lords', he may even have been responsible for drafting the protector's side of the correspondence that followed. On 6 October, fearing an armed coup, the protector moved the king and his remaining supporters from Hampton Court to Windsor, and his control over Edward quickly became the only card left in his hand. The negotiation that followed was conducted mainly by Cranmer and Paget from Windsor, and Warwick from London. Whether Cecil made any input, either as a scribe or adviser, we do not know, but when a bargain was finally struck on 10 October, it involved the removal of all Somerset's servants from 'about the king's person'—presumably including his secretary.

Cecil's own memory of what then happened appears to have been clouded by time, or perhaps it was simply too painful. When he jotted down a few notes years later, he recalled that he had been committed to the custody of the lord chancellor on 27 September, and sent to the

Tower in November.[16] In fact, he appears to have been fully oper-
ational in the first few days of October, and was only arrested when Sir
Anthony Wingfield reached Windsor on 11 October. At that point
Smith, Stanhope, Thynne and Edward Wolf, a gentleman servant of
Somerset, were committed to the Tower of London, along with the
fallen protector, and Cecil was placed in the custody of Lord Rich.
Whether this was preferential treatment, and if so what occasioned it,
we do not know. It may be that a good word from the Earl of Warwick
was responsible, but either the earl changed his mind or Rich became
tired of his company, because by the end of November Cecil had
joined his colleagues in the Tower.[17]

What followed may have been a time of patient waiting or equally
possibly acute anxiety; but it would appear that Warwick's victory over
his conservative opponents, which took place during December and
resulted in his complete ascendancy in the council, was good news
both for Somerset and for his servants. Cecil and Wolf were among a
group who were released on 25 January 1550 upon recognisances
(bonds) of 1000 marks (£666 13s 4d), to be forthcoming to the council when called upon.[18] They none of them seem to have been summoned, and the episode was regarded as closed. Somerset himself had
been similarly released and by April had been restored to the council.
The protectorship was quietly abandoned and Warwick styled himself
lord president of the council. He subsequently proceeded to make his
own mistakes, but ignoring the council was not one of them.

Apart from the bare facts of his imprisonment and release, we do
not know very much about Cecil's activities early in 1550. His old
friend the Duchess of Suffolk had written to him in prison twice, on
both occasions expressing sympathy for his misfortune, but not great
anxiety about his fate. Parliament was in session, but was prorogued on
1 February, so it is unlikely that he took his seat during that session,
which had convened in November. The impression is that Cecil was
incarcerated more for form's sake than because any action against him
was intended. Presumably he returned to his place in Somerset's
household, because the latter had not been convicted of any offence,
and his lands and properties had not been affected by his loss of office.
The duke himself had been released on 6 February, without penalty
but under a heavy recognisance and certain constraints upon his
movements.[19] Uncertainty appears to have lingered for a couple of

months about his reinstatement at court, and at some time early in March Cecil seems to have written to the Duchess of Suffolk asking for her good offices. His letter does not survive, but her reply does, expressing her good will, and continuing, 'But of my greater fear you have quieted me …Wherefore I trust that my journey shall be less needful, for the great good I could have done for my Lord was to have offered my counsel in case he had been anything unquiet at their unkind dealings.'[20]

By the time this letter was despatched, all anxiety had been further allayed by the news that Somerset was to be recalled to the council. Whether there had ever been any real threat to his security, or whether Cecil was imagining terrors, we do not know. It would not have been like him to be over-apprehensive. Catherine wrote several times over the next few months. From her letters it appears that the real threat came not from the intentions of the council, but from the hostile rumours that continued to circulate—the detritus, no doubt, of the events of the previous autumn, which targeted not only Somerset but also his associates, including Cecil. Who was responsible is not clear, but opponents of the now dominant party of religious reform should probably be suspected. Cecil's sympathy with the cause of moderate Protestantism was now well known, both in the court and outside it.

Far from being the covert enemy to Somerset that he was later represented to have been, Warwick seems at this time to have been again his friend. The duke's big problem, once he had been reinstated, was to resist the temptation to seek a return to something like his former authority. With that in mind, he began to press for the release of the imprisoned bishops of Winchester and London, Gardiner and Bonner, and (perhaps inadvertently) began to attract a following among the conservatives. This threatened a challenge to Warwick's authority that he could not afford to tolerate. The one thing that must not happen during a royal minority was that the regency council should split. That had been narrowly avoided during the crisis of October, and could not be risked now. So Warwick started dealing both with Richard Whalley, who was Somerset's chamberlain and relative by marriage, and with Cecil to persuade Somerset to back off. A letter from Whalley to Cecil of 26 June is very revealing in this context. It sets out how Warwick had lamented to Whalley the 'unadvised' attempts by Somerset to secure Gardiner's release. 'Thinks he to rule

and direct the whole council as he will, considering how his late government is yet misliked.' If he would desist, the king (that is, Warwick
himself) would still be his 'good lord'.[21] The only reason the earl could
have had for being so open with a servant was to use his good offices,
and it appears that he was also using Whalley to recruit Cecil to the
cause. 'He declared in the end his good opinion of you in such sort as I
may well say he is your very singular good lord … for he plainly said,
you have shown yourself … a faithful servant and most witty councillor unto the King's majesty and his proceedings as was scarce the like
within this realm.'

It may well be that it was Cecil rather than Whalley who was the
real object of Warwick's solicitations at this point. Letters are known to
have passed directly between them, and some survive, notably one of
4 July concerning articles of submission to be offered to Gardiner.
Warwick had been away from the council through ill health, and in his
absence it appears that Somerset's influence had grown. Warwick
needed to reassert himself, and appears to have asked Cecil to draw up
the relevant document. If this is correct, it was not only an extraordinary gesture of confidence, but also indicates that upon this central
issue William's ideas were closer to Warwick's than they were to Somerset's.[22] The articles were refused, and Gardiner remained in prison.
In the light of this it is not surprising that on 5 September 1550
William Cecil was appointed principal secretary in succession to
Nicholas Wotton, and exchanged the Duke of Somerset's service for
the king's. There does not appear to have been any rupture with his
former employer, and indeed petitioners were still soliciting his good
offices with the duke after his change of service. However, he had now
effectively entered the service of the Earl of Warwick, because
although in theory royal service emancipated a man from the need for
any other lord, in practice the earl was keeping a close grip on such
strategically important appointments.

Nor was Warwick Cecil's only patron. We do not know when his
friendship with Princess Elizabeth began, or what occasioned it,
although it is tempting to see an intellectual association—a sort of
tutor/pupil relationship. We know that they were acquainted as early
as August 1548, when the princess's governess, Catherine Ashley,
wrote asking for his intercession with Somerset for the release of a
prisoner, a letter to which Elizabeth added a note in her own hand.[23] A

year later he was exchanging letters with Thomas Parry, Elizabeth's 'cofferer', effectively treasurer, about the management of her affairs and receiving further gracious messages from the young lady herself. The estates that had been allocated to the princess in her father's will were finally allocated by patent on 17 March 1550, to an annual value of over £3000.[24] This grant marked her final emergence from the shadow of Thomas Seymour and her establishment as a grandee in her own right. She was now 16 and discreet and self possessed beyond her years. Cecil was probably appointed her surveyor at once, because he was already acquainted with both her and her business. When Parry referred to his position in a letter of July 1550, he had obviously been in the post a little while, because he confirmed that Elizabeth was happy that Cecil should continue to discharge his office by deputy.[25] He seems to have been an avuncular figure—a councillor rather than a practical servant—and the nature of their relationship remains shadowy, but it was well established by the summer of 1550. In theory, a surveyor should have been a lawyer and an accountant as well as a general man of business, but in this case the title seems to have been a pretext to maintain a more personal relationship. There is little evidence that Cecil soiled his hands with the day-by-day management of the princess's lands.

As secretary Cecil was the junior partner to Sir William Petre, an experienced diplomat and royal servant some 15 years his senior. They were already well acquainted and clearly fitted comfortably together as a partnership. However, it was a partnership that left Cecil with much of the routine grind, particularly attendance at council meetings, at which he was famously assiduous.[26] A large archive of incoming correspondence survives, but little of specific interest, and Cecil's own letter book (if he kept one) is missing. His old friend the Duchess of Suffolk wrote to congratulate him on his appointment, and added (somewhat mysteriously), 'I am content to become your partner, as you promised me, and will abide all adventures in your ship, be the weather fair or foul, although I cannot help you with costly wares to furnish her, yet I shall ply you with my old safety, which shall serve her for ballast ... '[27]

Whether this refers to some actual commercial venture, or the language is metaphorical, is not clear. What is clear is that their old bantering friendship continued, although Catherine did not cease to twit him about his lack of zeal in radical religious causes. What is equally clear is that both of them drifted away from their former friendship with Somerset. The duchess began to complain of the duke's 'unkindness', and Cecil's role as a trusted intermediary disappears. It seems that both were alienated by Somerset's somewhat devious attempts to regain a major say in the formulation of policy, probably in the same way that Warwick began to find him both tiresome and threatening. When Warwick forced a showdown in 1551, both of them chose to support him.

Everyone who left any record of their feelings seems to have been pleased by Cecil's appointment. Sir John Mason, an experienced diplomat then in France, was particularly effusive: 'I know what service you are able therein to do to the realm, and for that also I trust to the continuance of your good friendship ...' It is quite likely that, as secretary and in daily touch with the council's business, Cecil saw the great bulk of the correspondence that came into that body. Some are annotated in his hand. However, his job was as a facilitator, and to give advice when it was called for; he was not a policy shaper at this stage. Nevertheless, his voracious and systematic mind collected information from all quarters and, as his capital in that respect grew, so his services became more valuable. Warwick and Cranmer, and to a lesser extent Somerset, were the chief architects of policy at this time, and one of their great virtues as statesmen was the quality of the auxiliaries whom they recruited, mostly drawn from the Cambridge humanist circle of the 1530s and 1540s—Sir Thomas Smith, Sir John Cheke, Sir John Mason, Richard Morrison, Roger Ascham and, of course, Cecil himself. The way in which shared intellectual interests could draw such men into friendship and collaboration can be seen particularly in the relationship between Cecil and Morrison. The latter was a keen Greek scholar, and their correspondence is littered with subtle allusions that would have been lost on the less educated. Greek was also an enthusiasm of Mildred Cecil, and she was an equal partner in their friendship. While Morrison was on a mission in Germany in 1550 and 1551, his and William's correspondence was as much about their shared passion as it was about diplomacy.[28] Morrison was also a zealous Protestant, a factor that somewhat inhibited his effectiveness at the court of Charles V, whose ambassador in England described him as 'a great heretic'—a description that he also applied to Cecil.

Meanwhile, and in spite of Cecil's well-intentioned efforts, relations between Somerset and the Earl of Warwick continued to decline. Warwick's first reaction had been to seek constructive reconciliation, and on 3 June his son and heir (also John) married Anne Seymour, the duke's daughter. By the autumn, however, mutual suspicion was rising inexorably.

Somerset's aims are something of a mystery. He was rumoured to be seeking alliance with the religious conservatives, and even with the traditional nobility of northern England; but at the same time he was promoting the cause of the radical Bishop of Gloucester, John Hooper, and if he had any close links with the northern aristocrats such as the Nevilles, Cliffords or Dacres, they have never come to light. He deeply distrusted Warwick's policy of seeking the friendship of France, regarding the French as untrustworthy allies, and would have preferred an attempt to build bridges to Brussels, as he had done while protector. He was also opposed to Warwick's essentially pragmatic policy of supporting the gentry in their innumerable conflicts with socially conservative 'Commonwealth men', who opposed enclosure and agitated in print to preserve old rural ways. Those who accused Somerset in 1551 of attempting to ride back to power on the support of the common people were probably not far wrong. He also found the role of junior partner galling and clearly entertained hopes, from time to time, of overthrowing Warwick's authority.

In what seems to have been a calculated preparation for his strike, Warwick arranged for Somerset to be summoned back to court on 30 September in order to witness a series of peerage promotions. Warwick himself became Duke of Northumberland, while the Marquis of Dorset was elevated to Duke of Suffolk, and the Earl of Wiltshire to Marquis of Winchester. Although these were ostensibly by the king's command, the endorsement of the only other duke in circulation was clearly desirable. At the same time, on 11 October, William Cecil was knighted, and a few weeks later, in early November, received a significant grant of lands.[29]

Somerset's actual destruction was engineered largely by fraud. Jehan Scheyfve, the Imperial ambassador writing from a not very well-informed position in mid-November, believed that it had been Cecil who had 'first got wind' of the duke's alleged intentions, but the king's journal tells a different story. What Edward was told was that the first denunciation had been made by Sir Thomas Palmer on 7 October, and involved intentions going back to the previous year, including a wild tale about Somerset's plot to invite Warwick and Northampton to a banquet, and there to 'cut off their heads'. In spite of the (allegedly) horrendous crimes intended, Northumberland waited until after the peerage creations—perhaps seeking corroboration, or perhaps not—before informing the king on 13 October.[30] It was only then that the king's secretary found out what was afoot. He did not, however, warn Somerset that 'a plot was laid for his life', which creates the suspicion that he was already a party to it. On 14 October the duke sent for his former secretary and confided that 'he suspected some ill', to which he received the chilly reply that if he was innocent he had nothing to fear, but if not 'he had nothing to say but to lament him'. Although this is not first-hand evidence, it seems clear that Cecil had by then abandoned any attempt to mediate between Somerset and Northumberland, and had joined the latter's camp.[31]

Cecil's friends were simply relieved that he had not been in any way compromised, a reaction that may tell us that he had kept up his mediating efforts until very late in the day. Since none of them had any democratic inclinations, it is likely that Somerset's reputation for 'popularity' also told against him as they weighed their loyalties in the autumn of 1551. Somerset was eventually tried, acquitted of the more extravagant charges of treason and convicted of felony—of which he was technically guilty.[32] In other circumstances, that might well have been pardoned, but Northumberland had no intention of allowing such an escape. His one-time friend and eventual rival went to the block on 22 January, with sundry of his servants who had not turned their coats in time—Sir Michael Stanhope, Sir Ralph Vane, Sir Miles Partridge and Thomas Arundel—all sharing the same fate a few days later. It is not surprising that William Cecil's friends were disposed to congratulate him!

Cecil was not called upon to testify and appears to have played no part in the climax of these proceedings. By the end of 1551 he had returned to his habitual role as the administration's workhorse. Most of the evidence, once again, is incoming letters, but there are some memoranda in Cecil's hand, including an intriguing report of a council discussion on relations with the emperor, which Cecil started and the king finished. This should not lead us to suppose that the king was on intimate terms with his secretary, whom he probably regarded as part of the furniture of the court, but he may well have recognized a diligent servant when he saw one. Cecil must have dealt with the Duke of Northumberland on an almost daily basis during the last 18 months of the latter's ascendancy, but the chatty letters of the kind written two years previously no longer survive—if any such were written. The duke visited Burghley on one occasion on his way north, apparently at the secretary's invitation, but called in only briefly and was received by the aged Richard rather than by William.[33] There is no evidence at all of how their personal relationship developed (if it did) after the end of 1550. Cecil, like most of his friends, was inclined to be anti-French, but these opinions were seldom allowed to intrude into the discharge of their official duties and it would be wrong to suppose that such views created any tension with the duke or with the king, who shared his mentor's views in that respect. He drafted memoranda that others were to sign, and seems to have been mainly responsible for a long discourse on the establishing of a mart (trade staple) in England. His knowledge of such matters was great, but he remained a functionary. Although his duties gave him an immense fund of knowledge and experience that was later to stand him in good stead, as long as Edward was alive that knowledge was simply deployed in the service of his political masters.

In the second parliament of the reign, which was convened on 5 January and met on 1 March 1553, Cecil sat for Lincolnshire. This was probably the result of his increased status as secretary rather than of any falling out with the borough of Stamford; indeed, they heeded his advice over who should replace him. By this time, the king's health was giving cause for concern. He had failed to throw off what was thought at first to be a heavy cold, and by March had developed what we now know to have been pulmonary tuberculosis. At the same time the regime was under another cloud because of deteriorating relations between an impatient Northumberland and a more cautious Archbishop Cranmer over the pace of religious reform. By the spring of 1553 Cranmer had largely withdrawn from the council. Cecil undoubtedly sympathized with the archbishop in this confrontation, and their relations continued to be friendly, but there is no overt sign of any resultant strain with the duke.

By this time Cecil had a house at Wimbledon in addition to his normal 'duty' residence at Cannon Row, and in the latter part of April he withdrew there to sort out some private business. There is no suggestion that he intended to be away long, and such brief 'vacations' were not unusual. Early in May, however, he was taken ill. Edward's precarious condition, and the likely consequences should he die, made Northumberland suspect Cecil of malingering, but according to Cecil's own account he was not only genuinely, but even seriously, sick. 'Your companion here,' the duke wrote reproachfully, 'doth bear out the burden with as much pain as anyone can ...'[34]

News of the young king was up and down. Early in May he was poorly, but by 17 May he had recovered sufficiently to receive the French ambassador, and on the 21st he blessed the marriage of Northumberland's son Guildford with Lady Jane Grey, the Duke of Suffolk's eldest daughter, although he did not attend. Then, in the first week of June, he collapsed. At that juncture, on 11 June, the very day that the Imperial ambassador was reporting that Edward's life was despaired of, Cecil returned to duty.

If he had really been malingering, then his timing was extraordinarily inept, because he walked straight into the storm over Edward's plans to divert the succession. Back at the beginning of the year, before any crisis was in sight, the king had drafted a speculative document on the succession. It was little more than a school exercise, to address the hypothetical question—what if he should die without heirs of his body? This document revealed that he regarded both his half-sisters as illegitimate, and that he had a deeply rooted aversion to any female succession. He clearly regarded his father's succession act, which named Mary, followed by Elizabeth, as heirs to the throne should Edward died without male issue, as unsatisfactory and intended to repeal it.[35] Meanwhile, with a long time span in mind, he wrote of male heirs to be born to ladies who were not yet married. It was seriously meant, but it was not real politics. However, in early June it was all there was. As it stood, it was no use, because all it spoke of was boys yet unborn; however, by inserting the words 'and her' between 'the Lady Jane' and 'heirs male', it could be converted into an instrument naming Lady Jane Grey as the immediate heir. True, she was a woman too, but her religious inclinations and connection to the regime were far more palatable than Mary's. This was certainly done with the king's approval, although the alteration is not in his hand. It also suited Northumberland, who was now Jane's father-in-law, and inevitably gave rise later to the charge that he was trying to divert the crown into his own family. Edward may well have realized that he would not have time to alter the Act of Succession, so he commanded that this instrument be drawn up for the Great Seal. There was anguished debate in the council, the lawyers pointing out that, as it stood, the king's document was illegal.[36] Pressure built up during June for it to be signed and sealed, that being the most that could be achieved. Eventually Edward charged his advisors on their allegiance to carry out his wishes, and they consequently felt that they had no option. It was treason to reject the king's direct command. So the instrument was drawn up in due form, and signed by everyone, although there is no evidence that it was ever sealed.

Cecil was in the middle of this battle and as anguished as any. According to his own later self-justification and a memoir written many years afterwards by his servant, Roger Alford, he contemplated flight, put his London affairs in order and even prepared himself for a spell in prison.[37] He was determined, he claimed, to resist so unlawful an extension of the king's prerogative. 'I ... determined to suffer for saving of my conscience ...' When it came to the point, however, he signed with the rest. Perhaps, like several others, he consoled himself with the thought that it could not be an offence to obey the king's explicit order—and that when that king was dead, other considerations might apply.

When Edward did die, on 6 July, Cecil ducked and wriggled to avoid associating himself with the new regime—or so he claimed. He declined to draft Jane's proclamation, claiming that it should be done by one of the law officers, and avoided writing any official letters, although that would normally have been a part of his duties. It seems that none of the surviving drafts is in his hand, so his claim may well be correct. He did not, however, seek to resign. Perhaps that was not a realistic option in the circumstances, or perhaps he was waiting on events. After all, most observers thought that the Duke of Northumberland, and with him Queen Jane, would prevail.[38] Famously, that did not happen, and on 19 July the council split, the majority declaring for Mary, who was swept to power on the nearest thing to a demonstration of popular enthusiasm that the 16th century witnessed.

According to Cecil, he did not merely join the successful party, but was a prime mover in it. 'I practiced with the Lord Treasurer to win the Lord Privy Seal [the Earl of Bedford] that I might by the Lord Russell's means, cause Windsor Castle to serve the Queen [Mary].' It may have been so, but we have only his word for it. Once Mary had been proclaimed, Northumberland and his core followers, particularly Suffolk and Northampton, were left high and dry. The rest hastened to submit to the new queen, and Cecil performed what was to be his last action as secretary (for the time being) by bearing their submission and a memorandum of urgent business for Mary's consideration.[39] He caught up with her at Ipswich as she made her way towards London.

Mary knew quite a lot about Cecil. When she had had a particularly bruising encounter with the council in 1551, and read the king's letter which they had brought with them, she observed as she read it, 'Ah, good master Cecil took much pain here', implying that Edward had probably never seen his alleged epistle. According to his anonymous biographer, 'When Queen Mary came in, she granted Sir William Cecil a general pardon. And in charging her Councillors, she had also so good a liking to him as, if he would change his religion, he should be her Secretary and Councillor ...'[40]

He certainly received a general pardon, but whether any such conditional offer was made, we really have no idea. He was not appointed to any office, and shortly after was required to surrender the seals of the Garter Order, which he held as chancellor.

## CECIL SURRENDERS THE SEALS OF THE GARTER, 1553

A FTER OUR HEARTY *commendations. The Queen's Highness pleasure is, that you [Cecil] shall immediately upon sight hereof send unto her highness all such seals as remaineth in your custody belonging to the Order of the Garter, sealed either in some bag or otherwise as the same may come most safely to her Majesty's hands. Whereof we pray you fail not. From St. James's 21st September 1553*
  *Ye shall send therewith the old register*
Your loving friends<br>
Ste. Winton, Cancell.,<br>
Winchester, Arundel, William Paget.<br>
J. Rochester, Will Petre, sec.

Making a good case for his subject in the very different circumstances of the late 16th century, his biographer continued, 'like himself, he wisely and Christianly answered [to the Queen] he was taught and bound to serve God first and next the Queen. And if her service should put him out of God's service, he hoped her majesty would give him leave to chose an everlasting rather than a momentary service ...'

It is hard to imagine Mary taking such an innuendo in good part, but he was permitted to retreat in good order, and never called to account for signing Jane's instrument. After all, quite a few of her trusted councillors had done the same. What is clear, however, in spite of his biographer's implications, is that Cecil conformed to the Catholic Church, however minimally or reluctantly. It may well be that he was protected to some extent by old friends who conformed with easier consciences, like Lord William Paget and Sir William Petre, but if he had not at least gone through the motions he could hardly have escaped trouble. He was not an easy man to overlook and his example would have been taken seriously. John Clapham believed that he was regarded with grave suspicion by some councillors, but supported by others, who regretted his absence and believed him to be 'a very meet man' to have been used in the weighty business of the realm.[41] Clapham was probably right, because in November 1554 Cecil was one of those who accompanied Lord Paget to Brussels to 'bring home' the cardinal legate, Reginald Pole. Sir William seems to have developed an easy relationship with the cardinal, whom he cannot have met before. That was probably due to their shared scholarly interests rather than to any theological empathy, but neither his temperament nor his position would have permitted Pole to fraternize with a man seriously suspected of heresy.

In spite of his lack of office, Cecil remained a public figure. He served on commissions of the peace, and even, ironically, on one for the detection of heretics. He also served both Pole and Paget in a secretarial capacity during missions abroad, although he does not feature in any of the official correspondence and commentators never remarked on his presence.[42] He seems, for example, to have acted as Paget's treasurer on the mission to welcome Pole, although the only evidence we have for that comes from his own notes. He did not sit in any of Mary's first three parliaments, and that can hardly have been on account of any lack of local standing. It is tempting to suspect that it was the chancellor, Stephen Gardiner, who was managing the elections to those parliaments, and he was (for sufficient reason) one of Cecil's enemies within the council. By the autumn of 1555 the chancellor's health was in terminal decline, and he may well not have managed the October elections. When that parliament convened on 21 October, Sir William was back in his seat for Lincolnshire.

The fourth parliament of the reign was tense, not because (as the Venetian Michieli believed) it was more dominated by independently minded gentlemen, but because of Mary's personal tragedy. Although the queen herself would not entertain the idea, following her failed pregnancy in July 1555, it was now clear to her husband, King Philip, and to most of her subjects that the prospect of a direct heir was over. The queen's health was now also questionable and the king, perhaps hoping to overturn his marriage treaty, was pressing for an English coronation.[43] Mary also wanted a subsidy, and it was being rumoured at Westminster that the money would be sent to Philip to bolster his war chest—of which it had great need. In the event the subsidy was passed, although not without a lot of grumbling and some resistance, and the coronation was not mentioned in public.

Insofar as there was actual conflict, it centred on a bill ordering those who had left the realm without licence (mostly religious refugees) to return on pain of forfeiting their real property. The existing penalty for such departure was the confiscation of moveable goods, which were usually minimal if proper precautions had been taken, and opposition to the extension of the law was great. This was not so much because members sympathized with the cause of those in exile, although that may have been so in some cases, as because the forfeiture of real property was a penalty traditionally confined to those who had been tried and duly convicted of felony or treason. Resistance to this somewhat arbitrary extension of so drastic a penalty was fierce, and eventually successful.[44] The bill was voted down in a turbulent division, and the queen was furious. An enquiry followed, and several of the leaders of the victorious opposition were imprisoned. The fact that she had succeeded in returning 'First Fruits', those traditional ecclesiastical revenues, to the Church after an almost equally stormy passage and a similarly turbulent division did nothing to mollify her anger. The leaders of this troublesome group, who had been active against both measures, were Sir Anthony Kingston, Sir William

Courtenay, Sir John Chichester, and a number of others who were identified as having met at Arundel's tavern, near London Bridge, to concert their plans.

Another member, who was not apparently present at Arundel's, was Sir William Cecil. No individual voting records survive, and we are dependent for our knowledge of this on his later biography, but there is no reason to doubt its substantial truth. According to this source:

> IN THE PARLIAMENT *time there was a matter in question for something the Queen would have pass. Whereas Sir Anthony Kingston, Sir William Courtenay, Sir John Pollard, and many others of value, especially Western men, were opposite. Sir William Cecil being their speaker, and having that day told a good tale for them, when the House rose, they came to him and said they would dine with him that day. He answered they should be welcome, so they did not speak of any matter of the parliament* ...*[45]*

The council, acting on the queen's orders, sent for all these dissidents and committed them, but Cecil ended up in front of Paget and Petre — which may have been fortunate chance or may have been contrived. He apparently requested his interrogators not to deal with him as they had with the rest, to commit him without hearing, but rather, 'first to hear him, then to commit him if he were guilty'. 'You speak like a man of experience, quoth my Lord Paget'—not without irony, one suspects. The upshot was that Cecil cleared himself, 'and so escaped both imprisonment and disgrace'.[46] The story cannot be substantiated, but since Kingston and the others were also released after a brief imprisonment, it is quite probably true. Sir William's own diary merely notes that he participated in the debate 'at some risk', adding piously but somewhat irrelevantly that it was better to obey God than man.

Cecil's religious conformity certainly saved him trouble with the authorities, but it may also have strained his conscience and additionally earned him reproach from some of his friends and relations who had gone into exile. In February 1556 Sir John Cheke wrote from Strasburg, commending him for what he had heard of his performance in the House of Commons, but reproaching him in roundabout and convoluted terms for his apostacy—clearly fearing that he had lost all sense of right and wrong.[47] There are signs in his diary and other later documents that these reproaches troubled him deeply, but he was not made of the stuff of martyrs. Also, by the beginning of 1556 there were other good reasons for keeping his powder dry. Although the queen and her half-sister loathed each other, Princess Elizabeth was not only the heir in law, but also in fact. Philip had by then got the message that the English were not going to crown him, and that he had better come to terms with the fact that, if Mary should die, his interest in England would cease. His most sensible course, therefore, would be to extend the hand of friendship to Elizabeth, the dubious nature of whose religious conformity he was prepared to overlook. When Elizabeth had been suspected of involvement in Thomas Wyatt's rebellion, early in 1554, she had been imprisoned, interrogated and put in fear of her life; but when the Dudley conspiracy was broken up in March 1556, a similar opportunity was conspicuously not taken. The aim of the conspirators was roughly the same—to depose Mary and put Elizabeth in her place—but this time, although several of her servants were questioned and her dearly loved mentor Cat Ashley was removed from office, no threat was made against the princess herself. On Philip's insistence, she was merely admonished that her name had been taken in vain.[48]

How close Cecil was to Elizabeth remains something of a mystery. His biographer alleged that his devotion to her brought him into suspicion, and that his enemies in the council tried to use the fact of his service against him. However, by the time he was writing that was an obvious thing to say. Cecil continued to act as her surveyor through bad times and good, and may well have done more of the work himself now that his other preoccupations were less. In that respect he would have been a member of her council, and in regular communication. However, no exchanges between them survive and he was not considered to be close enough to her to be questioned, either at the time of Wyatt or that of Dudley. In fact, the only real evidence that we have of his continuance in office is the regular entry of his fee in his account book. When the time came in November 1558, he may have been the obvious man to recall to office, and the bond between them may have been no stronger than that. However, their shared intellectual interests, to say nothing of their common religious circumspection, must have brought them together in some more personal sense. They were, after all, both living in the same relatively small world.

As the months went by, although Elizabeth was watched, her friends in the council became more visible, and these were also Cecil's friends—pragmatists such as Paulet, Paget and Howard, who were not in any sense disloyal to Mary but simply watching their backs. While Elizabeth spent the last two years of her sister's reign fending off the pressing marriage proposals that represented Philip's idea of solicitude — and were, of course, his way of establishing control over her—Sir William maintained a low-key public career. He did not sit in the parliament of 1558 (perhaps the experience of 1555 had warned him off), but he did continue with his local duties, and remained in touch with like-minded colleagues, both within the administration and outside it.

An intriguing letter from Sir Thomas Cornwallis, the treasurer in Calais, illuminates a little corner of this activity. Writing to 'The Right Worshipful and my very assured friend, Sir William Cecil at Cannon Row, Westminster', on 5 March 1556, he conveys Lord Wentworth's thanks for the watching brief that Cecil had apparently been holding over a lawsuit between his lordship and one Record.

> YOU BEING PRESENT, *replied against Record, and said that you were well able to clear his lordship of many articles against him objected by the said Record. Whereunto I answered that I could well witness the same, for when I was in England I saw how you attended at Westminster Hall to hear the matter* ...[49]

Whether Wentworth had in any sense engaged Cecil in this work, or whether he was doing it speculatively to keep his fences in repair, we do not know. It was probably the latter, because Cornwallis continued, 'This doing of yours is so well accepted that my Lord thinketh himself much in your debt, which (in this time of his credit with the Queen's highness) may stand you in good stead ...'

Both Wentworth and Cornwallis were members of the privy council, and their friendship was well worth having. Perhaps 'running on little errands for the ministers of State' was one of the ways in which Sir William protected himself against those who were always trying to use his suspect religion against him.

Unlike Wentworth, the Earl of Bedford was not *persona grata* with the regime. After being in and out of trouble for the first two years of Mary's reign, in 1555 he was given leave to travel abroad and, after an enforced stay in the Low Countries, moved on to Italy, where in 1556 he became involved in the shady events surrounding the Earl of Devon, whose death in Italian exile may—or may not—have been murder. By the summer of 1557 he had made his peace with Mary, or at least with Philip, and had joined the army which was to fight at St Quentin. From Calais he wrote to Cecil on 26 July. The letter is of no great consequence, except that it reveals that Bedford had committed his wife and children to Cecil's care during the uncertain period of his absence. They would not have been short of money, so care in that sense was not called for, but they might well have stood in need of a friend with the right connections, because Bedford was a notorious Protestant, and that dexterous amphibian Sir William Cecil may well have seemed ideal. The earl could trust him, in a way in which he could not have trusted Arundel or Pole, not to bring pressure on his children to undergo a Catholic upbringing, and yet he had enough friends in high places to make that sort of protection effective. These letters are only fragments in an otherwise barren archive, but they do give some indication of how Cecil survived the lean years when he had no official clout whatsoever.

At the same time, not all his old friends were reproachful, and with his father-in-law Sir Anthony Cooke he seems to have kept up an amicable correspondence, very little of which has survived. Cooke was a bibliophile as well as a scholar—he bought books and conferred with like-minded friends wherever he went. In January 1558 he wrote to Sir William from Strasburg, lamenting that he was unable to find a work that Cecil had been asking for. 'The book that ye wrote of, to my knowledge I never saw ...' He had passed on commendations to 'Mr [Sir Thomas] Wroth and his Lady, who take them in very good part', and he was astonished and distressed to hear of the fall of Calais to the French.[50] Again, a single letter is of no great significance, but Cooke comments gratefully upon the warm and loving tone of his son-in-law's last communication, and we get a glimpse of a man who was extraordinarily good at getting and keeping friends. One other such was Sir Philip Hoby, with whom he kept up a lively exchange, and who was always urging him to visit Bisham Abbey, his seat in Berkshire. With Hoby he may well have had a slightly different affinity, because both had been keen Protestants under Edward, as well as serving the regime with some distinction, and both conformed under Mary, although Hoby was somewhat more successful at keeping out of the public eye. There were cautious and rather surreptitious gatherings of these former Edwardians from time to time—Hoby, Sir Walter

Mildmay, Lord John Grey, the Countess of Bedford, even Lord Paget—but we cannot be certain that Cecil ever joined them. He had no desire to give hostages to fortune.

Some idea of his domestic life during these fallow years can be gleaned from his surviving accounts.[51] His sister Elizabeth was married in September 1555 and cooks had to be hired to supplement the household staff. He paid for music lessons for his children and ran an account with William Seres, the London bookseller. He paid £26 16s 8d towards his county's 1555 subsidy to the queen, which suggests he was assessed at about £800, and Mildred spent nearly £100 on clothes when Henry VIII's fourth wife Anne of Cleves's effects were sold in 1557. He seems, with a fine contempt for 'commonwealth' orthodoxy, to have spent both time and energy developing his land for grazing purposes, and had a brush with the law when one John Johnson went bankrupt. As Conyers Reed pointed out, his antics in the latter connection, during which he pleaded ignorance of the law and took refuge behind his mother's role as executor, 'does not reflect that nice sense of moral integrity upon which Cecil always prided himself'.[52] It is a relief to find that even this model of probity could on occasion have feet of clay. It may also be that Cecil's domestic economics explain rather better than his public utterances while in office how he became estranged from the Duke of Somerset. The duke himself was not blameless when it came to estate management, but it seems that Cecil was a great deal worse, and perhaps it was his activities as an encloser that caused him to sympathize with the Earl of Warwick rather than his patron when it came to social policy.

As September turned into October 1558, it became clear that Mary was seriously ill. Her health had fluctuated since the fiasco of July 1555. At first that had left her prostrate and exhausted, but she had recovered during the autumn, and through most of 1556 had seemed to be her usual self, aided, perhaps, by what she increasingly regarded as Philip's neglectful behaviour. Inadvertently, he put her on her mettle. Although Philip's return in 1557 was in pursuit of his own ends, the temporary resumption of her married life also had a beneficial effect on the queen. However, several months after his departure she again became convinced that she was pregnant, and that was a bad sign.[53] Not only did nobody take her seriously, but there were no obvious symptoms, and concern about Mary's physical and mental wellbeing returned strongly at the beginning of 1558. By March of that year it was obvious that her pregnancy was another delusion, and she became weak and depressed. A summer fever was thrown off, but by mid September it was becoming clear that something more serious was amiss. A dropsy was spoken of, and it is likely that the queen was attacked by cancer of the womb. Such a condition could not have been diagnosed, let alone treated, at the time and her physicians became increasingly worried. Even Philip showed signs of concern, although (as the French pointed out) he had every incentive to find another wife.[54] By the end of October it was clearly a question of when, and not whether, the queen would die. Some of Philip's servants urged him to come to England, but even if he had been so inclined, there were good reasons not to. If he had actually been in the country when Mary expired, his honour would have required him to claim the throne, and that he had no desire to do, knowing perfectly well that it would cause a civil war. So in early November he sent his trusty adviser, the Count of Feria, on a special embassy. Feria reached London on 10 November and, although Mary knew him and was pleased to see him, she was too weak to transact business. Just a few days earlier, and under extreme pressure, she had acknowledged Elizabeth as her heir, a bitter defeat that must have sapped what little energy she had left.

Having paid his respects and offered what comfort he could, Feria took himself off to Hatfield to see Elizabeth. He had done this several times during his last mission, back in the summer, and had established a good relationship with the princess. This time, he reported to Philip on the 14th, he found her changed; more reserved and less forthcoming. She was, he judged, very close to the threshold of power, and very conscious of it. A clever woman, obviously her father's daughter, and probably a heretic.[55] The existing council, he wrote, were frightened to death of her, and received him as they would one 'who came with bulls from a dead Pope'. Much of his despatch was filled with speculation about who the new queen would favour. Heath, Paget, Petre and Mason, he judged, would be in favour, Boxall, Gage and Pole would definitely be out. Arundel was a joke. Clinton, Bedford and Lord Robert Dudley would also be favoured, and, 'I have been told for certain that Cecil, who was King Edward's secretary, will also be secretary to madame Elizabeth. He is said to be an able and virtuous man, but a heretic ...'[56]

Many of Feria's predictions were wrong, but in this case he was to prove spot on. Sir William's favour at Hatfield was obviously notorious, and points to the fact that Elizabeth had assembled something of a 'shadow council' around her in the last weeks of Mary's life. She knew who her friends were in the existing council, and she would bear that in mind, but Elizabeth was also determined to recruit new faces to the most confidential positions. In such a context, Cecil was both a new man and an old. He was uncontaminated by association with Mary's regime but experienced in office. He was also famously discreet and wise. At 37 he was too young to be a father figure to the 25-year-old queen—but an elder brother? Probably.

# CHAPTER 3

# Secretary to the Queen

MARY'S DEATH HAD been protracted, and it is likely that most of those who were to form the new queen's council were aware of the impending change well before 17 November. It would not have been proper for men like Sir John Mason or Lord William Howard, who were members of the existing council, to have danced attendance at Hatfield, but those such as Cecil and Sir Nicholas Bacon, who were to form the core of the new regime, were almost certainly in conference there. Feria knew that Sir William was to be secretary, but he probably did not know what that was to mean. Mary had built her government around the traditional offices of lord chancellor and lord privy seal. For confidential advice, she had turned first to Simon Renard, then to Philip, and finally to Reginald Pole.[1] Her secretaries were busy officials, but not really councillors in the proper sense. It may have been for that reason that Sir William Petre had resigned in 1557. Under Edward a similar order had prevailed. Somerset, notoriously, did not listen to advice, and although Northumberland had listened, he had been the principal shaper of policy himself. It was not since the earlier days of Thomas Cromwell's influence that the secretary had been a major statesman.

Elizabeth, it seems clear, intended from the beginning to go back to what she probably regarded as the best days of her father's reign. She kept both the Great Seal and the Privy Seal in her own hands, and immediately made it clear that her principal councillor would be her secretary. The famous charge (plate 17) that she is alleged to have given to him at a meeting on 20 November could have been addressed to any privy councillor.[2] That Elizabeth chose to direct it to Cecil indicates that he was already selected to be her councillor in a special sense; it was probably recorded after the event in recognition of that fact.

## ELIZABETH'S WELCOME TO CECIL, 1558

I GIVE YOU *this charge, that you shall be of my Privy Council and content yourself to take pains for me and my realm. This judgement I have of you, that you will not be corrupted by any manner of gift, and that you will be faithful to the state, and that without respect of my private will you will give me that counsel that you think best, and if you shall know anything necessary to be declared to me of secrecy, you shall shew it to myself only. And assure yourself I will not fail to keep taciturnity therein, and therefore herewith I charge you.*

['Words spoken by her majesty to Mr. Cecil', from Hatfield House, 20 November 1558. TNA SP12/1, NO.7 (copy). *See also* plate 17.]

Reginald Pole had obligingly died a few hours after Mary, giving the new queen an extraordinarily clear field. Archbishop Heath of York, the highest-ranking ecclesiastic after Pole, was neither a zealot nor a leader of men. He was to stand his ground creditably enough in the later debate over the royal supremacy, but he neither believed nor claimed that a heretic could not be a legitimate queen, and was shunted into a more or less comfortable retirement.[3]

The one thing that Cecil was not was a potential husband for his royal mistress. He had been securely married for 15 years to a woman who was a true soul mate. Various names were immediately canvassed, including Sir William Pickering, Lord Grey of Wilton, the Earl of Arundel and King Philip of Spain, but none of these was seriously considered and, for the time being, Cecil was free from rivals of that sort. It was only several months later that Lord Robert Dudley (plate 8) emerged as a serious contender for the royal ear. When that happened Cecil was for a time beside himself with anxiety, but it did not happen at once. Years later, with all the benefit of hindsight, his position was described:

O NLY A SECRETARY *hath no warrant or commission in matters of his own greatest peril but the virtue and word of his sovereign, for such is the multiplicity of occasions and the variable motions and intents of foreign princes and their daily practices, and in so many points and places, as secretaries can never have any commission so large and universal to assure them ...*[4]

and again,

THE PRACTICE *of the place of a secretary … consisteth partly in
dealing with her majesty, and partly with the rest of her Highness's
most honourable privy Council.*

In other words, the secretary was omni-competent, the only councillor without a specific brief, and as such uniquely placed between the
monarch and all the problems, both foreign and domestic, that
demanded her attention. He was also Elizabeth's masculine face, and
expected to translate the workings of the queen's essentially feminine
mind to the sceptical male audience who constituted the entire political world in which she was forced to move.[5] This was doubly important because he was also, in political terms at least, her principal contact
with the nation. It was the secretary who was supposed to keep lists of
all the noblemen and gentlemen, county by county, to know their
affiliations and their religious inclinations and to be personally
acquainted with as many of them as possible. He was also supposed to
keep maps and to be familiar with the topography of the coasts; to be
in regular contact with the City of London; and to keep his finger on
the pulses of the universities.

William Cecil also doubled the role of principal secretary of state
with that of private secretary to the queen, which gave him privileged
access to the otherwise female world of the privy chamber. As such, he
took over responsibility for the Privy Purse, which in Henry's time
had been the job of the principal gentleman, and also held the stamp of
the royal 'sign manual', that is, the stamp of Elizabeth's signature.
Elizabeth clearly judged that it was safe to allow him such access, and
she was right. Not only was he happily married, he was also of a sober—
not to say pompous—cast of mind. No hint of impropriety ever crept
into his relations with these ladies and the queen herself, who was an
inveterate flirt, never forgot herself so far as to make a pass at him.

The two matters that first confronted the new queen were the formation of a religious settlement and the resolution of conflicts with
France and in Scotland. Cecil's role in both these issues was so important as to merit separate chapters, so no more will be said about them
here. We know that Cecil had been in consultation with Mary's officers before her death—which was no doubt how Feria found out
about his impending appointment—but the shape of the new regime,
as it emerged between mid-November and Christmas, bore the stamp

of Elizabeth's priorities rather than his. At court she changed her lord chamberlain and vice-chamberlain, but the lord great chamberlain and the treasurer of the chamber continued, as did the lord steward and the treasurer of the household.[6] A few of Mary's more zealously Catholic partisans retired, probably by their own wish as much as the queen's, but neither the chamber nor the household was purged. The privy chamber, however, that uniquely personal retreat, was cleared out entirely, and Mary's most confidential servant, Susan Clarencius, soon followed her youngest Lady, Jane Dormer (the new Countess of Feria), into exile in Spain. In her place came Elizabeth's equally long-serving confidante, Catherine Ashley, supported by a number of the kindreds of Boleyn, Seymour and Dudley.[7] All the queen's ladies, as Feria sadly observed, were definitely heretics.

Her council, on the other hand, was carefully balanced. That ancient and dutiful conformist the Marquis of Winchester continued as lord treasurer, while both Nicholas Heath and William Paget were dropped. The earls of Pembroke, Arundel and Shrewsbury provided further continuity, while many of the lower-ranking councillors who had comprised Mary's somewhat oversized board disappeared in favour of men such as Sir Nicholas Bacon and the Earl of Bedford. Altogether, Elizabeth just about halved the size of her council, tightening it as an advisory body at the cost of abandoning Lord Paget's expedient of using minor councillors (who seldom attended meetings) to stiffen local commissions in the crown's interests.[8] The new queen seems to have relied particularly on her secretary to make sure that commissions were staffed by 'sound' men who would perform their tasks as required. It would be no exaggeration to say that Elizabeth deliber-ately chose men whom she believed would place their loyalty to her-self above any religious allegiance, and ended up with a balance of Henrician Catholics and moderate Protestants. This created problems of its own, but nothing compared to the trouble that would have resulted from a more overtly ideological approach.

Cecil's religious circumspection not only matched his mistress's, but also served to rein in any tendency that he might show towards evan-gelical enthusiasm. While John Foxe put the best face that he could on Elizabeth's conformity, he never found it necessary to mention Cecil's.[9] As was also to become apparent over the next few years, a history of expedient conformity was not the only culture that the queen shared with her minister. Both were equally endued with the rhetorical and political wisdom of classical antiquity, a wisdom that Cecil had learned at Cambridge and Elizabeth from her Cambridge-educated tutors.

When Cecil returned from Scotland at the end of July 1560, he was immediately confronted with an important item of business that seems to have been on hold awaiting his leisure. The coinage had been in a terrible mess since about 1545, when it had dawned on Henry VIII that he could make some desperately needed money by debasing it. This had meant (roughly) adulterating the silver currency, particularly shillings and testons (six-penny pieces) with alloy and reissuing them at the same face value. The gold currency was relatively little affected, but over the next five years the silver content of the shilling and the teston fell to as little as 33 per cent, the difference between the face value and the real metallic value representing the crown's profit.[10] The full value of silver coins was restored by Northumberland, but the 'full value' coins inevitably went abroad to alleviate what had been a col-lapsing exchange rate, while the older debased coins continued to cir-culate at home. Cecil served on a royal commission in 1559 and was the main figure behind the government programme to redeem the alloyed coins with the newer ones in the hope of stabilizing prices. By April 1561 some £700,000 worth of coin was recycled: a considerable achievement that brought credit on Cecil. The crown made a profit of about £50,000, but other factors (such as population growth) under-mined the anticipated fall in prices.

While all this was going on Cecil was talking and writing, appar-ently seriously, of walking out on his public career altogether. In the light of the other things that he was doing, it is hard to understand these letters, but they are earnest, and even at times desperate. The cause was the queen's relationship with Lord Robert Dudley. Robert was about a year older than Elizabeth, and they had known each other since they were children. Robert was the third son of John Dudley, Duke of Northumberland and Edward VI's last mentor. As adolescents they were both about the court, but there is no evidence of any attach-ment between them; and indeed, in 1550, at the age of 18, Robert had married Amy Robsart, the daughter of a Norfolk neighbour, Sir John Robsart.[11] Robert had been convicted for his part in his father's scheme to divert the succession, and spent about 18 months in prison. For a part of that time Elizabeth had shared his incarceration, but there is little chance that they could have met in the Tower. Eventually Robert and two of his brothers were pardoned, and he retired to the relative obscurity of his Norfolk estates. At some time between 1555 and 1558 Robert and Elizabeth had renewed their acquaintance, and Robert is reported to have loaned the princess money—presumably when she had some sort of a cash-flow problem, because her resources were far greater than his. When Mary died, Lord Robert was sufficiently in favour with the new queen to be appointed master of the horse within a few days; as we have seen, Feria noted that he was likely to be favoured.[12] This was not a position of much political significance, except in one respect: it guaranteed regular *ex officio* access to the royal person, and that was what Elizabeth apparently had in mind. Robert was an accomplished horseman and jouster, and a bit of a soldier—just the kind of dashing, slightly dangerous man to excite a young woman.

At first, no one thought too much about this. When there was talk of marriage (as there was almost at once), the names being canvassed were her brother-in-law Philip and the Archduke Ferdinand. Less seriously, the Earl of Arundel appears to have entertained ambitions, and there was talk of Sir William Pickering as a fine upstanding fellow. However, by the spring of 1559 the gossip was beginning to focus on Lord Robert. Feria wrote to Philip, 'The Lord Robert is come so much in favour that he does whatever he likes with affairs, and it is even said that her Majesty visits him in his chamber, day and night ...'; and on another occasion, 'They say that she is in love with Lord Robert, and never lets him leave her.'[13] They say—but who are they? It seems that court gossip may have been running a little ahead of itself because, although Robert was elected to the Garter in April, the fact that he was already married cooled speculation, except among those such as Feria who was anxious to mine any sleazy seam that seemed to bring some discredit upon the heretics.

Cecil was as keen as anyone to get Elizabeth married, but apparently his rather straight-laced mind did not run to the possibilities of extra-marital sex and he was puzzled rather than alarmed by her proceedings. In his own puritanical upbringing, and distinctly orthodox marriage, he had never encountered this sort of female high jinks. In any case, he had other things to worry about. However, when he got back from Scotland, he found a situation that jolted him out of his complacency. The Treaty of Edinburgh, his great achievement in the north, got scarcely a nod of acknowledgement. He could not even be sure that it had been good political sense and not sheer indifference that had caused Elizabeth to accept his doings. She appeared to have no mind to anything except dalliance with Lord Robert. It may therefore have been pique, as much as alarm, that caused Cecil to write to the Earl of Bedford,

THE COURT *is as I left it, and therefore do I mind to leave it as I have too much cause, if I durst write all. As soon as I can get Sir Nicholas Throgmorton placed, so soon I purpose to withdraw myself* ...[14]

Later he wrote of his purposes to Throgmorton himself but without, apparently, raising the possibility of his becoming a replacement. His friends, notably Sir Ralph Sadler, sought to dissuade him, pointing out (truthfully enough) that many careers and many good causes depended upon his remaining in office. The word 'ingratitude' occurs several times in these letters, and it really seems that the cool reception accorded to his great triumph in Scotland was as much to blame for his rather extravagant despair as Lord Robert. Bishop de Quadra, the Spanish ambassador, who loathed England and all things English, did his best to exaggerate the tension and discontent. Being out of favour, the secretary did not have his usual access to his mistress, so he besought de Quadra to convey these warnings to her.

## CECIL VERSUS DUDLEY, 1560

I [BISHOP DE QUADRA] *met the Secretary Cecil, whom I know to be in disgrace. Lord Robert [Dudley], I was aware, was endeavouring to deprive him of his place. With little difficulty I led him to the subject, and after many protestations and entreaties that I would keep secret what he was about to tell me, he said that the queen was going on so strangely that he was about to withdraw from his service. It was a bad sailor, he said, who did not make for port when he saw a storm coming, and for himself he perceived the most manifest ruin impending over the queen through her intimacy with Lord Robert. The Lord Robert had made himself master of the business of the state and of the person of the queen, to the extreme injury of the realm, with the intention of marrying her, and she herself was shutting herself up in the palace to the peril of her health and life. That the realm would tolerate the marriage he said that he did not believe. He was therefore determined to retire into the country although he supposed they would send him to the Tower before they would let him go. He implored me for the love of God to remonstrate with the queen, to persuade her not utterly to throw herself away as she was doing, and to remember what she owed to herself and to her subjects. Of Lord Robert he said twice that he would be better in paradise than here … He told me the queen cared nothing for foreign princes. She did not believe she stood in any need of their support. She was deeply in debt, taking no thought how to clear herself, and she had ruined her credit in the city. Last of all he said that they were thinking of destroying Lord Robert's wife. They had given out that she was ill, but she was not ill at all; she was very well and taking care not to be poisoned. God he trusted would never permit such a crime to be accomplished or so wretched a conspiracy to prosper.*

[Letter from Bishop de Quadra to Philip II of Spain, 11 September 1560. Taken from the *Calendar of State Papers, Spanish, 1556–1567*, pp. 174–5.]

The ambassador was not only intent on making mischief, he was also determined to display his own favour and the key role that he believed himself to be capable of playing in the shaping of English policy. That Cecil was threatening to resign was almost public knowledge, and it is possible that he was trying to use de Quadra to convey a warning to Elizabeth that her people were becoming restive at her behaviour, but it is grotesquely unlikely that he was seriously proposing to dispose of Lord Robert. Moreover, Lady Dudley really was ill, probably with breast cancer, and was found dead at Cumnor just a few days later.[15]

Amy's death administered a salutary shock to all concerned. The queen, in particular, awoke from her emotional daydream to find her favourite being blamed on all sides for having murdered his wife. He had to leave the court while the circumstances were investigated, and although the separation caused great distress to Elizabeth, she was not so infatuated that she could not see the necessity. Lord Robert himself was shocked. He had been an extremely neglectful husband, but he was not guilty of homicide. Had he even contemplated such a course, it must have occurred to him that the queen could not possibly marry a man who was so compromised. In his bewilderment he turned, rather surprisingly, to Cecil. If de Quadra had been right, the hatred between them should have been visceral and profound, but in fact it seems not to have been so. Cecil was bitterly opposed to the queen's flirtatious favourite and possible husband, but in other respects they were political allies, and at court rivals rather than enemies. With the crisis upon him, Robert even wrote a friendly letter to Cecil, soliciting his good offices.[16] For a month or more the conflict between Elizabeth the woman and Elizabeth the queen raged unabated. Her health began to suffer, and de Quadra contemplated with relish a situation in which she would succumb to her emotions and be consigned to the Tower by her indignant subjects. Of course, it did not happen. By October the queen had emerged triumphant, and Cecil was back in his privileged position. Exactly how this happened we do not know. The talk of his resignation evaporated and we cannot be certain that it was ever more than a shock tactic to make Elizabeth realize the error of her ways. Dudley was eventually exonerated, returned to court, and even to his old intimacy, but the passionate spark had gone out of their relationship—they were just good friends—and Cecil no longer felt either threatened or excluded.

Thereafter the queen's favour to Dudley remained real, and sometimes became playful, but the cold winds of political reality had blown away the romance. Even if domestic reactions had not convinced her, reports of the laughter and contempt that her infatuation had provoked abroad, and which Cecil's friends made sure were vividly reported, would surely have had the same effect. 'The Queen of England is to marry her horsemaster', Catherine de Medici had sniggered, and the thought of such mockery was unendurable to a proud young woman.[17] Dudley, who was nothing like as bright as his mistress, became disorientated. He seems to have believed that, once the first shock of Amy's death had worn off, he would be able to pick up the threads where he had been forced to lay them down. The queen, he was convinced, still loved him, and in a sense he was right. It took him years to come to terms with the fact that it was a love that was doomed to remain for ever unconsummated. This was partly because Elizabeth's messages of estrangement were at first too subtle, and early in 1561 Dudley decided to try a new tactic. He approached de Quadra, offering his services to Philip in return for the king's backing for his suit. This was not quite as outrageous as it sounds, because he was not proposing to drag the queen back into the Catholic fold if he married her.[18] He must have known Elizabeth too well to believe that he could do any such thing. Rather, he was offering to promote the pope's efforts to persuade Elizabeth to send representatives to the reconvened Council of Trent. Pius IV was endeavouring to persuade all established Protestant churches to do the same, ostensibly in search of a general reconciliation but probably to give him a pretext to proceed more rigorously against them if (or when) they refused. The English council knew that such an invitation was on its way, and was divided over what advice to offer. Cecil and the more strongly Protestant members favoured concerting a response with the French and German evangelicals. The more conservative believed in unilateral action, and as a first step admitting the papal nuncio (the Abbot Martinengo) who was bearing the invitation.[19] What Dudley was offering to do was to use his influence on the conservative side, and probably to argue for accepting the invitation.

By March Cecil knew that the Germans would boycott the Council, and that the French representatives would come from Catherine de Medici and not from the Huguenots. He also knew of Dudley's approach to de Quadra, probably because Elizabeth herself had told him about it. He talked to de Quadra in conciliatory terms. Let Philip write a letter in Dudley's favour, which could be placed before a representative group of the Lords and Commons of the parliament; no doubt that would do the trick. Meanwhile he would also argue for participation in the Council, provided that certain conditions were observed. In April de Quadra believed that Martinengo would be admitted, the invitation accepted, and an announcement about the royal wedding made at the Garter ceremony on the 23rd. His lodgings were thoughtfully moved to Greenwich, to get him away from the hostile London mob.[20] Apart from his move, he was doomed to disappointment on all fronts, and it is hard to avoid the conclusion that Cecil comprehensively outwitted him. In the first place the conditions that were attached to attendance at Trent were completely unacceptable to either the pope or Philip; but far more important, a Catholic plot was uncovered.

One John Coxe, a Catholic priest and chaplain to the Marian councillor Sir Edward Waldegrave, was arrested en route to Flanders with money and letters. His testimony implicated his master and another Marian councillor, Sir Thomas Wharton, in a plot to encompass the queen's death by witchcraft and to overturn the Protestant settlement with Spanish assistance. Waldegrave and Wharton were immediately arrested, along with several priests, and a full-scale panic ensued. It is quite likely that Elizabeth was taken by surprise, not least by the scale of the alarm that Cecil and his friends had succeeded in creating. Martinengo was not admitted, so the invitation to Trent was not even considered, and when the Earl of Sussex proposed a petition in Dudley's favour at the Garter assembly, it was decisively defeated in favour of a bland and general petition to the queen to marry. When Cecil wrote to Sir Nicholas Throgmorton in May, he was able to record with much satisfaction:

> WHEN I SAW *this Romish influence towards about one month past I thought necessary to dull the papists' expectations by discovering of certain massmongers and punishing of them ... I take God to record I mean no evil to any of them, but only for the rebating of the papist's humours which by the Queen's lenity grow too rank. I find it hath done much good ...*[21]

Much good, indeed! Elizabeth's commitment to the Protestant cause had not only been reaffirmed but publicly demonstrated, and if she had ever thought of going back upon her decision not to marry Dudley, that was now impossible. The queen metaphorically shrugged, and was soon able to joke about her passion for Lord Robert. He remained a force to be reckoned with at court, and soon after in the council, but he was no match for Sir William Cecil.

At about this same time, Mildred bore William a son. They had been married some 16 years, and had two daughters, so this was an event of some note. As it happened, William lived only a short time, but it was long enough to persuade his father that it was time for his first born, Thomas, now 19, to see the world. He sent him to France, heavily briefed and under the conduction of his secretary, Thomas Windebank.[22] The project was a failure for a number of reasons that will be investigated in due course, and the main consequence was that Sir William abandoned any hope he might have had that Thomas would follow in his footsteps. He would be his father's heir in the legal sense, but not in any professional capacity. Fortunately Mildred was still young enough (just about) and resilient enough to throw off the disappointment of William's premature death, and on 1 June 1563 she bore a second son, who was named Robert. Robert was not as robust as

Thomas, but a great deal more so than the late William, and was to survive to fulfil his father's highest expectations.

Robert's birth, and survival, was not the least achievement of these years, but it was by no means the only one. Cecil was in the position, which they had both probably anticipated from the beginning, where he was playing continuous political chess with his mistress. Sometimes he won, as over the intervention in Scotland or the invitation to Trent; sometimes he lost, as over marriage and intervention in France; some-times, notably in ecclesiastical affairs, their games were drawn. For Cecil any political action at national or international level must clearly be underscored and complemented by the true worship of God, while for Elizabeth that true worship was most fully expressed in the exercise of her own supremacy. The important thing is that both of them knew the rules by which they were playing, and consequently Cecil could suffer setbacks, and even have his most cherished advice rejected, without ever feeling again (as he had in 1560) that complete with-drawal might be the only option.

One of their subtlest and longest-running battles was over the suc-cession. At one level, this was a disagreement about marriage. Cecil was insistent that the queen should marry—as long as it was not Dud-ley—and threw all his weight behind the Habsburg negotiations, first with Ferdinand and then with Charles.[23] He seems to have remained convinced that the obvious difficulty over religious allegiance could be resolved with good will on both sides, which was probably wrong but was never ultimately put to the test. However, at another level it was an urgent matter of providing immediate cover. In the autumn of 1562 Elizabeth nearly died of smallpox, and it was forcibly brought home to everyone that there was no 'plan B'. De Quadra's well-known account of the frantic debates in council tell only part of the story. In fact, there were three possible candidates: Mary of Scotland, the heir by strict hereditary right; Catherine, Countess of Hertford, the heir by Henry VIII's will; and Henry Hastings, Earl of Hunting-don. The latter's claim was remote, but he was the only male in sight.[24] Mary had much general support, but little within the council who were, according to the ambassador, divided between Catherine and Henry. Cecil did not, apparently, declare himself, but he was probably one of those who favoured an interim solution while further thought was taken.[25] The immediate crisis quickly passed, because Elizabeth made a full and speedy recovery, but it focused minds, particularly those in the House of Commons, which was summoned in November to meet in January 1563. Although the queen's main purpose was to obtain a subsidy, Cecil knew perfectly well that the succession would be raised, and equally well that Elizabeth would stall. Inevitably, Cecil did most of the spadework in preparing for the session, and may even have tested the water by causing the opening preacher, Dr Alexander Nowell, to raise the question at length in his sermon. If he did, and if the intention was to remind the queen how strongly her people felt about the issue, then he was wasting his time. Perhaps he realized that that would be the case, because although he was prominent in negotiating the subsidy and in introducing legislation on other issues of a routine nature, he does not feature in the preparation of a petition to the queen on the subject of the succession. Her response was gracious but totally non-committal, and the graciousness at least may have owed something to Cecil's influence. But on the substantive issue, she would not budge.

Parliament was prorogued on 10 April, no response having been received to its petition on the succession. However, the issue would not go away. In 1560 Catherine Grey had secretly married Edward Seymour, Earl of Hertford, son to the former protector. Because she was of the royal blood, she should have obtained the queen's consent to this marriage, which she had conspicuously failed to do. Elizabeth was extremely annoyed, imprisoned the countess and had her marriage declared unlawful.[26] Faced with the fact that her two grandsons were now bastards, in 1563 the formidable Ann, the dowager duchess and the earl's mother, waded into the fray. Lord John Grey of Pyrgo, Catherine's uncle, and his servant John Hales also became heavily involved, and all these were long-standing friends of Cecil's, who claimed kinship with him via Mildred. While the parliament was in session, John Hales had obtained legal opinions favouring Catherine's marriage, and had written a tract denouncing the succession pretensions of the Queen of Scots and declaring that the Countess of Hertford was the undoubted and lawful heir. It is hardly surprising that such actions caused ructions, and in letters to Sir Thomas Smith in the spring of 1564, Cecil lamented this 'troublesome, fond matter'. Hales was in the Fleet 'and like to go to the Tower', the Earl and Countess of Hertford were in the custody of separate councillors, and Lord John

Grey was also in custody.[27] Cecil was troubled because, as he said in November, 'I have been noted also a favourer of my Lady Catherine's title', but in spite of that, and of his kinship with some of the delinquent group, his favour with Elizabeth seems not to have suffered. Guzmán de Silva (who was de Quadra's successor as Spanish ambassador) believed in the summer of 1564 that Lord Robert was trying to use the queen's annoyance to get rid of Cecil, and of his friend and ally Sir Nicholas Bacon, and to steer the queen in a more Catholic direction. There were rumours that Sir Nicholas would be replaced by Sir Anthony Browne, a notorious conservative, and he seems to have been rusticated for the better part of a year. Perhaps Robert was responsible for Bacon's disfavour, as he may have been for a rumour that Cecil was the real author of John Hales's tract; but he made little or no impression upon the secretary's power or upon the anti-Catholic tone of the council, if that had ever been part of his intention.[28]

What he did do was to secure a more recognized position for himself. On 29 September 1564 he was created Earl of Leicester. The great advantage of this from everyone else's point of view was that it regularized his position. He was now a major peer in his own right and symbolically distanced from the queen. In practice he continued to depend heavily upon royal favour, but in principal he was no longer a maverick, and his appointment to the privy council soon after confirmed the same impression. He was now 'in the frame', and expected to abide by the normal rules of political discourse. From Cecil's point of view he became a known quantity. Although their rivalry continued, it was never as acute as the Spanish ambassador wished to make it appear and the formal courtesies were maintained between them.

In September 1566 parliament was reconvened, with Cecil continuing to occupy the senior county seat for Northamptonshire. The reason for the meeting was money, but Elizabeth knew that she would again have to run the gauntlet of representations about her marriage and the succession. Cecil, who realized how paranoid the queen was about the latter issue, concentrated his efforts on promoting the Austrian marriage, which was a live possibility at the time, while Leicester, affecting to be pro-French, bent his influence in the opposite direction.[29] Much of what we know about these discussions derives from what one party or the other saw fit to tell the ambassadors of France and Spain, and should be treated with caution. Cecil, who controlled the formal business of the Commons and whose notes also survive, says nothing of such matters, concentrating instead on the provision of a subsidy, the management of penal legislation and processes for the redress of grievances. It is likely that the main debate over the marriage took place in the council rather than in the parliament. The agenda was again Cecil's responsibility, and one of his typical 'pro and contra' memoranda reflects the way in which he was attempting to steer the discussion: 'To require both marriage and the establishment of the succession is the uttermost that can be desired. To deny both is the uttermost that can be denied ...'[30]

Following his own mind, Cecil concluded that the marriage should be pressed first and the succession only raised if that failed. Then, exercising all his considerable powers of persuasion, he convinced the Commons that they should petition on the former grounds alone. Carefully briefed, and surprisingly acquiescent, Elizabeth responded that she had every intention of marrying, but did not say to whom. The parliament was not satisfied, and tempers ran high. There were acrimonious exchanges between councillors and self-appointed leaders of the Commons. The queen prohibited further discussion and was then persuaded to withdraw.[31] There was talk of presenting a petition on freedom of speech, but it was not eventually delivered. Meanwhile Cecil strove to contain tempers and reduce levels of indiscretion, and was reasonably successful. Perhaps persuaded of the futility of trying to force issues on a sovereign who had no mind for them, parliament decided to be content with the answer that it had already received, and did not take the matter further. Given the level at which feelings were running by then, this was a considerable achievement by the secretary. When members attempted to return to the charge by incorporating the substance of their petition into the Subsidy Bill's preamble, Cecil succeeded again in transmitting Elizabeth's extreme annoyance and the offending passages were deleted.[32] A rearguard action delayed the bill by two days, but effectively the secretary had won again.

He was much less successful in trying to get an Act of Apparel. This was a subtle way of trying to resolve a difficulty that had been building up for some time over clerical dress—the so-called vestiarian controversy. Basically, this was an objection by puritanically minded clergy to being instructed by their superiors to wear a surplice when conducting services. There had been many discussions on the subject and Cecil, for whom it was an issue of discipline rather than doctrine, had more than once lost patience with the objectors. In many ways he was sympathetic to puritan calls for further reform, but not in this respect, and his intention was to get parliament to endorse the position that both Archbishop Parker and the queen had taken up. The bill went backwards and forwards, and was redrafted several times, but ultimately failed on its third reading on 23 December.[33]

By the time that this happened, Cecil had withdrawn, and that was no doubt one of the reasons why it failed. In late November, his old enemy the gout laid him low. He was not old, even by 16th-century standards, being about 45, but it was not the first time he had been so afflicted. He attributed this weakness in his constitution to the excessive rigours of study in his early youth, but in fact it was probably congenital, and was to get progressively worse as the years advanced. He was missed, because during December the Commons tried to push though a bill establishing the Thirty-Nine Articles of Religion, the fundamental doctrinal statements that would underlie the English Church, which so far had been approved only by convocation. The queen vetoed it, and Archbishop Parker attributed the setback to Cecil's absence from the court. By the time that he returned to his desk in early January, the parliament had been dissolved, leaving a lot of very dissatisfied people. The queen was pleased, because she had got her subsidy and given nothing of substance on any of the issues in controversy. In what sounds suspiciously like a set-up scene, she apparently accused Cecil, in the presence of the council, of orchestrating the marriage petitions against her—an offence of which she then allowed him to clear himself to everyone's satisfaction. As she must have known that he was innocent of any such purpose, we can only assume that this was her way of allowing him to outface his enemies in council.[34]

While these events were taking place, Elizabeth had become involved in piracy. England's maritime adventurers had started (or rather continued) making a lucrative business out of plundering merchantmen, particularly those of France and Spain. If the victims were English, redress lay through the admiralty courts, and although these were slow they were ultimately effective. To the unfortunate foreigner, however, both the courts and queen tended to turn a deaf ear. Sometimes the depredations were on a large scale, and major diplomatic incidents ensued, but the queen appeared to be incorrigible. She even invested directly in the strictly illegal trade in African slaves, which Sir John Hawkins was conducting with the Spanish New World. Cecil is not known to have managed any of these affairs, but he probably took the pragmatic view that the risks were worth taking because of the scale of the profits and the size of the royal share. In the spring of 1567 Hawkins was in the process of being conned by two allegedly Portuguese adventurers who invited him to prospect for gold in Africa, another illegal activity given the Portuguese claims to the area. He in turn interested the queen, and an expedition was duly set up. In September, however, before it could set off, the Portuguese got cold feet and disappeared. Not to be deterred, Hawkins then proposed that his preparations be redirected to his old Atlantic stamping ground, and Elizabeth, not wanting to lose her investment, concurred.[35] There is no mention of Cecil's involvement in these proceedings, but he could hardly have been unaware of them and it must be presumed that he also agreed. If he had not done so, it is almost certain that someone (not least Hawkins) would have noticed and commented. This was the expedition, which was famously ambushed at San Juan d'Ulloa in September 1568 and from which Hawkins returned with only a fraction of his men and profits. Thanks to Francis Drake (whom Hawkins accused of deserting him), news of this disaster sped ahead of him, liberally spiced with tales of Spanish treachery, and a few days after Drake's arrival, in December 1568, a golden opportunity arose to redress the balance.[36]

Genoese bankers had, for many years, been in the habit of lending large sums of money to the king of Spain. It was a risky business, because although the rates were high and the profits substantial, every so often Philip defaulted, resulting in heavy losses, and even bankruptcies. In November 1568 four small vessels were bearing a cargo of bullion from Spain to Flanders, amounting to some £85,000, to pay the army with which the Duke of Alba was squeezing the life out of the Dutch Protestants. Perhaps because their mission was supposed to be secret, they were not escorted, and when French privateers hove in sight, they took refuge in Plymouth Sound, being held there for some time by deteriorating weather.[37] The French made several attempts to infiltrate the sound, and the new (1568) Spanish ambassador Don

Guerau de Spes requested permission to transport the money overland to Dover, from whence the passage would be much shorter and safer. At the same time another Spanish ship, similarly freighted, arrived in Southampton. According to Cecil's official report, all the money was then brought ashore with the full cooperation of the captains of the vessels, and the captain in Southampton asked to be allowed to broach one of the chests to pay his current expenses. When the relevant chest was opened, documents were found inside demonstrating that the money was still the property of the bankers and 'not the proper treasure of the King of Spain'. Elizabeth needed the money and was only too willing to inhibit the activities of the Duke of Alba, so she decided to borrow it herself. According to Cecil, the bankers were entirely happy with this arrangement, provided they got their interest. It is possible that this idea originated with Benedict Spinola, who represented the bankers in London, but equally possible that Cecil himself was responsible.[38] There was nothing illegal about such a transaction, and it appears that Elizabeth embraced the suggestion with some enthusiasm.

De Spes got wind of what was afoot about Christmas. He challenged the legality of the new loan and urged Alba to take immediate countermeasures, adding for good measure that both Cecil and Leicester were spoiling for a fight with Spain. In fact it was de Spes himself who was spoiling for a fight, and war was not on anyone's agenda in England—least of all the queen's. Consequently in early January 1569, when the duke inhibited trade between the Low Countries and England and seized every English ship and merchant that he could lay hands on, the reaction of Elizabeth and her council was one of outrage. She replied in kind, but Alba quickly realized that he had listened too credulously to de Spes, and had overreacted. Within a fortnight he had sent representatives to London to open discussions.[39] Moreover, it quickly became apparent that he had shot himself in the foot, because the English owed a lot of money in Antwerp, which the merchants and bankers there could not now recover. At the same time the unsettled conditions in the Netherlands had already prompted the merchant adventurers to seek other markets that were not under his suffocating control, and this embargo was therefore nothing like as damaging as it would have been ten years earlier. Time might well be on Cecil's side. In the meantime he was perfectly capable of being disingenuous, writing to both Henry Norris in France and Henry Sidney in Ireland on 3 January, deploring Alba's reaction and claiming that no decision had been made about the destination of the money. On that point at least, de Spes appears to have been right. In theory, all direct trade with Spain was inhibited as well, and some Spanish merchants in London were placed under restraint; but in practice much exchange seems to have continued and, since Spanish trade in England was a good deal more valuable than English trade to Antwerp at this time, the English were in no hurry to settle. At the end of February Cecil wrote again to Sir Henry Sidney:

THE ARREST *betwixt us and Flanders continueth still in one state, saving that daily ships of King Philip's with merchandise come in so plentifully as in policy it may tempt somewhat otherwise to be done than was meant in the beginning. I myself like peace best for though in wars I hazard not myself, yet my labours and pains be as great as whosoever taketh most.*[40]

All this time de Spes was under restraint in his Greenwich lodgings and was as mad as a snake. The particular object of his venom was Sir William Cecil, whom he represented as the greatest heretic in England, the principal enemy to his master and a miserable parvenu into the bargain. The best remedy for the dreadful state of England would be to get rid of him and bring in some genuine noblemen who would be more sympathetic, both to the Catholic faith and also to the Queen of Scots, now a fugitive from her kingdom and lurking uneasily in Elizabeth's custody.[41] As far as heresy was concerned, and profound suspicion of the intentions of foreign Catholics, de Spes was not far wrong. At about this time Cecil penned (and published) *A Short Memorial of the State of the Realm,* dwelling on the intention of both the French and the Spaniards to restore papal authority in England and declaring that the English would deserve no less if they did not buck up their ideas of God's service: 'The service of God and the sincere profession of the Christian religion is much of late decayed, and in place thereof partly papacy and partly paganism and irreligion are crept in ...'[42]

He went on to dwell on the weakness and poverty of the kingdom, the threat from Mary of Scotland and, in short, to give the impression of being thoroughly paranoid. Apart from improving the sincerity of their religion, the only remedy he had to propose was a Protestant league, in which the kingdoms of Scandinavia and the Protestant princes of Germany should be brought into a confessional alliance. As far as we know, he never took any practical steps in that direction. Perhaps Elizabeth would have none of it, and she may well have been the real target of his diatribe.

However, it was not only de Spes who believed that Cecil was leading the queen and the country into unjustifiably perilous courses. There are several versions of what happened, but they are agreed in stating that there was a plot against Cecil in which the Duke of Norfolk, the earls of Northumberland, Pembroke and Leicester, and perhaps the aged Marquis of Winchester were involved. 'They conspired therefore secretly to cast him into the Tower ... [thinking that] once imprisoned means to undo him would not be far to seek.'[43] This is extremely reminiscent of a similar plot by the council against Thomas Cranmer in 1543, and it is impossible not to wonder if the storytellers were aware of that.

The outcome, too, was remarkably similar. In February 1569 a crescendo of complaint was audible at court. Cecil's severity towards the Catholics was causing unnecessary stress, both abroad and at home; he had blundered over borrowing the Spanish money and provoked a completely unnecessary crisis with the Netherlands; he was authorizing secret aid both to the Huguenots and to the Dutch, thereby upsetting both England's most powerful neighbours. The queen, so the stories run, became alarmed and tried to convene her council to discuss the complaints, but many councillors made excuses and absented themselves. Versions of the story then diverge over what happened next. According to Camden (who may well have got his version from Cecil himself), Elizabeth found out what was afoot and, taking advantage of the presence of a number of noblemen in her privy chamber, rebuked them publicly and reaffirmed her confidence in her secretary's judgement.[44] According to a French version, the Earl of Leicester took advantage of a similar gathering on 22 February to denounce Cecil to the queen, with the support of several other noblemen, and received such a tongue-lashing for his pains that he and his accomplices were forced to abandon the whole project.[45]

The stories differ mainly as to whether Elizabeth was forewarned of the plot or discovered it only from Leicester's action. Camden's version is the more convincing, because Cecil had eyes and ears everywhere at court and it is highly unlikely that he was unaware of what was going on. It is entirely likely (if he *was* Camden's source) that he was himself responsible for warning his mistress, and equally likely that he would have been unwilling to acknowledge the fact. Quite probably both the main versions exaggerated and dramatized what was in fact quite a minor scuffle, but all are agreed that the queen's reaffirmation of confidence in her secretary killed the movement against him stone dead. It also seems to have converted the Earl of Leicester from a slippery opponent into an almost equally slippery ally. In the aftermath of these events, Cecil was able to make his peace both with Leicester and with Norfolk, and wrote with some complacency to a friend in Ireland:

I AM IN QUIETNESS *of mind as feeling the nearness and readiness of God's favour to assist me with his grace to have a disposition to serve him before the world. And therein have I lately proved His mere goodness to preserve me from some clouds and mists, in the midst whereof I trust mine honest actions are proved to have been lightsome and clear …*[46]

There was, however, no peace, even for the pious, and scarcely had he exchanged friendly greetings with the Duke of Norfolk than the latter was in trouble again. Rumours had been circulating for some months that he was planning to regularize the Scottish queen's anomalous (and troublesome) position by marrying her. It may have been part of his intention to neutralize her, but he may also have had his eye on the crown matrimonial. Cecil probably picked up these rumours early on, and may even have seen some advantages in the plan, but the queen, it soon became apparent, was adamantly opposed to any such scheme. She summoned the duke and made her mind abundantly clear. He, in turn, denied any such purpose. He was not, however, telling the truth, and the plans continued to be discussed, drawing support from both the French and Spanish ambassadors.

Cecil played his cards very carefully, allowing it to be thought in the right quarters that he supported the match, while keeping a wary eye open for any change of mind on Elizabeth's part. Her attitude was critical, and it was by no means certain that events in Scotland or elsewhere would not alter her position. In conversations with Norfolk Cecil took the line that openness was the best policy, and that the duke should go frankly to the queen, putting forward his arguments as persuasively as possible in the hope that she would have second thoughts. Several opportunities arose to do that, but Norfolk could not summon up the courage to take them. His hesitancy put Cecil in a very strong position, not only in respect of the duke, but also of the Earl of Leicester and other councillors who were backing him. These same men had attempted to destroy him in the spring and, although that was all supposed to be over and forgiven, such reconciliations had a habit of unravelling. Cecil dropped dark hints to Elizabeth, and when it became clear that her mind had not changed — indeed that she loathed the very thought of the Queen of Scots—he advised Norfolk to back off.[47]

Ostensibly the duke did just that, but in secret he persevered with his intentions. This was now, by late September 1569, becoming a seriously risky strategy. Stories began to circulate that he intended to release Mary and use her against the queen. These soon reached Elizabeth, perhaps via Cecil, and she reacted with alarm. Mary's custody was strengthened and Norfolk was summoned to court and informed categorically that his intended marriage must be abandoned. Meanwhile several of his supporters, notably the earls of Arundel and Pembroke, were arrested and interrogated. Shortly after, the duke left the court without licence, thus heightening suspicions of his intentions. He seems to have been genuinely torn between the desire to submit (and be forgiven) and the desire to rebel in the name of the nobility of England—or something. In the event he submitted, and was incarcerated in the Tower. By October, Cecil was completely in control. Leicester had submitted on his knees and been forgiven (again); Pembroke and Arundel had been released without penalty, but were seriously out of favour; and the secretary's caution had been vindicated without openly falling out with any of them. Those who had denigrated him only a few months ago were now suitors for his intercession in the hope of recovering their positions.[48]

Before Cecil had time to draw breath, however, another and much more overt crisis broke out. The earls of Northumberland and Westmorland had been parties to the plot against Cecil and supporters of the Duke of Norfolk. When the duke was arrested, they returned to the north. Their real intentions are not clear, and may not even have been clear to themselves. It seems that they wanted to make some demonstration against what they saw as the secretary's inordinate power and mistaken policies. They also wanted to secure Mary's recognition as heir to the throne, and probably the withdrawal of the Church settlement. Rumours began to circulate, particularly in County Durham, of an intended 'stir', and these were connected with the earls and their alleged purposes. The Earl of Sussex, the president of the council in the north, summoned them to York, but allowed himself to be convinced that the rumours had no foundation. Elizabeth was not satisfied. She had Mary moved further south, and summoned the northern earls to court.[49] They declined to come, and the fat was in the fire. On 13 October Cecil wrote to the Earl of Shrewsbury (Mary's custodian) of 'a fond rumour' stirred up in the North Riding and in Durham, and called it 'but vain smoke, without any spark of any account'. This time he was wrong, and the same day the earls of Northumberland and Westmoreland were proclaimed traitors. By the end of the month the rebel forces were too strong to be contained locally, and by the middle of November they had taken Durham and restored the mass in the cathedral.

Within a week, Cecil was heavily involved in the mobilization of troops. On 16 November Lord Hunsdon was sent north with a commission as governor of Northumberland and Newcastle (an *ad hoc* appointment with no precedent), and armies began to assemble in Lincolnshire and Warwickshire. The secretary worked out in detail the county levies that were to contribute to these armies, and arranged for money and munitions to be sent to the north. It soon became apparent that, although the rebels were numerous, they were neither united nor well equipped. Unlike the general discontent exhibited in the so-called Pilgrimage of Grace 30 years before, there was also no sign of substantial sympathy with the dissidents in the south or the midlands. What was worrying was the fear of French, or more particularly Spanish, involvement. For that reason, a substantial army was deemed necessary in the southwest and another for the safeguard of the queen's person.[50]

Somewhat unrealistically, a general rising of Catholics seems to have been feared, perhaps more a reflection of Cecil's personal anxieties than an assessment of the real threat. In fact, the earls were hardly in control of their own rebellion, because their desire for a conservative and anti-Cecilian demonstration had been effectively hijacked by more radical followers such as Christopher Norton, who wanted to involve the Duke of Alba, depose or murder Elizabeth and put Mary on the throne at once. It was this radical group that sent an appeal to the pope for his help, but they had relatively little support, even in their own camp.

By 2 December, when Cecil reported developments to Sir Henry Norris, the situation was largely under control. The rebels, he reported, had advanced south, but had no more than 4000 foot and 1000 horse. Against them, the Earl of Sussex had mustered Yorkshire, Lord Scrope the West March, and Clinton and Warwick were leading the forces of Nottinghamshire and Derbyshire. Clinton and Warwick had between them 12,000 men, and the royal armies altogether totalled more than 30,000.[51] The young gallants of the court, anxious to demonstrate both their mettle and their loyalty, were flocking to the standard. Sir Thomas Cecil was one who offered his services, and Sir William sent his ward, the young Earl of Rutland, to wait on the Earl of Sussex. By 10 December the rebel advance had petered out at Bramham Moor, not far from Leeds, and the royal armies began to advance. There was no serious fighting, and by 19 December Sussex was in Newcastle, having re-established control over Durham. In fact, emulation between the various royal commanders was a more serious problem than rebel resistance. Both Warwick and Clinton apparently behaved with a high hand, arresting suspects and confiscating property, which they had no commission to do, and Sussex (whose patch they were on) complained vigorously to Cecil: 'Mr. Secretary,' he wrote on 1 January, '... if I weighed not the quiet of my good queen more than any other matter, I would have stopped them from crowing upon my dunghill, or carrying one half penny out of my rule ...'[52]

Hunsdon supported him vigorously, but because Leicester was a party with the delinquents, the queen would do nothing against them, and Cecil became (not for the first time) deeply frustrated by her attitude. Fortunately the situation was a temporary one, because there was no justification for keeping large forces or many senior commanders in the north after the New Year, and when the officers returned south, the problems faded away. A belated intervention by Leonard Dacre in February was easily coped with by Hunsdon and the forces that remained at his disposal.

Even before that happened, Cecil was able to turn his main attention to the punishment of the rebels and the opportunities that that presented for redeploying the royal authority in the area. 'It were a pity but some of these rascals were hanged by martial law,' he wrote, 'but the richer should be but taken and attainted, for otherwise it is doubtful how the Queen's Majesty shall have any forfeiture of their lands and goods.'[53]

The alarm had been exaggerated and the actual conflict slight, but the traditional loyalty systems of the north were now exposed to Tudor rationalization in a way that had never happened before; and the man who saw and grasped this chance was William Cecil. Those who had been guilty of treason could expect no mercy. But the queen had no interest in tarring all Catholics with that brush, and in that she was right. However sympathetic the northern conservatives may have been to the rebel cause, the majority had done nothing to aid them. She issued a declaration specifically refuting the rebel claim that she intended draconian measures of Protestant enforcement, 'no such thing did appear or was any wise by us meant or thought of'. Cecil may not have entirely agreed—he still had some puritanical edge at this point—but he drafted and issued the declaration. The earls fled into Scotland, whence Westmorland eventually made his way to the continent; Northumberland, less fortunately, was traded after some hard diplomatic bargaining and executed at York on 22 August 1570. The Percy and Neville inheritances fell to the crown by attainder, and it was this that enabled the restructuring of landholding to take place in the northern marches. Initially, some 700 executions were ordered by martial law, in addition to those who were indicted, but it seems clear that far fewer than that actually suffered.

In one sense, the rebellion and its collapse had settled nothing. Mary had not been implicated, and what might have happened if the rebels had succeeded in reaching her remained speculation. She still had strong support—not indeed as queen, but as heir—and by the summer of 1570 that support was again being led by the Earl of Leicester. To them Cecil was adamantly opposed, but he did not succeed in associating the rebels with her cause, and the queen remained in two minds. The Duke of Norfolk was released from his confinement and, although his ambitions appear to have become terminally confused, his eventual fate had nothing to do with the rebellion.

In other ways, however, the action of the earls was decisive. Their appeal to Pius V did not go unheeded, and although his response came far too late to do them any good, it was decisive in its way. They had asked for clarification of the conflict of allegiance in which they believed themselves to be caught between the English crown and the Holy See. The papal bull *Regnans in Excelsis,* issued in the spring of 1570, did that in full. Elizabeth, it declared, was a heretic and a usurper. No allegiance was due to her and all her so-called subjects were released from any such obligations. She was declared deposed from her pretended titles and an enemy to the Catholic Church.[54]

This was a declaration of war, and bitterly unwelcome to the majority of English Catholics, who had been struggling to think of themselves as good subjects and obedient churchmen. Now they could be one or the other. It was equally unwelcome to Elizabeth, who had been trying very hard to avoid any kind of showdown with the religious conservatives whom she realized perfectly well made up the bulk of the country's population. To Cecil and those who thought like him, however, it cleared the air. Any priest, and anyone who accepted the ministrations of a priest was now potentially a traitor rather than simply a non-conformist. The immediate result was a stiffening of the laws against Catholics, and recusancy (avoidance of church attendance) began to be an identifiable problem.

This had the further effect of strengthening the secretary's hand, and by the end of 1570 his position was universally recognized as unassailable. Between 1568 and 1570 he had seen off challenges that had for a while seemed certain to lead to his downfall. He had triumphed over the Norfolk marriage and he had triumphed over the northern earls. If Elizabeth had ever had any doubts about where she should repose her main confidence—and we cannot be certain that she ever had—those doubts were resolved by 1570. In February 1571, the queen raised Sir William Cecil to the peerage as Lord Burghley. It is alleged that he declined an earldom because of the lack of means to sustain such a dignity, but this is probably embroidery. He was a seriously wealthy man, a fact revealed by the scale of his housekeeping, and several earls would have been grateful for his disposable income.

# CHAPTER 4

# Reconciling Church and State

CECIL'S FIRST MEMORANDUM of 'things to be done' dates from the very first day of Elizabeth's reign, and consists mostly of routine matters such as arranging for the proclamation of the new queen, notifying ambassadors abroad and securing new commissions for the peace emissaries at Cateau-Cambrésis, where Anglo-French and Franco-Spanish treaties were signed (confirming, among other things, the English loss of Calais).[1] However, he also noted the need to make a careful selection of the first official preacher at Paul's Cross, 'that no occasion [be given] by him to stir any dispute touching the government of the realm'. In other words, he was reminding himself not to select some zealot who might question the new queen's religious credentials. His choice eventually fell on the diplomatic William Bill, who was Elizabeth's chaplain and who had remained quietly in England during Mary's reign. On 20 November the chronicler-diarist Henry Machyn cautiously noted that Bill 'made a goodly sermon'.[2]

Unlike her sister, the new queen did not chose to make any open display or announcement of her allegiance, but she did send out some clear signals. As Feria quickly noticed, the members of her privy chamber and her closest advisers were all either open heretics or strongly suspected of being such. As he told Philip even before Mary's death, the religious climate of the new regime was likely to be hostile. A settlement was obviously urgent. Two further bishops died before the end of the year, in addition to Archbishop Pole's earthly departure in 1558, so Canterbury was vacant and so were several other sees that had not been filled because of strained relations with the papacy.[3] There were also a number of Protestants in prison; some had already been convicted and their execution stayed only by Mary's death; some awaited examination. In respect of these the queen did act, or rather allowed Cecil to act on her behalf, and it quickly became known that the persecution of heretics had ceased. Those still in custody were to be released.

Otherwise, Elizabeth sat on her hands, in conformity with the best advice that she was receiving. Several memoranda addressed to the queen at this juncture survive, apparently offered as spontaneous counsel. One is by Sir Nicholas Throgmorton, one by Armigal Waad, and two others are anonymous. None are by Cecil, but the two known authors were both his friends and all four came from a position close to that which he was known to occupy.[4] All were Protestant, to varying degrees, all urged caution, and each argued for a parliamentary settlement to precede any decisive action on Elizabeth's part. This unanimity is suspicious, because it might have been suspected that someone would have made a strong case for the status quo, while another could well have argued for an immediate declaration of godly intent.

Had all this advice really been spontaneous, that is probably what would have happened, but clearly it was not. Someone was orchestrating a careful campaign, and it is fairly obvious that that person was William Cecil. Several years later he acknowledged that Feria had realized what he was up to, and had even accused him. 'I must confess,' he wrote 'that I am thereof guilty, although not at fault.'[5] Cecil was clearly proud of what he considered to have been a significant achievement, but it is possible that he was deceiving himself, because in matters of such importance, it was the queen who made the decisions, not her secretary; and by accident or design, this campaign was very much what she wanted to hear. By the time that parliament met on 23 January 1559, Elizabeth knew what she wanted to achieve, and two separate bills were prepared, one restoring the royal supremacy, more or less as Henry VIII had exercised it, and the other restoring the Protestant uniformity of her brother's reign, with a few minor concessions of a conservative kind. These bills were drafted by a council committee in which Cecil played a prominent part, but it was one thing to draft legislation, and quite another to get it through, even when the queen was known to support it.[6]

The House of Commons in this first parliament of the reign was no more 'packed' than most. Councillors used their influence to secure favourable elections, and those who were eligible sat themselves, but about a third of the members had sat in Mary's last parliament, which meant that the ratio of 'old' to 'new' parliament men was about the same as usual. Those gentlemen who had gone into exile for their faith had not, for the most part, yet returned, and even their clerical friends were still scarce. In these circumstances the lack of serious opposition to the government's religious programme is truly remarkable. Either the Roman Church was not as popular as it has been represented, or its popularity was at a lower social level.

The House of Lords was a different matter. There the surviving bishops, ably marshalled by Nicholas Heath, mustered a solid and principled resistance to both supremacy and uniformity. But the churchmen had been in a minority ever since Henry VIII had removed the mitred abbots, and in January 1559 they were further depleted by death and non-appointment. They numbered only some 13 or 14 in a House of about 60, so their effectiveness in opposition depended upon the number of lay peers who would support them. Over the Supremacy Bill these numbered no more than half a dozen (including the Marquis of Winchester) and the measure passed without a division. Uniformity—that is, the measure introducing full Protestantism—was, however, a different matter. Here the conservative lobby numbered about 20, and the Bill was in serious danger of defeat when parliament was prorogued for Easter. William Cecil masterminded the debates on these measures in the Commons, and Nicholas Bacon (as lord keeper) in the House of Lords. Each was the subject of complex debates and discussions, which kept Cecil endlessly busy, but as Easter approached it looked seriously as though an impasse had been reached.[7] Would Elizabeth accept supremacy without uniformity and dissolve the parliament—or would she try again? Acting on the advice of her chief councillors, she decided to try again, which was why parliament was prorogued instead of being dissolved.

During the recess, something had to be done to shift opinion in the House of Lords, and a conference of divines was set up at Westminster. Whether this was Cecil's idea, or Bacon's, or the queen's own is not clear, but Cecil drafted the announcement, and Bacon presided over the debates. Elizabeth, it was declared, 'having heard of diversity of opinions in certain matters of religion' had chosen a number of 'the best learned of either part' to confer together and to reach some 'amicable agreement'. It appears that Nicholas Heath, as the leading incumbent bishop, supported the scheme, perhaps because he was deceived by the specious rhetoric or perhaps because he was anxious to shift responsibility.[8] He did not take part himself. Given the circumstances, it is unlikely that amicable concord was either looked for or expected. The intention was to discredit or reduce Catholic opposition in the House of Lords, and that was achieved after a couple of days by tempting the Catholic disputants into a procedural indiscretion. Having agreed to submit certain responses in writing, they then demurred, apparently suspecting a deception. After being duly summoned to obey the rules, and still refusing, bishops White of Winchester and Watson of Lincoln were consigned to the Tower for contempt, and the debates ended inconclusively.[9]

For some obscure reason, Feria believed that this constituted a Catholic victory, and declared that it had 'greatly encouraged' them, while 'throwing the heretics into some confusion'. The source of his information is not known, because the tangible outcome of the fiasco was that when parliament reconvened after Easter, two of the most prominent Catholic protagonists in the Lords were missing. Opposition to the Bill of Uniformity continued, but Bacon now felt that he could take the risk of putting it to the vote. It passed by the narrowest possible margin, and its opponents, shifting the debate from parliament to the council, did their best to persuade the queen to veto it. Since it represented her own wishes, there was never much chance of that, but we are told that the protagonists on either side were Winchester and Cecil.[10] While the debate raged, parliament continued to sit, preserving at least the appearance that the discussions in council were real and that the queen might change her mind. If that was the case, Cecil and his friends prevailed in council as they had done in the House, and when parliament was eventually dissolved on 8 May, Elizabeth gave her assent to both religious measures. Cecil's old friend the Duchess of Suffolk was bitterly disappointed by what she saw as a compromise, 'Wherefore I am forced to say with the prophet Eli, how long halt ye between two opinions …'[11]

Catherine was entitled to her rebuke. She had been in exile for her faith while Cecil had sat quietly at home, but in terms of the politics of early 1559, she was wrong, while he (and the queen) were right. They had created a settlement that, with a lot of effort and a certain amount of good luck, could be made to work.

By instinct or sound information, the duchess thought that she knew who was responsible for that settlement and realized that, whatever the underlying realities, it would be Cecil who would now have the main say in staffing the new church and setting the process of conformity on its way. There was a good deal of mutual suspicion between the secretary and the returning exiles who were, by the summer of 1559, mostly back in England. This was partly because of unspoken reproaches about his Nicodemism and partly because the new church, although undeniably Protestant in doctrine, had 'as to ceremonies and maskings ... a little too much foolery'. In other words, the liturgical concessions in the *Book of Common Prayer*, which Elizabeth had made partly to suit her own taste and partly as a gesture to prevailing conservative opinion, were unacceptable to 'the hotter sort'.[12] This meant that Cecil would have to exercise all his famous powers of persuasion and tread delicately.

Typically, he set about his task by drawing up lists. The first, which has been dated between March and May 1559, consists of a list of 'Spiritual men without promotion' and a list of bishoprics and other benefices; the second, similarly dated to late June, consists of a list of 16 bishoprics, most of them with a valuation, and a list of 19 names headed by 'Dr. [Mathew] Parker'. Neither of these documents is written in Cecil's distinctive italic hand, but he annotated the second and was clearly responsible for both.[13] Meanwhile a royal visitation was in progress, the main purpose of which was to extract subscriptions to the Acts of Supremacy and Uniformity. The new Prayer Book came into compulsory use on 24 June and the visitation was conducted by a variety of local commissions, the personnel of which were in theory selected by the council, but in practice largely by Bacon and Cecil. As a result 15 sees were vacated by deprivation between June and October 1559, and a number of deaneries, prebends and other senior appointments similarly became available.[14] Among rank-and-file clergy the subscription rate was much higher and only about 300 ordinary benefices were vacated in the same way, some of them held in plurality by senior clerics. Meanwhile, the traditional revenues of First Fruits and Tenths returned to the Church by Mary were resumed by the crown, and the religious houses that had reappeared under the Catholic queen were dissolved, thus annulling a large part of the late queen's will and bringing a landed income of some £3000 a year to Elizabeth.[15]

Elizabeth's intentions with regard to the new episcopate need to be distinguished from her attitude towards the Church as a whole. In general a process of Protestant evangelization was both desirable and necessary, and the queen seems to have raised no objection to Cecil's mobilization of his university friends, particularly his 'Cambridge mafia'. As Brett Usher noted recently, one of the characteristics of the men on Cecil's lists, apart from their Cambridge links, was the fact that most of them had been noted preachers in Edward's reign.[16] What therefore happened, almost as soon as the parliament was over and well before the deprivations really began at the end of June, was that Cecil began to negotiate with potential nominees, trying not only to obtain their acquiescence in the new order but also to set up financial packages that would be acceptable to them.

As early as 29 May it was being noted that Parker had been 'marked out' for Canterbury and Grindal for London. Several *congés d'élire*, i.e. royal licences providing for the election of new bishops, were issued on 22 June, but they were only the beginning of the story, because Parker at first refused nomination. When John Aylmer issued his *Harborowe* against Knox's *First Blast of the Trumpet,* he spelled out the compromise position that the secretary was aiming for:

> COME OF[F] *you bishops, away with your superfluities, yield up your thousands, be content with hundreds as they be in other reformed churches, where be as great learned men as you are. Let your portion be priestlike and not princelike* ...[17]

This could be described as modified episcopacy and was probably realistic. Elizabeth wanted bishops, but she wanted them 'good cheap', while Cecil, starting from the same position was forced by his labours at the coal face to recognize that good men were not to be recruited by such parsimony. He was also confronted with the need to find candidates who were acceptable to her majesty. About a quarter of the July list, assuming that to have been the basis for the original suggestions, appears to have been rejected. By October Cecil had only five bishops in place, none of whom were yet consecrated. The only redeeming feature was that one of those five was Canterbury. However, even that was not much gain if he could not be consecrated, and at the end of September Cuthbert Tunstall finally rejected the Oath of Supremacy, thus making Parker's consecration in accordance with the existing statutes impossible. Cecil was under pressure from all sides, because the queen now chose to believe (perhaps rightly) that she had been misled by her secretary over the issue of episcopal income and now found herself faced with no option but an ignominious retreat. This was finally effected by a letter to the lord treasurer and barons of the exchequer on 26 October and, although the issues of Exchanges and First Fruits did not go away, they became thereafter manageable.

The next critical issue was to secure the consecration of Parker as archbishop, so that other installations could proceed with some semblance of due form. A commission set up in October eventually came up with a new set of statutes, and it was under those that his sacring was eventually achieved on 17 December, with the assistance of such duly ordained bishops as were prepared to be available — Barlow and Scory, who had held Hereford and Bath and Wells under Edward and were nominated to Chichester and Hereford respectively, and Miles Coverdale, who had formerly held Exeter but did not feature further under the new regime.[18]

Meanwhile, Cecil struggled to fill the remainder of the bench. He produced at least two more lists, one in October and one in December, and these gained a few more nominations. The negotiations were complex and frequently frustrating, but Cecil persevered, dealing with the queen, his fellow councillors and the nominees themselves with infinite skill and patience. William May was duly elected to York in August, but by the time that happened he had already been dead for five days. The secretary's relative lack of activity in this ongoing matter during 1560 is probably explained by the crisis created by Robert Dudley, which we have already noted. Even when Elizabeth was concentrating on business, filling her bench of bishops did not usually have a high priority and, since it was virtually impossible to blame her directly, Cecil found himself saddled (even by Archbishop Parker, who should have known better) with responsibility for the very situation that he was straining every nerve to correct.

The first Elizabethan bench, which was largely completed by 1561, was a very mixed bag. Some were first-rate scholars and excellent pastors, others were conformists or men of obscure pedigree; some had been prominent exiles, others had remained in England. The one thing that they all had in common was a willingness to serve the Church upon the terms that were laid down. Parker was a good choice for Archbishop, as was Grindal for London or Horne for Winchester. Others, such as John Parkhurst at Norwich, became famous for their ineptitude, while William Alley at Exeter was virtually a Lutheran and was theologically out of step with his colleagues and a constant embarrassment to his superiors.[19] The management of this diverse team in an ecclesiastical sense was the responsibility of the archbishop, when Elizabeth did not pre-empt him or take the wind out of his sails. But insofar as they were landlords, patrons, commissioners of the peace, members of the House of Lords or secular administrators, they remained the concern of the privy council, and most particularly of the secretary. He dealt with the exchequer on their behalf, found securities when they were unable to do so, and conveyed the queen's temporal instructions as tactfully as he was able.

Cecil also had an evangelical position in respect of the episcopate, which gave a degree of ambiguity to his relationship with them. While he supported them in principle and recognized their legitimate financial concerns, he was opposed to what he called 'prelacy'—that is, any hint of pomp or display in the discharge of their duties. He believed that 'worldliness' was a snare into which several erstwhile zealous evangelicals had fallen. Years later he wrote to Archbishop Whitgift, 'I see such worldliness in many that were otherwise affected before they came to cathedral churches chairs, that I fear the places alter the men … few there be that do better being bishops … than being preachers they did …'[20]

Part of the trouble was that Parker was a shade too conservative for him. That quality in the archbishop that made him most agreeable to the queen frequently set him at odds with her secretary. By 1566 there was a clear division on the bench, with the more evangelical bishops, such as Grindal and Horne, equally out of sympathy with Parker's policy. The archbishop chose to make an issue out of the wearing, or rather not wearing, of vestments, and in March of that year suspended 37 incumbents for non-conformity. This conflict centred on London. Parker called a conference at Lambeth, to which he summoned all pastors and curates within the City. Bacon and Cecil were also invited, because the course upon which he was determined could have left many London benefices without incumbents and that would have been a matter of direct concern to the civil authorities.

## THE VESTMENTS CONTROVERSY, 1565

S IR, I [ Archbishop Parker ] send your honour [ William Cecil ]
a book of articles, partly of old agreed on amongst us. And partly of
late these three or four days considered, which be either in papers fasted
on as ye see, or new written by secretary hand. Because it is the first
view, not fully digested, I thought good to send it to your honour to
peruse, to know your judgement, and so to return it that it may be fair
written and presented. The devisors were only the bishops of London,
Winchester, Ely, Lincoln and myself. [ i.e. Edmund Grindal, Robert
Horne, Richard Cox, Nicholas Bullingham ]

This day in the afternoon we be agreed to have conference with
[ Richard ] Sampson, [ Lawrence ] Humphrey and four other of the
ministers in London, to understand their reasons etc., if your honour will
step over to us, as it please you.

To be prescribed in preaching, to have no matter in religion spoken of,
is thought far unreasonable, specially seeing so many adversaries as by
their books plentifully had in the court from beyond the seas, do impugn
the verity of our religion.

... I earnestly pray your honour to obtain a private letter from the
Queen's Majesty to my Lord of London, to execute laws and
injunctions, which he sayth, if he be so charged, he will out of hand see
reformation in all London; and ye know there is the most disorder, and
there is the matter almost won through the realm. I pray you earnestly,
expeditiously to procure these letters, for he is now in a good mood to
execute the laws, and it will work much more than ye would think etc.

This third of March [ 1565 ]
Your honour's
MATTEU. CANTUAR.

[ Taken from J. Bruce (ed.), *The Correspondence of Mathew Parker*, 1853, p. 233.
The Articles referred to are the 'Advertisements, partly for due order in the
public administration of Common Prayer and using the holy sacraments, and
partly for the apparel of all persons ecclesiastical', published by Edward Cardwell
in *Documentary Annals of the Reformed Church of England*, I (1839), p. 287. ]

The assembly was then confronted with an ultimatum—either sub-
scribe to the 'advertisements', i.e. the articles covering apparel and
other Church matters, or not. Sixty-one subscribed, and the thirty-
seven who refused were suspended.[21] Disorders followed and an

intense pamphlet warfare. Cecil's duty to the queen impelled him to declare for obedience, whatever his private feelings. The dissidents appealed to the theologian Heinrich Bullinger, Zwingli's successor in Zurich, but he advised them not to disrupt an essentially godly church for a matter so intrinsically unimportant. His words carried weight, and in August 1566 Edmund Grindal (himself no great enthusiast for vestments) was able to write to Bullinger:

> IT IS SCARCELY *credible how much this controversy about things of no importance has disturbed our churches, and still in great measure continues to do. Many of the more learned clergy seemed to be on the point of forsaking their ministry. Many of the people also had it in contemplation to withdraw from us, and set up private meetings; but however most of them through the mercy of God, have now returned to a better mind.*[22]

Those who did not return, however, now moved in the direction of open non-conformity, and on 19 June 1567 over a hundred gathered at the Plumbers Hall in London to hold a conventicle. The ringleaders were interrogated, and they made it clear that from their standpoint, vestments were not 'things indifferent', but were directly contrary to scriptural injunction. In so doing they were placing the authority of scripture in direct opposition to the authority of the monarch. When it was put like that, of course, Cecil had no option. Under the royal supremacy, secular and ecclesiastical discipline became one and the same thing and, although he would gladly have avoided the confrontation that Parker had provoked, once it had happened he defended the archbishop's authority as the representative of the queen in that context. Although he continued to sympathize with those who sought for further reform in the church, those who separated from it became a small but persistent headache.

The big problem remained the Catholics, and in that respect the series of crises that erupted between 1568 and 1571 proved ultimately beneficial. The incident of the Genoese treasure and of the Low Countries trade embargo clarified relations with Spain, which was now identified as the greatest potential threat abroad. Mary Queen of Scots, an ambiguous figure on her first arrival in England, had become, via the Norfolk marriage negotiation and (as we shall see) the Ridolfi plot, an unambiguous threat.[23] And the English Catholics, through the rebellion of the northern earls and the bull *Regnans in Excelsis,* were now (however reluctantly) a subversive element. These developments served to clarify both protestant identity and the unity of the council and to give what Stephen Alford has called 'a providential edge' to all the secretary's political thinking. After 1569 Cecil's position as the queen's most trusted and confidential adviser was never again challenged, and both Archbishop Parker and the Earl of Leicester acknowledged that fact. As a result, in terms of ecclesiastical policy they were closer together in 1571 than either before or afterwards. Archbishop Thomas Young of York had died in the summer of 1568 and Elizabeth (as usual) hesitated over his replacement. Parker had begun to canvas Grindall's claim as early as June 1569, but it was not until April 1570 that he was formally translated.[24]

The move was symbolic of the ascendancy that the 'evangelical party' had now achieved in government, and when the Earl of Sussex was replaced as president of the council of the north two years later by the Earl of Huntingdon, what Patrick Collinson has called 'the need for the kind of administrative resolution which was only to be looked for from committed protestants' had at last been fully recognized.[25] In other words, Cecil's view that only those 'whose convictions remained firmly wedded to the idea of further reform' could most effectively defend the established Church. His vision of the Church was dynamic rather than static, and in that he differed from his mistress, who regarded the settlement achieved in 1559 as definitive. She was also totally committed to the view that God had entrusted the guidance of his Church in England to her personally, and that it was she who would have to render account for that stewardship. That her will must ultimately prevail in all issues of controversy was thus a matter of conscience rather than convenience, and by 1570 Cecil had recognized that fact. It would continue to inform his responses after the consensus of 1570 had disappeared.

Grindal's translation to York meant that London was now vacant, and London was the most demanding of all episcopal assignments, excepting only Canterbury itself. Parker seems to have favoured John Aylmer, but both Leicester and Cecil were vehemently opposed. John Jewel, who would probably have been their first choice, was already a sick man—he was to die the following year—and could not have coped with so demanding a place. This left Edwin Sandes of Worcester as the front runner, and the only candidate upon whom both the brokers could agree. Perhaps impressed by their unanimity, Elizabeth appears to have given her consent without difficulty. Sandes, however, did not appreciate the honour which was being done him and declined the promotion.[26] Both Leicester and Cecil were extremely annoyed; indeed, the secretary seems to have been incandescent with rage. He had, he pointed out (perhaps mendaciously), taken the trouble to obtain the 'calling and consent' of the people of London, or at least of some of them. What he had actually done is not clear, but some sort of a 'calling' had been obtained, and this was obviously a matter that Sandes took very seriously. Leicester's anger he might have endured, or even a hostile wag of the royal finger, but to upset Cecil and disappoint the people of London was more than he could live with. So he allowed himself to be persuaded, and his election received the royal assent on 1 July.[27]

The domino effect of Thomas Young's death now required that the see of Worcester be filled, and again Leicester and Cecil worked together. Their preferred choice, James Calfhill, was academically able and may have been in exile during Mary's reign. He had also preached openly against Parker's 'advertisements' as recently as February 1566, but he was not beneficed in London and no action had been taken against him.[28] He was offered the see of Worcester in July, and apparently accepted, but he then died at Bocking in Essex during August without going anywhere near his diocese. The somewhat limp response to this misfortune was yet another translation, this time of the ageing Nicholas Bullingham from Lincoln. Unlike Calfhill, and more particularly Sandes, there is no documentation to tell us who was responsible for this—or why. It does not fit with any forward policy for which either Leicester or Cecil might have been responsible and it looks suspiciously as though Bullingham had petitioned the queen directly to be relieved of so large and troublesome a see, and this was her response. Bullingham was a Worcestershire man and that may also have been a consideration. He compounded for his first fruits in February 1571 and was shown no particular favour.[29] His move, however, now left Lincoln in need of an incumbent.

The elevation of Thomas Cooper, a scholar and reformer who was already Dean of Christ Church, may well have been Elizabeth's own choice in spite of the fact that he was not only married but at odds with an unsatisfactory spouse. Irrespective of her well-known utterances in favour of clerical celibacy, the queen did not show any particular reluctance to promote married men to the bench.[30] Cooper was later to be famously (and unfairly) pilloried by Martin Marprelate.

The remaining episcopal appointments of the next two years—Richard Barnes to Carlisle, William Bradbridge to Exeter, Edmund Guest to Salisbury and Edmund Freke to Rochester—all reflected in different ways Cecil's successful manipulation of the ecclesiastical agenda. Only Barnes was in any obvious way a client of his; and he testified himself that Cecil was his 'only preferer' to Carlisle, where his appointment was confirmed on 1 July, within weeks of the death of John Best.[31] In 1577, when he was translated to Durham, he wrote to Cecil, who was by then lord treasurer, 'I have served my seven years, and I trust discharged the promise you then made unto her highness on my behalf...' Barnes was an able and energetic man, and not afflicted with the angular personality that characterized some of his colleagues. Bradbridge was an old man, and his promotion may have had more to do with the desire to shift him out of the deanery of Salisbury, where he had been something of a drag, than with any expectation of a fruitful (or long) incumbency in the west. If Brett Usher is right, Edmund Freke's appointment to Rochester, and subsequent translation to Norwich (1575), may have had more to do with the forceful personality of his wife than with any qualities of his own.[32] In terms of any evangelical agenda the picture is a confused one, because at Rochester he was an active supporter of the 'prophecyings' that were shortly to be so controversial, whereas he suppressed them in Norwich and generally gained the reputation of being a strict disciplinarian. As one of his victims in Norfolk was to declare, 'worldly dignity and vainglory [had] led him to do against his own conscience, and wished him to look if it were not so.'[33]

Freke was not the only person to be confronted with that delicate predicament. The task of trying to maintain some evangelical momentum within the confines laid down by the queen's preferences and by her own highly personalized interpretation of her function as supreme governor was one of the greatest that her secretary had to perform. However, in this connection his old hostility to the Earl of Leicester was forgotten, just as the latter put his flirtations with the Spaniards behind him. They did not always agree over individual cases, but their agenda was now the same, and this led to a large measure of cooperation.

One of the clearest manifestations of this was that the earl made no attempt to undermine Cecil's efforts at the exchequer on behalf of newly appointed bishops. Left to himself, Lord Treasurer Winchester probably would have done so, because raising revenue was his priority. However, such was the secretary's influence with Elizabeth that for about 15 years after 1561 the strict provisions of the act for First Fruits and Tenths were virtually abandoned. During that time the only bishop required to produce sureties was Richard Cheyney of Gloucester, and that may have been because he held the see *in commendam* with Bristol.[34] The largest concession, in financial terms, was that given to Sandes when he eventually accepted London, because his first fruits — which were worth about £1000 to the crown — were also remitted.[35] It is unlikely that the bishop would have had any success if he had tried to persuade the queen directly that this was the price of his acceptance, so it seems that Cecil was again the intermediary, and his pleasure at Sandes' acceptance may have been somewhat reduced by the scale of the necessary concession. The only translation of these years not so sweetened was that of Grindal to York, because he was charged the full amount, and in six monthly instalments rather than the annual ones that were granted to the others. This lack of generosity was not caused by any hint of disfavour from Cecil, Leicester or the queen, but rather (it would seem) because he had only recently been exonerated from the balance of the debt (about 25 per cent) that he still owed after having originally compounded for London.[36]

One of the most remarkable features of the changes from Catholicism to Protestantism in England, both in 1549 and in 1559, is the absence of persecution. In the first case the king was a minor, and the government may well have felt that it was taking sufficient risks without provoking unnecessary resistance. But Elizabeth's regime was no weaker than Mary's had been at the same stage, and their policies were completely contrasted. Neither wasted any time in securing parliamentary endorsement for their chosen course, both removed unsympathetic bishops from the bench and both prompted a few prominent individuals to take refuge in flight. There the similarities come to an end. No one died for their faith in the first five (indeed the first ten) years of Elizabeth's reign, whereas Mary's holocaust is notorious. The persecution that did ensue later in the reign, which was real enough, was almost entirely political in its inspiration and owed its incidence partly to the threat posed by Mary Stuart and partly to the papal bull of 1570. This contrast must be largely attributed to the different personalities of the two women in charge, but it was also partly due to their advisers. Stephen Gardiner felt that he had a point to prove, and demonstrated his zeal by blaming the heretics for everything that went wrong, from Northumberland's conspiracy to the Wyatt rebellion. He felt no threat from extremists on his own side, because he was as extreme as any. Cecil's attitude was quite different, although it might be thought that he had the same point to prove. He set about a patient game of persuasion, using the laws (which were not, in any case, very severe) only when necessary. One of the first things that he did was to commission John Jewel, almost before he had had time to settle as Bishop of Salisbury, to write an Apology for the English Church. In May 1561 he wrote to Nicholas Throgmorton, 'I have caused an Apology to be written, but not printed, in the name of the whole clergy, which surely is wisely, learnedly and gravely written, but I stay the publication of it until it may be further pondered.'[37]

It was printed the following January and some, including Throgmorton, found it disappointing. As a refutation of popish arguments, it was fine—but the Protestant radicals got scarcely a mention. Unlike Gardiner, Cecil was constrained to fight his war on two fronts because, although Rome was the main enemy, the zealots on his own side were also an embarrassment. Vestments were to become the focal issue, but they were not the only one, and the perpetual clamour of zealous preachers against those whom they considered to be inadequate, whether in the Church or in the government, became a considerable nuisance. Of course, it was also these troublesome preachers who were his most effective allies in dealing with the conservatives. Cecil, by virtue of his position, was bound to put obedience first, and when he could persuade one of these zealots into even the most minimal gestures of conformity, he was often willing to promote him.

In this he did not necessarily see eye to eye with the queen, for whom the imperial powers of the English crown were the most important principle in the religious settlement. She was equally afraid of 'papists', but much less suspicious of conforming conservatives. Being more concerned than her secretary not to upset such people, she was even more suspicious of the 'radical left', and often seems to have blocked Cecil's efforts to use them in what seemed to him appropriate circumstance.

We are, however, talking about tactical disagreements rather than strategic ones. Archbishop Parker frequently found himself unable to get on with his job in the way in which he would clearly have preferred. It was part of his terms of appointment that he was answerable to the supreme governor, and she was not always sympathetic to his methods, but he also found himself constrained to deal with Cecil and, to a lesser extent, with Robert Dudley.[38] It was Cecil who wrote to him in August 1561, expressing the queen's disturbance at clerical behaviour in Essex and Suffolk, behaviour that had been encouraged by the episcopal vacancy at Norwich. The archbishop was given the unenviable task of trying to placate both the queen and the clergy. He chose, inevitably, to placate the queen, and then wrote to Cecil complaining that his clergy found him 'too sharp and earnest' whereas Elizabeth had accused him of being 'too soft and easy'.[39] It was a dilemma that was to plague him throughout his incumbency, but at least he felt that he could bend William Cecil's ear as one who was familiar with the same problem.

Parker and Cecil were both equally the queen's servants, both bound to advise and obey. They found her baffling and elusive, but the evidence suggests that she did listen to them, and often did as they suggested, although that could never be guaranteed. Neither felt forced by his conscience either into resignation (as we have seen Cecil contemplated over a different issue) or into the kind of calculated defiance that eventually put paid to Archbishop Grindal's career. Parker, however, had only the ecclesiastical side of his mistress's eccentricities to deal with. For Cecil the Church and its fate were perpetually interwoven with questions of the queen's marriage—and through that issue with just about every option in foreign policy that was open to the queen and her council. Whether he liked it or not, Cecil was bound to take what has been dubbed a 'holistic' approach to the affairs of state.

# CHAPTER 5

# French Suitors and
# the Queen of Scots

IN NOVEMBER 1558 England was at war with France. Both sides were financially exhausted and peace negotiations were already under way. They were temporarily suspended when the news of Mary's death arrived, because the English commissioners' mandate had expired with the passing of their sovereign, and it was not known whether Elizabeth would renew it. She had very little option, because England could not afford to be stranded if Spain settled without her, and Sir John Mason, Mary's treasurer of the chamber who still retained his job, wrote to Cecil within days of Elizabeth's accession, 'the first and principal point is to think upon the peace'.[1] At first, the queen seemed to be in an awkward frame of mind. She would dearly have liked to start her reign by redeeming the fortress town of Calais, which her sister had lost. However, as Mason pointed out, it was idle to 'stick upon Calais as though we had the Frenchmen at commandment' and, although Philip was willing to argue for its return, he was not going to lose his peace for the sake of his allies. Elizabeth blustered, but had to accept the loss of the town, albeit with a face-saving formula about its eventual return—which nobody took seriously, least of all the French. So at the end of March 1559 the Treaty of Cateau-Cambrésis with France was signed, and England was officially at peace.

However, war was only the most extreme form of foreign policy, and the new queen was given very little time in which to decide what her attitude was going to be to the rest of England's neighbours. Mary of Scotland (plate 14) and her husband the Dauphin Francis (courtesy king of Scotland) immediately laid claim to her throne, quartering the arms of England with their own.[2] In theory that claim was abandoned at Cateau-Cambrésis, but it remained as a potential threat—especially when Francis succeeded his father as king of France in July 1559. It quickly became apparent in a Europe that was increasingly divided along confessional, rather than dynastic, lines that the English religious settlement would be crucial.

Elizabeth faced the logic of this with reluctance. Having made peace with France, she had no particular desire to fall out with Philip, or with the queen regent of Scotland. Cecil, however, embraced it, if not with enthusiasm then at least with conviction. As his frequent notes and memoranda make clear, he saw the state of Britain clearly in relation to Europe, and the fate of England depending upon its faith in the true reformed religion.[3] The hostility of the pope he took for granted, especially after the English ambassador Edward Carne's credentials were withdrawn in February 1559. Although historians may neatly divide policy into 'foreign' and 'domestic' for convenience of study, no such division in fact existed. The queen's marriage, her religious settlement, relations with Scotland, France, the Empire and Spain, the threat of Catholic insurrection at home and the perennial problem of Ireland were all interwoven. The council had to discuss and to offer advice on all these issues and it is important to realize that, although they were divided, there were no factions, either there or in the court, either at this time or later. There were personal rivalries, even animosities, but no settled groupings, and men who might be at variance on some issues would be in agreement on others.[4]

Even before the war with France was concluded, the situation in Scotland was pressing. The history of English intervention north of the border since James V's death had been an unhappy one. Henry's so-called 'rough wooing' of the Scots, designed to impose on them a marriage between Mary Stuart and Prince Edward, had not only failed in its purpose, it had also strengthened Scotland's 'auld alliance' with France and the hand of the Scottish Cardinal David Beaton against the Protestants—who were now generally seen as an English fifth column.[5] Protector Somerset's victory at Pinkie had resulted indirectly in the assassination of Cardinal Beaton, but had produced no other favourable developments from an English point of view. The French ascendancy in Scotland did not make them loved, but it could not be challenged, least of all by any pro-English party, and when Mary of Guise (mother of Mary Stuart) became regent in 1554, it looked as though a revitalized Catholic Church would also overcome

[1] JANE CECIL (*c.*1500–88), née Heckington, wife to Richard Cecil and the mother of William Cecil. She is depicted in her later years, about 1580, in this anonymous portrait in the Anglo-Dutch style from Burghley House.

[2] WILLIAM CECIL (1520–98), later 1st Baron Burghley (*below*), in an unattributed contemporary portrait. He devoted his life to government service, putting the Cecil family at the centre of national life.

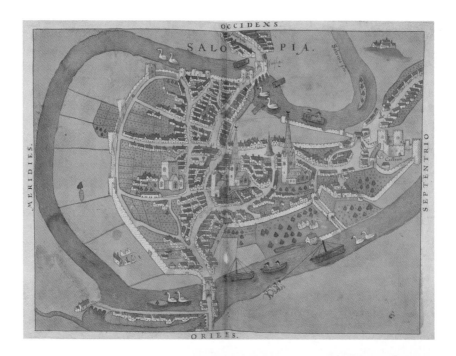

[3] THE TOWN of Shrewsbury near the Welsh border. With Welsh antecedents himself, William Cecil commissioned this map for his copy of Christopher Saxton's *Atlas* (1579), for which he gave Saxton access to government records.

[4] WILLIAM CECIL, around 1560. The somewhat primitive portrait belongs to New College, Oxford, and depicts Cecil in unusually robust health.

[5] EDWARD SEYMOUR (c.1506–52),
Earl of Hertford and later Duke of
Somerset, the 'lord protector' to
Edward VI, who promoted William
Cecil to his service. The portrait is
attributed to Holbein the Younger.

[6] THE BOY KING Edward VI (*right*),
striking a manly pose in the year
of his accession (1547). The artist
is unknown.

[7] ELIZABETH I, regal icon. This
so-called 'Pelican Portrait', *c.* 1575–
80, is by Nicholas Hilliard. The
enduring if complex relationship
between the queen and William
Cecil was fundamental to the
nature of her reign.

[8] ROBERT DUDLEY, Earl of
Leicester (1533–88), portrayed by
Steven van der Muelen, *c.*1565.
He was a courtier and member of
the council, but more importantly
Elizabeth's influential favourite,
a position that often vexed
William Cecil.

[9] WILLIAM CECIL, Lord Burghley (*below*), presides over the Court of Wards and Liveries, a function he carried out from 1561 until his death. It was a lucrative position which passed to his son Robert Cecil.

[10] MILDRED CECIL (*c.*1522–89), née Cooke, the first Lady Burghley and the austere second wife of William Cecil and mother to Robert. The portrait is attributed to Hans Eworth (*fl.*1540–73).

[11, 12] Burghley House in Stamford, Lincolnshire (*above and above right*). Inherited by William Cecil from his father, it later passed to Thomas Cecil. It was embellished mainly to William's designs between 1555 and 1587, and the clock tower bears his coat of arms.

[13] William Cecil, Lord Burghley (*below*), in his finery as lord treasurer, in a painting attributed to Marcus Gheeraerts the Younger (*c.*1561–1635).

[14] AN UNUSUALLY delicate and full-faced Mary, Queen of Scots (1542–87), attributed to François Clouet (c.1510–72). Mary was Elizabeth's rival, tormentor and eventual victim.

[15] A CONTEMPORARY sketch of seating arrangements for the trial of Mary, Queen of Scots, at Fotheringhay Castle, September 1586 (left). The outcome ended the prospects of the woman long regarded by William Cecil as a danger to the state.

Classis Hispanica celeberrima, quæ anno celeberimo. CD.LXXXVIII. inter Galliam Britanniamq Venit. & perÿt.

Graveling     Cais

[16] AN EVOCATIVE depiction of the English fleet in action (*above*) at the Battle of Gravelines (1588), the principal engagement and decisive battle of the Spanish Armada,

from *The Holy Bull and Crusado of Rome* published in the same year. Weather, luck, Spanish disorganization and English tactics all contributed to saving England from invasion.

[17] THE TEXT of Queen Elizabeth's famous charge to William Cecil in 1558 (*below*) on creating him her secretary (*see* transcription on page 54) [TNA SP12/1, NO.7].

the Protestant challenge. This had not happened, partly because the old church had made too many concessions to retain any credibility and partly because England reverted to Catholicism, thus ending the association between the reformers and the old enemy.[6] Paradoxically, Mary of Guise had encouraged Protestantism by her attempts to be judicious and fair minded—and Protestants were not minded to reciprocate. Shortly after Mary Tudor's death the reformers, led by Lord James Stuart and the 5th Earl of Argyll, began to press for further concessions to be made in the parliament, and this time the regent resisted.

The atmosphere became tense, and when an attempt was made in May 1559 to accuse several preachers in Perth of heresy, there was an explosion. John Knox preached an inflammatory sermon, and there was an outburst of iconoclasm. Perth, Angus and the Mearns were in uproar, and the regent had little choice but to treat the movement as a rebellion.[7] This was welcome news to Cecil who, in spite of the fact that Scotland had been included in the peace with France, was looking with acute anxiety at the French presence in Scotland and had been taking pains to strengthen the northern border from the moment that he had assumed responsibility for such matters. The best thing that could happen in Scotland, from an English point of view, was that the Scottish Protestants should seize control of the government and expel the French, preferably without any help from south of the border.

It was partly this thought that inspired Cecil to speed John Knox, who was on his way back from Geneva in April 1559, to his homeland —that and the fact that he was *persona non grata* in England thanks to his outburst against female monarchy. Knox was not particularly grateful, but he knew the politics of the situation. On 11 April he wrote from Dieppe:

> MY ONLY THIRST IS, *in passing to my country, to communicate with you and with some others such things as willingly I list not to commit to paper, neither yet to the knowledge of many ... And this, I suppose, should be no less profitable to her Grace [ Elizabeth ] and to all godly within England, than it would be pleasing to me ...*[8]

His contempt for Cecil as a former conformist was but thinly veiled, but the secretary was in no mood to take offence, particularly when he appreciated the effect of Knox's return and understood that the Lords of the Congregation of Jesus Christ, as the rebels called themselves, were anxious to talk to him. It soon transpired that such talks might well be necessary because, in spite of their momentum and the distinguished nature of their leadership, the Protestants were by no means carrying all before them. The principal stumbling block was the presence of several thousand French troops, who provided solid support for the regent and encouraged the loyalists to rally to her. On 14 June Sir James Croft wrote from Berwick that virtually all the Scottish nobility had joined together to promote the word of God; but the truth was never that simple, and various well-placed Scots were soon talking of the need to confer with Cecil and were asking discreet questions about what sort of assistance they might expect in their worthy cause.[9] There was talk of bringing the young (and Protestant) Earl of Arran back from France and little hints that Elizabeth might consider marrying him.

Cecil's main line of communication at this stage was via Sir Henry Percy to Sir William Kirkaldy of Grange who spoke (somewhat indirectly) for the Scottish lords. The secretary disingenuously sought clarification of the lords' aims, and assured Kirkaldy discreetly that, 'rather than see an ancient nation oppressed by foreign power, when her nobles seek to maintain Christian religion', then England would come to their aid. Meanwhile he wrote to Croft to say (off the record) that England would provide first encouragement, then money and finally arms, provided the lords could keep their cause alive.[10]

## CECIL EMBOLDENS THE SCOTTISH LORDS, 1559

I MUST NEEDS CONFESS *upon the consideration of the same [your letter of 19th July] ... the two principal points intended by your proceedings be such as all good ... Christian men ought to allow, first to abandon idolatry, next to maintain the liberty of your native country from the thraldom of strangers ... We see here how these miseries have afflicted you, we see how Godly a deed it is to succour you, we perceive also what ways you take therefore; partly you attempt some things yourself, partly you require some promise of aid ... You know your chief adversaries, I mean the popish kirkmen, be noted wise in their generation. They be rich also, whereby they make many friends: by their wit, with false persuasion, by their riches, with corruption. As long as*

*they feel no shortness, nor offence, they be bold, but if they be but once*
*touched with fear, they be great cowards ...*

*   Will you hear of a strange army coming by sea to invade you and seek*
*help against the same and yet permit your adversaries, whom you may*
*expel, keep the landing and strength for the others. Which of these two is*
*easiest, to weaken one number first, or three afterwards? ... Will they*
*favour you in Scotland that burn their own daily in France ... [ 28th*
*July 1559]*

[Extracts taken from TNA SP52/1, NO.77 ]

So far, Elizabeth seems to have concurred with the line that her secretary was taking, but it remained to be seen whether she would continue to do so if such pledges needed to be redeemed. After a flying
start, by August the lords were on the back foot, having been forced to
retreat from Edinburgh. The death of Henry II also significantly altered
the position, because Mary Queen of Scots was now also queen of
France and the likelihood of French reinforcements arriving had greatly
increased. At the same time Cecil backtracked slightly, reminding
himself that military intervention in the north would be a breach of
the recent peace.

The Scottish lords withdrew to regroup, and emerged with a
slightly different strategy—and propaganda to match. Without abandoning their Protestant identity, they shifted their emphasis onto
expelling the French, and the Earl of Argyll offered Cecil the help of
his highlanders in dealing with the perennial problem of Ulster.[11]
Argyll also appealed to the Scottish nobility in general, invoking their
'ancient liberties'—that is, the traditionally aristocratic nature of Scots
government—against what was represented as French tyranny. This
increased his appeal beyond the limited Protestant franchise and had
the additional merit of being more appealing to Elizabeth.

The queen was being less than honest. To the French she disclaimed
any intention of intervening, but by the end of August she was already
sending money to the lords. Cecil, as usual, debated the issue with
himself on paper and came down in favour of intervention. His determination was put to the test early in December, when Maitland of
Lethington arrived at the English court with a plea for armed English
assistance and Argyll's offer of help in Ulster. It may well have been this
offer that settled Cecil's mind, because when the privy council

debated the matter on 27 December, he led the case for intervention. There was a vigorous debate because several councillors, notably Arundel and Winchester, strongly opposed this. Elizabeth hesitated, and then accepted the majority advice.[12] Early in January William Winter was despatched, and the English fleet's arrival in the Firth of Forth on 22 January caused the French, who had been besieging St Andrews, to beat a hasty retreat to Leith. A formal agreement with the Lords of the Congregation then followed, and in February the Duke of Norfolk was sent north with an army to their support.

In achieving this victory, Cecil had made much not only of the needs of English security, but also of the crucial importance of Argyll's assistance in Ireland. In this he was also assisted by Sir Nicholas Throgmorton who, writing from France, placed much emphasis upon the Irish situation, again in the context of the queen's general security. Several factors contributed to the eventual success of this alliance, but the most important had nothing to do with either Scotland or England. The rising domestic tension in France, and particularly the widely resented influence of the Guise brothers, made it virtually impossible for Francis to send assistance to his mother-in-law in the north, so the French troops that she had were all that she was likely to get. Second, Mary of Guise herself fell ill. This combination of circumstances made the failure of the Anglo-Scottish siege of Leith almost irrelevant.

Cecil, of course, had no control over this, but in one respect his wise guidance was extremely important. In spite of Elizabeth's feelings to the contrary, he kept every hint of English imperialism out of the propaganda and discussions.[13] It had been Henry's and Somerset's claims to authority over Scotland that had wrecked English intervention in the north in the 1540s and been fatal to the anglophile party. By insisting that the queen's sole intention was to enable the Scots to govern themselves, Cecil succeeded in laying that ghost and in making a genuine alliance possible. That alliance was not free from mistrust on both sides; each believed that the other might settle with the French and leave them in the lurch, because it was the latter who controlled the agenda. Even before the siege of Leith on 7 May Francis had decided to cut his losses, and a representative had arrived in London to negotiate—or at least propose—a peace.

By the end of May the determination to settle was general to all parties, assisted by the terminal condition of the queen regent's health. Commissioners were appointed to meet either in Newcastle or in Edinburgh, and the English team was led by William Cecil.[14] This was fitting, as the Scottish campaign had been very much his show, but his prospective absence from court raised some anxieties. 'Who', Throgmorton wrote, 'can as well stand fast against the queen's arguments and doubtful devices? Who will speedily resolve the doubtful delays? Who will make despatch of anything?'[15] This was a male perception of Elizabeth's style of government, but as a tribute to Cecil's perceived importance it could hardly be bettered. The secretary, meanwhile, summarized his purposes and prospects in a memorandum. The English were concerned primarily to get the French out of Scotland. The state of government and religion in that country they would leave to the Scots themselves; but they would not settle separately.

> O UR COMMISSIONERS *shall, if they see it needful, and that the Scots cannot obtain to live in freedom of their conscience, persuade with the French that they may so do, or at least that the laws may be suspended against such as live according to their conscience … and so to remain until the end of the next parliament in Scotland. Whereunto, if the French will not be induced and the Scots will not therein accord with the French, then our commissioners shall forbear to conclude with the French.*[16]

After some preliminary discussions in Newcastle, the venue was transferred to Edinburgh to convene on 17 June. News had arrived that the queen regent was at the point of death and that the French in Leith were talking of surrender. By the time that the commissioners met again, Mary of Guise was dead and a temporary truce had suspended hostilities at Leith. Thereafter, the French were conducting a damage-limitation exercise, and Cecil sent blow-by-blow accounts of their progress, both to the queen and to the council in London. The secretary, it seems, was ploughing a lonely furrow; not only was he leading the English delegation, but he was also constantly preoccupied with bolstering their confidence to get the job done. However, since that understanding is derived largely from his own letters, it should perhaps not be taken at face value.

By 5 July the treaty was ready for signature, and both the English and the Scots had got pretty much what they wanted. The French would leave Scotland, and the English would repatriate them; Francis and Mary would cease to use the arms of England; and the Scots (saving their allegiance to their queen) would govern themselves both in secular and religious matters as they thought fit. The English would also leave, and no word was spoken of any claim to overlordship.[17] Elizabeth, hearing which way the wind was blowing, almost sabotaged her representatives' efforts by demanding a large sum in compensation and the return of Calais, but her letter arrived only on the 9th, after the treaty was signed—as it may have been intended to do. As Cecil pointed out in his response, to have raised either of the issues that the queen had now aired would have meant aborting the negotiations. The queen affected to be displeased, and may in fact have been so, because when her secretary returned to court on 28 July, fresh from one of the great negotiating successes of his life, he found his mistress firmly in the arms of Robert Dudley and with thought for nothing else. The consequences of that we have already seen.

Francis and Mary were supposed to ratify the treaty within 60 days, but first neglected and then declined to do so. In the event their displeasure was purely symbolic, because the French had left Scotland and the Scots wasted no time in setting up a system of government to please themselves. They also took advantage of the complete demoralization of the Scottish Catholics to establish an official Protestant kirk, which quickly commanded the allegiance of the Lowlands and, through the influence of the Earl of Argyll, of the southwestern Highlands also. Argyll was rapidly emerging as a key ally in the Anglo-Scottish polity that Cecil, as soon as he picked himself up after the Dudley fiasco, was busily promoting. Elizabeth showed no interest in marrying the Earl of Arran, but that was hardly unexpected and did little to affect the amity that was now developing. Of course, that amity was also preserved by fear that Francis, having refused to ratify the Treaty of Edinburgh, might now be entertaining ambitions of a military return to the north.

In December 1560, however, Francis died and was succeeded by his young brother, Charles IX. The queen mother, Catherine de Medici, became regent, and at the age of 18 Mary Stuart had become a dowager and something of a liability.[18] Both English and Scottish policy now became focused upon the likelihood of her return to her native land; there was not very much else that she could do. Maitland was not alone in viewing the prospect with apprehension. 'Whenever she comes,' he wrote to Cecil in February 1561, 'I believe here will be a mad world. Our exactness and singularity in religion will never concur with her judgements. I think that she will hardly be brought under the rule of our discipline.'[19] Cecil's immediate reaction is not known, but it seems that his main concern was to preserve the amity by strengthening the kirk. Indirectly, the effect was to persuade him to redouble his efforts to persuade the queen to marry. Only by securing the succession in that way could the threat that Mary still presented as a potential heir be removed. His anxiety was not misplaced, because the Scottish Catholics were visibly reviving with the prospect of Mary's return and even sent a mission to her, urging her to come 'with force' and they would meet her with 20,000 men in arms.[20] Whether they could really have mustered even a tenth of that number is immaterial. The threat was there, and was known.

In the event, Mary's actual arrival at Leith on 26 August was something of an anti-climax. The English fleet intercepted her galleys but let them pass, and the Scots were not expecting her. She came ashore under a lowering sky, and John Knox was quick to exploit the symbolism of the Scottish weather. Once settled in Edinburgh, however, Mary at first conducted herself with notable wisdom and discretion. She agreed to keep her religion private and came to terms with the politically dominant Protestant nobles. Cecil kept a close eye on these developments through the English ambassador in Edinburgh, Thomas Randolf, who was accredited to Mary in August 1563. He was in no position to interfere in Scotland's internal politics, but the top item on the agenda was one of international significance — Mary's second marriage. Randolf's instructions bear witness to this priority; 'we have already opened our mind therein,' Elizabeth wrote to her principal secretary, Lethington. Mary shows no sign of having resented the advice of her 'good sister', and indeed appears to have solicited it.[21] Although Elizabeth was in a similar situation, the younger woman expressed her gratitude. The two planned to meet and, although this never happened, relations for several years appeared to be cordial.

There was a general expectation in Scotland that Elizabeth would 'provide' a husband for Mary. 'Divers here have been in hand with me,' Randolf wrote to Cecil at the end of December 1563, 'to know whom the Queen's majesty will give in marriage to the Queen.' By March

1564, however, the latter was growing coy. The memory of her late
husband 'is yet so fresh', she lamented—and in any case, why did
Elizabeth not take her own advice? At the beginning of April the
queen of England came up with a surprising suggestion—why should
not Mary marry Lord Robert Dudley? The idea appears to have grown
upon her during the summer, and may well have been in mind when
she created him Earl of Leicester on 29 September. Hardly had the
ermine settled when she formally proposed him as a husband for the
Scots queen, offering at the same time to recognize Mary's right to the
English succession if she should accept him.[22]

Cecil's role in this development is not very clear, because his letters
to Maitland of Lethington, which constitute our principal source, are
allusive and discreet. His priorities were to preserve the Protestant
ascendancy in Scotland, and with it the friendship that had been
achieved in the wake of the Treaty of Edinburgh (still unratified by
Mary). He was therefore suspicious of the growing strength of Mary's
party, and doubly suspicious of any plan—of which there were several
—to marry her to a Catholic prince. Dudley was (at least in this context) a useful ally, and there might also be advantages in prising him
away from Elizabeth. So reading between the lines we may conclude
that he supported the idea. The Queen of Scots, however, was not
amused at the thought of being fobbed off with her 'dear sister's' ex-
lover. Indeed, she regarded the suggestion as insulting, and relations
between the two women cooled.

Cecil, it seems clear, was deeply suspicious of Mary and her purposes, even when she took firm action against the rebellious Catholic
Gordon family, earls of Huntley, during her progress to Aberdeenshire
in 1562.[23] She went so far as to issue a proclamation forbidding the
public saying of mass, and put several bishops on trial in May 1563 for
ignoring it. However, the secretary's cherished plans for a 'British'
solution, involving Scotland too, to settle tribal disputes in Ulster came
unstuck at about the same time. This was, in a sense, his own fault. He
failed to secure the active support of the Earl of Sussex, the lord lieutenant of Ireland, and thus to mobilize the Dublin government against
the dissident O'Neills.[24] By the time Sussex was replaced by Sir Henry
Sidney in 1565, it was too late. The Earl of Argyll had intervened by
establishing and supporting a MacDonald plantation in Ulster, but he
could not suppress the rising power of Shane O'Neill, and the

lieutenant, who could have done so, did not. When the O'Donnells and the MacDonalds were defeated at the Battle of Glentaisie in 1565, the whole Gaelic world was destabilized and Argyll, disgusted with the lack of support that he had received, withdrew his cooperation.[25]

Meanwhile, Mary's search for a suitable husband went on. Despite pious comments about her husband's memory, by 1564 the Scots queen, four years widowed and still only 22, needed a man. The name of Henry, Lord Darnley, seems to have been first canvassed in 1562, but neither Randolf nor Cecil thought at that time that Mary was seriously interested. Darnley was the son of Mathew Stuart, Earl of Lennox, and his mother was Margaret, daughter by her second marriage to that Margaret who had been the elder daughter of Henry VII. He was thus (in a remote sense) a prince of the blood. His father had been long exiled in England, but in February 1565, thanks to Elizabeth's indulgence and the complexities of Scottish politics, he was able to return home. Darnley, then aged 20, went with him. As soon as they met, Mary fell hopelessly in love with this extremely tall and handsome young man.[26] Over the next few weeks, all her carefully fostered good will, both in England and in Scotland, was dissipated. On 1 May the subject was discussed by the privy council in London:

THE QUEEN'S MAJESTY, *finding by the Laird of Lethington of his mistress, her good sister's intention to marry with Lord Darnley, which she thinks very strange, has communicated the same to her council, who having advised thereon, with one assent think that it would be unmet, unprofitable and perilous to the sincere amity between the Queens and their realms ...* [27]

Nicholas Throgmorton was immediately despatched to Edinburgh with instructions (drafted by Cecil) to threaten all kinds of dire consequences should the marriage go ahead, and on 2 June Cecil drafted another minute on the subject ahead of a council meeting:

FIRST THE MINDS *of all such as be affected to the Queen of Scots either for herself or for the opinion of her pretence to this Crown, or for the desire to have a change of the form of religion in this realm, or for the discontentation they have of the Queen's majesty or her succession, or of the succession of any other besides the Queen of Scots, shall be by this marriage, credited, comforted and induced to labour how to bring their desires to pass ...* [28]

In other words, a first-rate security crisis threatened. Musters were ordered in the north, the Earl of Bedford was despatched to Berwick, the Countess of Lennox was placed under restraint, and the lieutenant of Ireland was replaced. Only the Earl of Leicester seems to have favoured the match secretly — probably because it got him off a singularly uncomfortable hook. In the event, however, Mary was her own mistress, and in no mood to be either advised or intimidated. On 29 July 1565 she married her 'long lad', and on the same day he was proclaimed King of Scotland. The match, Randolf wrote with some exaggeration, was as unpopular in Scotland as it was with the English government. Apart from his appearance, Darnley had few redeeming features, 'his pride intolerable, his words not to be borne'. 'God,' Randolf concluded prophetically, 'must send him a short end.'

In one respect, the match was a great success: within two months, Mary was pregnant. However, apart from Randolf's hyperbole, the opposition was real enough, and within a couple of months Mary's opponents were begging the English council for support, on the grounds of the 'utter subversion' of religion, the perpetration of 'daily enormities' and the fact that 'Davy' [David Rizzio] the Italian now controlled everything. Cecil was sympathetic to their situation and Elizabeth was persuaded to send the Earl of Murray some financial assistance, but it made little difference. However unpopular Darnley may have been in some quarters, Mary was in control of the situation. In September the Scottish queen wrote to Elizabeth asserting her willingness to discuss her differences with her 'dear sister' by envoy, but declaring roundly that she would not tolerate any interference in Scotland's internal affairs.[29] The French offered to mediate, but the last thing Cecil needed was their renewed involvement in the north and the offer was politely declined.

Elizabeth was rather less polite about Mary, but there was little that she could do. It soon transpired, however, that the Queen of Scots was quite capable of self-destructing. Rizzio's influence was much resented, not least by the Duke of Albany (as Lord Darnley had become). The Earl of Murray and a number of his supporters were exiled in England, and relations between Mary and her husband were becoming increasingly strained. On 19 February 1566, Mary expelled Thomas Randolf from Scotland, and a week later the Earl of Bedford wrote to Cecil from Berwick, 'I have heard of late of a great attempt to be made by such advice as the Lord Darnley hath gotten of some noblemen of Scotland, whereby he thinketh to advance himself unto that which by other means he cannot attain [the crown matrimonial] ...'[30]

Randolf had informed him of 'their whole intent' and 'knowing the certainty of these things we thought it our duty to utter the same to you, Mr. Secretary, to make declaration thereof as shall seem best to your wisdom.' De Silva heard that the whole plot was laid in England, but if that were so, then Cecil was not a party to it. On 9 March David Rizzio was murdered in the queen's presence by a gang led by her husband. For about a week there was turmoil, but at the end of that time, with one of those extraordinary twists of which Scottish affairs were so capable, Mary was back in control, the Earl of Murray was reconciled to her, the plot leaders, Morton and Ruthven, had fled to England, and Darnley was totally discredited.[31] If either Elizabeth or Cecil had sought to manipulate Scottish discontents to their advantage, then they had burned their fingers and simply had another bunch of Scottish fugitives on their hands. Mary protested about this in mild terms, but took advantage of her great triumph—the birth of James on 19 June—to invite both Leicester and Cecil to the christening. The birth even ostensibly reconciled Mary to her husband and, after the crisis month of March, Anglo-Scottish relations appeared to have settled down in a kind of suspicious truce.

At the beginning of January 1567 Cecil was depressed and afflicted by gout. Parliament had just risen and on the 11th he wrote to Henry Sidney, 'Lack of money is the principal sickness of this court, and although counsels be so well given, if the sinews be defective the counsels must languish ... at this time I feel all my body well but my sinews, and by their weakness I am but as a dead body.'[32]

If, however, he was inclined to be self-indulgent, the volatile Queen of Scots soon put any such thoughts from his mind. On 10 January, before dawn, the house at Kirk o' Fields just outside Edinburgh in which Darnley was staying was blown up and Darnley was killed. Mary claimed that it was a failed attempt on her own life, but most of her subjects thought differently. Her relations with Darnley had deteriorated again after James's baptism, partly for political reasons and partly because there was a new man in her life—the dashing and completely unscrupulous James Hepburn, Earl of Bothwell. By the time of Darnley's death, Mary was completely, and rather publicly, infatuated.

Bothwell was immediately and plausibly blamed for the murder, to which Mary was generally held to be a party. As a gesture to her critics, Bothwell was tried for the murder, but as none of his accusers dared to appear, he was acquitted, to the satisfaction of no one. So strong was Bothwell's position that many of his critics fled, and Kirkaldy of Grange wrote to the Earl of Bedford in April, 'she [Mary] cares not to lose France, England and her own country for him, and shall go with him to the world's end in a white petticoat ere she will leave him …' As if to confirm his opinion, Bothwell summarily divorced his wife, and on 15 May married Mary with Protestant rites — in total violation of her supposed principles — thus ensuring that she forfeited any significant support from the Scottish Catholics, hitherto her last and strongest defenders.[33] The capacity of a passionate young woman to ruin herself for sexual reasons has never been more convincingly demonstrated.

Scotland was again in turmoil, and this time Mary did not succeed in riding the storm. She and Bothwell were defeated at the battle of Carberry Hill on 15 June. He escaped, but she was confined to Lochleven Castle. When the news reached England a few days later, Cecil and Elizabeth had no option but to accept the *fait accompli*, but their agendas of reaction differed. The queen was concerned that Mary should be set at liberty and that Bothwell should be brought to justice; her secretary was relaxed about the Queen of Scots' imprisonment and interested mainly in preserving the Protestant ascendancy. Both, however, were exercised that no harm should come to young James, who seemed to be in some danger of being treated like a football. Nicholas Throgmorton was promptly sent on mission to Scotland, his instructions (as usual) drafted by Cecil. Throgmorton was to insist that Mary be set free and that Bothwell be brought to justice, otherwise the Scottish lords who were presently in command of the situation could look for neither support nor recognition from England. He was to suggest that James be sent south for his own safety. Superior powers, Cecil sternly reminded the lords (with an eye on John Knox), should be obeyed.[34] However, before the ambassador could even reach Edinburgh, Mary's captors had forced her to abdicate and, on 29 July 1567, crowned her son in her place. Elizabeth was chagrined beyond measure at what she saw as an act of open defiance. She blustered, and on 11 August Cecil wrote to Throgmorton:

THIS AFTERNOON ... *the Queen sent for me hastily and entered*
*into a great offensive speech that nothing was thought of for her*
*to do to revenge the Queen of Scots imprisonment and deliver her. I*
*answered as warily as I could, but she increased so in anger against these*
*lords that in good earnest she began to devise revenge by war* ...[35]

He concluded wryly, 'We prepare musters on our sea coasts in case the
King of Spain come by ...' In fact, there was no more danger of Elizabeth declaring war on Scotland than there was of a Spanish invasion,
but Elizabeth hated being made a fool of. The Scottish government
settled down under the regency of the Earl of Murray, and Cecil was
well enough pleased: '[he] doth acquit himself very honourably to
the advancement of religion and justice without respect of persons ...'

However, Scotland was now divided, ironically in much the same
way that Elizabeth was divided from her secretary. The majority
accepted the Earl of Murray as regent for the young James VI, but a
determined minority continued to recognize Mary, claiming that her
abdication was invalid because it had been coerced. On 2 May 1568
Mary escaped from Lochleven and summoned her followers to defend
her cause. It took about five days for this news to reach Cecil, and he
responded with what was probably a verbal message, urging Murray to
dispose of her quickly. He knew perfectly well that Elizabeth would
have reacted very differently, but in the event it did not matter. Before
any English reaction had reached Scotland, Murray had defeated the
queen's zealous but motley army at Langside and, finding her escape
route to the west blocked, Mary had turned south. On 16 May she
crossed the Solway and landed in England.[36] The Queen of England, it
seems clear, was prepared to support her sister, but only on the condition that she did not summon aid from France. In the event, her reaction was irrelevant. As soon as the news of this unexpected (and
unwelcome) guest reached London, the council went into emergency
session. De Silva summarized the situation concisely:

THIS QUEEN *has always shown good will to the Queen of Scots,*
*and the Council or a majority of it have been opposed to her and leant*
*to the side of the Regent ... If this Queen has her way now they will be*
*obliged to treat the Queen of Scots as a sovereign, which will offend those*
*who forced her to abdicate, so that, although these people are glad enough*
*to have her in their hands, they have many things to consider* ...[37]

Cecil, inevitably, drew up a long memorandum of pros and cons for dealing with the Queen of Scots, concluding eventually that she should be held in custody and that the charges against her in respect of the death of Lord Darnley should be fully investigated. The council seem to have agreed with him, and since that is eventually what happened, it may be supposed that Elizabeth's declarations of sisterly sympathy and support were so much double talk. It is impossible that so important and sensitive an issue could have been handled by the council without the queen's connivance, so it must be concluded that her declarations of support were for consumption by the outside world rather than seriously intended.

It was soon to become clear that Elizabeth was in two minds about Mary, and for the time being it was Cecil's agenda that the government followed. Cecil regarded the Queen of Scots with rational and total hostility; she was a menace in several different disguises and he was to spend the next 18 years of his life in constant efforts to persuade his mistress to dispose of her. The danger that she represented was clearly demonstrated, not only by the Norfolk marriage scheme but also by the attitude of the northern rebels in 1569.[38] For the time being Elizabeth either could not, or would not, see it. In October 1569 Cecil summarized his position in a memorandum to the queen:

THE QUEEN OF SCOTS *indeed is and shall always be a dangerous person to your estate, yet there be degrees whereby the danger may be more or less. If your Majesty should marry, it would be less, and whilst you do not, it will increase. If her person be restrained, either here or at home in her own country, it will be less. If [she] be at liberty, it will be greater.*[39]

Scotland was not only England's closest neighbour, but both the progress of the Scottish reformation and the sensitive position of its queen placed it at the top of any foreign policy agenda that Cecil might draw up. It was not, however, his only concern. Mary's position was closely linked to the issue of Elizabeth's own marriage, and Cecil was very anxious to bring that about, if only to keep her out of the clutches of Robert Dudley.

Early in the reign there had been talk of a union with the Archduke Ferdinand, but he wed elsewhere, and by 1563 the focus had shifted to his brother, Charles. The Duke of Wurtemberg's offer to mediate a negotiation was accepted, but it proved a slow business. A Habsburg alliance was desirable for several reasons, but religion proved to be a serious obstacle. This was partly because Cecil instinctively regarded all Catholic powers as being parties to a conspiracy against England; partly because the queen, for all her overt conservatism and conciliatory words, would not compromise her Protestant principles; and partly because Charles's own position was at first misrepresented.[40] The duke had his own agenda for the formation of a Protestant league, and this was well understood in London. The Emperor Ferdinand was opposed to any marriage scheme, and as long as he lived open negotiations were impossible. However, he died in July 1564 and his successor Maximilian II was less hostile. For reasons that are not altogether clear, a proposal to send an English delegation to Vienna was dropped, but in the spring of 1565 a member of the Emperor's council, the Baron von Mitterberg, arrived in London.

It soon became apparent that there were misunderstandings about the archduke's religious position, which had been represented as flexible. The English understood that, although he could not be expected to become a Protestant, he might nevertheless conform to the established church in public and hear mass only in the privacy of his own closet. This, it transpired, was a good deal further than Charles was willing to go. Nevertheless, Elizabeth appears to have been in earnest about the negotiation. She informed Mitterberg that 'she was now resolved to marry, and that [he] might report as much to [his] Imperial majesty in her name.'[41] Her council meanwhile proposed a settlement based closely on that which had been agreed between Philip and Mary in 1554. English law and religion were to be protected, no foreign officers were to be intruded, neither the queen nor her children might be taken out of the realm, and England was not to be involved in any Habsburg wars.

Meanwhile the English council was deeply divided. Cecil, Sussex and Norfolk favoured Charles. Leicester was strongly opposed, and backed a rival French bid to marry the queen to the young Charles IX. When Elizabeth rejected the latter proposal on the grounds that she was too old, the French ambassador even attempted to revive her interest in Dudley as a means of checkmating the Habsburg negotiation. Cecil and his friends argued not only the archduke's (alleged) amenability over religion, but his suitability in age (he was seven years younger that Elizabeth), and above all his Imperial credentials: 'No Prince of England ever remained without good amity with the House of Burgundy; and no prince ever had less alliance than the Queen of England hath. Nor any Prince ever had more cause to have friendship and power to assist her estate.'[42]

## CECIL'S ARGUMENTS ON THE ROYAL MARRIAGE PROSPECTS, 1566

### REASONS TO MOVE THE QUEEN TO ACCEPT CHARLES

*Besides his person: his birth his alliance.*

I *She shall not diminish the honour of a Prince to match with a Prince.*

II *When she shall receive messages from kings, her husband shall have of himself by birth a countenance to receive them.*

III *Whatsoever he shall bring into the realm, he shall spend it here in the realm.*

IV *He shall have no regard to any Person, but to please the Queen.*

V *He shall have no opportunity nor occasion to tempt him to seek the Crown after the Queen, because he is a stranger and hath no friends in the realm to assist him.*

VI *By marriage with him the Queen shall have the friendship of King Philip, which is necessary considering the likelihood of falling out with France.*

VII *No Prince of England ever remained without good amity with*

### REASONS AGAINST THE EARL OF LEICESTER

I *Nothing is increased by marriage of him, either in riches, estimation [or] power.*

II *It will be thought that the slanderous speeches of the Queen with the Earl have been True.*

III *He shall study nothing but to enhance his own particular friends to wealth, to office, to lands, and to offend others.*

| | |
|---|---|
| *Sir H. Sidney* | *Middlemore* |
| *Earl Warwick* | *Colshill* |
| *Sir James Croft* | *Wiseman* |
| *Henry Dudley* | *Killigrew* |
| *Sir Fr. Jobson* | *John Dudley* |
| *Appleyard* | *ii Christmas* |
| *Horsey* | *Fostar* |

IV *He is infamed by the death of his wife.*

V *He is far in debt*

VI *He is like to prove unloving or jealous of The Queen's Majesty.*

*the house of Burgundy; and*
*no prince ever had less alliance*
*than the Queen of England hath.*
*Nor any Prince ever had more*
*cause to have friendship and power*
*to assist her estate.*
*VIII The French king will keep*
*Calais against his pact.*
*IX The Queen of Scots pretend-*
*eth title to the Crown of England,*
*and so did never foreign prince*
*since the Conquest.*
*X The pope also and all his*
*parties are watching adversaries to*
*the Crown.*

[From Cecil's minute, *De matrimoniae Reginae Angliae cum extero Principe*, April 1566, as appearing in Haynes, State Papers, I, p. 444]

Maximilian, however, rejected the English proposals and made it clear that his brother could not be expected to compromise his faith. When this response was received in July 1565, Elizabeth commented that 'two persons of different faiths could not live peaceably in one house', and that she would not marry anyone who differed from her in religion. Cecil, who shared her reservations, nevertheless did his best to keep the negotiations alive after this uncompromising stand-off. In March 1566 Thomas Dannett was sent to Vienna, ostensibly to bear the Order of the Garter to Maximilian, but in fact to bear some (slightly) revised suggestions in connection with the marriage negotiation.

The Emperor, however, was grown inflexible. He would settle for nothing less than that Elizabeth should bear the full costs of her consort's household and that the said household should have full liberty to practise the Catholic faith in public.[43] Dannett not only came back with his tail between his legs, but with a very pessimistic estimate of Charles's own religious attitude. When the queen renewed her general commitment to marry in an acrimonious exchange with parliament in 1566, this impasse was unresolved, and the most that Cecil and his allies had managed to achieve was that inconclusive diplomatic exchanges continued.

Parliamentary pressure, however, was not entirely fruitless, and for

that Cecil must take the main credit. As early as January 1567 Elizabeth
was persuaded to send the Earl of Sussex on another special mission to
Vienna, although in fact he had nothing new to say and the queen's
procrastination delayed his mission until the end of June. On arrival at
the imperial court, Sussex made haste slowly. Going well beyond his
instructions, he claimed not only that Elizabeth was more flexible in
religion than her own words would suggest, but also that the English
Church did not differ significantly from the Lutheran churches with
which Maximilian was familiar. The Emperor was sufficiently
impressed to summon Charles himself to the negotiation. By the end
of October Sussex believed that a satisfactory compromise had been
reached. The archduke would have his mass in private, from which
Englishmen would be excluded, but he would respect the laws of the
land with regard to public conformity. The earl wrote triumphantly to
Cecil that all obstacles had been overcome.[44] However, he rejoiced too
soon. By the time his reports reached London there had been another
furore over the mass, this time over supposedly private masses in the
Spanish ambassador's chapel which Englishmen had been attending.
This was dangerously close to the nub of the Habsburg agreement. On
10 December, Elizabeth wrote to Sussex rejecting any compromise
over the archduke's private mass—and that was effectively the end of
the discussions.

Although in a sense he had failed, in another way Cecil had been
very successful in this matter. By his constant mediation he had managed to keep the peace between the rival groups in the council, among
whom feelings had run high. Followers of Leicester and Sussex had
even at one point turned up at court wearing what can only be
described as 'party favours' until the queen, on Cecil's advice, had
summarily forbidden the practice. He was also scrupulously careful to
respect the queen's mood. While the French proposal was still alive he
wrote to Sir Thomas Smith:

THE EMPEROR'S *ambassador is not idle in this matter, but presseth
the match for the Archduke discreetly and diligently. One great
obstacle is that the queen's majesty will needs see before she marry.
And how that device may be performed, if she should assent either to
the French king or the Archduke, will prove hard ... what shall follow,
God knoweth.*[45]

Sir Nicholas Throgmorton, as was often the case, identified his role accurately in conversation with the French ambassador in July 1565. Cecil, he said, made a great show of mixing in nothing, but behind the scenes did everything, often through third parties. He vigorously but subtly promoted the suit of the archduke, using principally the intercession of the Earl of Sussex and the Duke of Norfolk. He was also principally responsible for the queen's decision to take the advice of her councillors separately in this matter, without calling them together.[46] As both de Silva and the French ambassador eventually realized, while Sussex and Norfolk were the chief spokesmen for Charles, Cecil was the mainspring. The Earl of Arundel apparently believed that Cecil was opposed to any marriage, because the advent of a king consort would inevitably reduce both his influence and his access to the queen, but most of the evidence is against such an interpretation; it was just that, in this case, he did not succeed.

French marriage proposals at this stage should probably be seen as no more than an attempt to countermine the Austrians, but they also serve as a reminder of how quickly Renaissance diplomacy could change. It was barely a year since the Treaty of Troyes had brought a state of war between the two kingdoms to an end in April 1564.

The main problem in dealing with France was that the country was unstable. Even before the death of Henry II in July 1559, the great houses of Guise, Montmorency and Bourbon had been at each other's throats, and during the brief reign of the rather feeble Francis II the situation had become markedly worse. There were a number of reasons for this. All the great noble families were anxious to turn back the advance of royal power that had taken place under Francis I (1514–47), and all had suffered heavy losses during Francis's and Henry's wars. Guise and Montmorency were Catholic; the Bourbons were Huguenot. Montmorency and Bourbon were bitterly hostile to the ascendancy that the marriage of Mary of Guise, to Scotland's James V, had brought to her brothers Cardinal Charles and Duke Francis, and each family was suspicious of any advantage gained by the others.

When Francis II died in December 1560, as we have seen the turmoil resulted in the abandonment of Scotland, but it also brought a fourth power group into play. The great nobles stalemated each other, and left the way open for the queen mother, Catherine de Medici, to secure the regency for her young son, Charles IX. Her priority was to protect (as far as possible) the authority of the crown from noble encroachment, and at the beginning of 1561 this meant an alliance with the Bourbons against the still overpowering Guise presence. This made her accommodating towards the Protestants at home, and anxious for the friendship of Protestant powers abroad. Even while Francis was still alive, in May 1560, Nicholas Throgmorton had written to Elizabeth suggesting that she might like to take advantage of the state of France to invade either Brittany or Normandy with the object of securing a bargaining counter for the return of Calais.[47]

She referred Throgmorton's letter to Cecil, who immediately expressed his alarm and dissent. Such an incursion would be an act of war and he had only just made peace with the French in Scotland. Elizabeth could not count on Huguenot support, whatever her pretext for intervention, and financially such a commitment would be a disaster—a 'bottomless pit'. The secretary's attitude was strictly pragmatic. He said nothing about the recovery of Calais, or about Protestant solidarity, merely pointing out that an English invasion would be the surest way of persuading the French to compound their internal differences. Thereafter for several months Cecil was preoccupied with the 'Dudley affair', and the situation in France did not significantly change. There was a suggestion that the English be invited to send delegates to the proposed colloquy at Poissy, but nothing came of it. Nor did proposed talks with the German Protestant princes come about. Elizabeth was trying to keep all her options open, and suspected a plot to pin her down.

Then, in the spring of 1562, there were developments. The Montmorencys and the Guises came to terms, and the King of Navarre, the senior Bourbon prince, went over to the Catholics.[48] Catherine, now considerably strengthened, urged Elizabeth to accept the invitation to Trent and to make common cause with her for a moderate settlement. The queen even got as far as naming a delegation of conservative councillors—albeit led by Cecil—but as we have seen, he managed to sabotage the invitation and no delegation was sent. Instead, in early April, civil war erupted in France.

Throgmorton immediately urged Elizabeth to intervene on the Protestant side, arguing that if they were crushed it would be to England's lasting peril. Within a month the Prince of Condé, the Huguenot leader, had also sent a mission to England, requesting both military intervention and a loan of 100,000 crowns. Cecil apparently urged Elizabeth to offer mediation instead, and to send a mission not to Condé but to the queen mother and the King of Navarre.[49] Sir Henry Sidney was duly sent, with very limited instructions (which Cecil drafted) and more than a hint that the main purpose of his mission was to prevent the Spanish from intervening on the Catholic side. His mission got nowhere and the situation in France became steadily worse, so that Throgmorton began to fear for his life.

Under the pressure of these events, Cecil's position shifted. By the middle of July he was urging armed intervention, but indirectly, paying certain German princes to send troops into France. On 16 July he wrote to Throgmorton, 'My device is to solicit them [the Germans] to offer contribution for an army to enter into France. Mr. Mewtas is gone by Dieppe to the prince [of Condé] ...'[50] He also complained (as usual) that Elizabeth seemed to be unable to make up her mind. This time, however, it seems that he did his mistress an injustice, because the very next day at a meeting attended by the queen, the council agreed to mobilize 10,000 men, call musters in all the southern and eastern counties, and prepare a dozen ships for the seas.

Ten days later Throgmorton was recalled.[51] What prompted this sudden change of heart is not known, but the influence of Lord Robert Dudley and his friends may be strongly suspected. For once William Cecil was behind the game, because he seems not to have known that there was already talk of the surrender of a cautionary town in return for English help and to serve as a base for the expeditionary force. All these discussions were very secret, but it was most unusual for the secretary not to be a party to them. It may be that he simply did not record his role, because he seems not to have objected to this sudden change of direction. On 20 July he wrote himself a note about 'the perils growing upon the overthrow of the Prince of Condé's cause', painting a graphic picture of a Europe dominated by the Guises, the Spaniards and the Catholic Church. 'Whosoever thinketh that relenting in religion will assuage the Guisans' aspirations, they are far deceived.'[52] Put like that, and given that no progress was being made in Germany, a policy of direct intervention became almost inevitable, whether it was his own idea or not.

Early in August 1562 the Vidame of Chartres, the commander of Le Havre, paid a secret visit to England. The records of his visit are scanty, but the one thing that is clear is that Cecil and Dudley were working closely together, and between them they seem to have conducted the English side of the discussions. By the end of August agreement had been reached, and on the 29th Cecil briefly summarized the terms: 'Newhaven [Le Havre] shall be delivered, and there shall be delivered to the Prince at Strasburgh 100,000 crowns, and further 40,000 to help Newhaven and Rouen, and Newhaven shall be restored when Calais shall, and the whole sum of 140,000 crowns.'[53] The inclusion of the recovery of Calais clearly points to the queen's priorities rather than Cecil's. The preparations took time, and the queen (of all people) became impatient. Yet Cecil was doing his best, and at the beginning of October 3000 men under the command of the Earl of Warwick landed at Le Havre, while a further 3000 were despatched to Dieppe. By the end of October the whole operation was in place.

However, success stopped with deployment. By the end of November, Catholic forces had captured Rouen. Shortly after Dieppe also fell, and the English retreated to Le Havre. The war that followed was a disaster for everyone, except possibly the queen mother. By the end of the year both Condé and the Duke of Montmorency had been taken prisoner; on the other side, in February 1563, the Duke of Guise and the cardinal were assassinated.[54] Condé came to terms on 10 March. These were not favourable, and Coligny, his deputy, was opposed to them. They completely ignored the English presence at Le Havre. Elizabeth's only option was to sit tight and see what advantage she could secure from her possession of the town. 'I can assure you,' Cecil wrote to Sir Thomas Smith on 29 March, 'here is full determination made to keep Newhaven, and if the French shall offer any hostility it shall not only be defended but they shall also feel more hostility by sea and land than they can bear.'[55] The council was gritting its collective teeth. Le Havre was reinforced, and as late as 20 May Cecil was still writing of the intention to recover Calais as a *quid pro quo*. However, the French, now united, were not disposed to negotiate on those terms.

Le Havre could be supplied by sea, and a prolonged stalemate might have ensued, but for one thing. Towards the end of June plague broke out among the garrison, and on 29 July the Earl of Warwick was authorized to surrender. He did so with as much dignity as he could muster and the remnants of his army were repatriated. The last chance of recovering Calais disappeared. Elizabeth had burned her fingers badly, and the lesson was not lost on her, but Cecil remained infuriatingly silent about the whole business. The peace negotiations were conducted under duress, with both Throgmorton and Smith in France receiving somewhat different instructions.[56] Dudley communicated mainly with Throgmorton, and Cecil with Smith. In the event it did not prove possible for either of them to obtain terms other than those that the queen mother was prepared to offer.

Fortunately, there was at this stage no temptation to military adventure in the other area of confrontation between the Catholic Church and its enemies, namely the Low Countries. Religious tensions had existed in the Netherlands since the 1530s, but they had become worse since Philip had taken over the government from his father Charles V (of Ghent) in 1555. The end of the Franco-Habsburg wars had also allowed French-speaking Calvinist preachers to cross from Picardy into Hainault. There were two main issues. The first was religious freedom, demanded by the Protestants and denied by the government wherever its arm could reach. [57] The second was local and aristocratic privileges. The Netherlands were accustomed to being governed by their own people in accordance with their own laws, but that did not suit Philip's centralizing and bureaucratic agenda.

By 1563 the provinces were seething with discontent, and Margaret of Parma, the governor, was convinced that the English were to blame. There was some truth in this, in that there were friendly contacts between the council in London and opposition leaders such as Count Egmont and William of Orange, but Elizabeth had not the slightest intention of intervening directly. On the other hand, English pirates were becoming a serious nuisance to trade between Flanders and Spain, and the English government appeared either unable or unwilling to do anything about it.[58] At the end of October 1563 Margaret of Parma closed all her ports to English ships for four months to persuade Elizabeth to take her complaints about pirates seriously.

This turned out to be a self-inflicted wound because, although Antwerp had been the chief focus of the English cloth trade for many years, the recently unsettled political situation had already persuaded the merchant adventurers to look elsewhere. Jan Utenhove, the minister of the Strangers' Church in London, had contacts in East Friesland, and as early as March 1563, at Cecil's suggestion, he was beginning to act as an intermediary with the countess there. It was some months before the negotiations actually took place, but it was on Cecil's initiative that this search for an alternative 'vent' took place.[59] Margaret extended her embargo beyond the original four months, and in May 1564 the cloth fleet (worth about £300,000) sailed to Emden. In the spring of 1564 various things changed. Cardinal Granvelle was eventually forced out of office and Philip accepted his resignation.

A new Spanish ambassador arrived in England to take the place of the deceased Bishop de Quadra, and this one, Guzman de Silva, proved a good deal easier to deal with. Nevertheless the negotiations dragged, and in September 1564 Cecil wrote to Sir Thomas Smith, expressing his concern at the lack of progress. In spite of the damage that was being inflicted on her merchants, Margaret was intransigent. However, she was not a sovereign, and the main negotiation was being carried on between Cecil and de Silva. On 26 November the former wrote to Smith, 'I send you the articles whereupon the Spanish ambassador and we are agreed, which he has sent seven days past to the Duchess of Parma. And upon the return of her answer we shall know what will take place …'[60] He added, 'We begin to find that our commodities will be well enough uttered though the intercourse should not open for the Low Countries, for we find the strangers ready to carry all our clothes …'

Margaret was apparently now coming to the same conclusion, because she accepted the articles in early December, and the markets reopened on 1 January 1565.

The disruption had caused a good deal of heart searching in England, and Cecil was not alone in concluding that the country had too many eggs in the one basket. At some time during 1564, at the height of the embargo, he wrote a long paper on the subject, setting out the pros and cons of reopening the trade to Antwerp and concluding that, if the worst came to the worst, the unemployed could always be sent off to Ireland![61] It was a thoughtful document, and one thing that came of it was Cecil's firm commitment in the future to all ventures designed to open new markets to English goods. This was to be one of the pretexts for the adventures of Hawkins, Drake, Raleigh, Frobisher and other 'sea dogs', and it may well have been Cecil's influence that prompted Elizabeth to be so famously supportive of such ventures in the future.

Meanwhile, the situation in the Low Countries continued to

deteriorate. Infuriated by their failure to win any significant concessions, the Calvinists of Flanders, Hainault and Brabant began a systematic campaign of smashing of Catholic symbols and the government
was in serious danger of losing all control. Antwerp was particularly
badly affected, and the merchants and bankers upon whom it
depended began to leave the city. In September Sir Thomas Gresham,
Elizabeth's long-serving financial agent, wrote to Cecil:

> Y OUR HONOUR *shall do very well in time to consider some other*
> *realm and place for utterance of our commodities ... whereby her*
> *majesty's realm may remain in peace and quietness, which in this brab-*
> *bling time is one of the chiefest things your honour hath to look unto ...*[62]

Gresham began to find it difficult to borrow money, not because there
was anything wrong with his credit but because no money was to be
had. However, there is no sign that either Elizabeth or Cecil contemplated getting involved in the troubles. In February 1567 a group of
reformed pastors wrote to the secretary, expressing their confidence in
his good will and godliness, but he is not known to have responded. In
order to save the rapidly dwindling Antwerp Bourse, Margaret was
prepared to make some concessions on religion, but Philip would have
none of it. He repudiated her agreement with the malcontents,
relieved her of her duties and sent the Duke of Alba with an army in
her place. The English council looked on these developments with
mounting concern, but did nothing. Instead Elizabeth was careful to
express her disapproval of rebellious subjects—at least for de Silva's
benefit—and ordered her subjects by proclamation to desist from any
involvement.[63]

This may not have been very strictly enforced, because anti-Spanish
feeling was growing in the country as a whole, fuelled, no doubt, by
atrocity stories about the behaviour of Alba's soldiers (which were
mainly true). There was a high-level spat during the summer of 1568,
when Philip expelled Dr John Man, the English ambassador in
Madrid. Elizabeth's response was subtle, but effective. While maintaining a public face of strict neutrality, she not only continued to turn
a blind eye to the doings of English pirates, but actively encouraged
them. John Hawkins, in whose voyages she was investing, was nothing
less than a pirate. As we have seen, it was Hawkins's misadventure that
led indirectly to the seizure of the Genoese silver in December 1568,

and all that followed from it. Whether rightly or not, Cecil was seen as the moving spirit in that exploit.

There is no doubt that Cecil was Elizabeth's most important councillor in her dealings with foreign powers, whether over her marriage or any other cause, and his general view of the world was dictated by the 'conspiratorial model'. The queen could marry a Catholic prince, but only if his religion was emasculated. Mary Queen of Scots was a menace because of her Catholic and Guisard connections as much as her English claim. The Duke of Alba was a threat because of his extreme intolerance towards heretics. In short, the pope was Antichrist. As Stephen Alford has observed, 'Cecil's notes often present an interpretation of the state of Britain and Europe in which the future of England depends upon faith and a true reformed religion ...'[64]

All political systems were directed to present needs, and because policy, both foreign and domestic, was a unity, Cecil's Protestantism was fundamental to all of his actions. Rather surprisingly, this strengthened his ties to Elizabeth whose own religion was equally firm—although perhaps rather more subtle. It also makes nonsense of the factional interpretation of Elizabethan politics. There were many differences of opinion within the council, and some members were much more conservative than others, but there was no 'Catholic group', clandestine or otherwise. Robert Dudley was a bit of a loose cannon, but in spite of his flirtation with de Quadra, his Protestantism was as strong as any, and he was, intermittently at least, on the best of terms with the secretary. Normally, they worked together, except over the Austrian marriage and Dudley's own pretensions, and it is a distortion to see them as regular enemies. When several of his colleagues thought that Cecil had overstepped the mark in the spring of 1569, it was the Earl of Leicester (as he then was) who alerted Elizabeth. During the first decade of the reign, Cecil's main problem was that he had not yet (or thought that he had not) learned to read the queen's mind. After 1570 that anxiety receded.

# CHAPTER 6

# Lord Burghley, the Lord Treasurer

ON 25 FEBRUARY 1571 William Cecil was raised to the peerage as Baron Cecil of Burghley. The creation took place in the presence chamber at Westminster, and the National Archives holds a detailed description of the 'rites and ceremonies' with which it was conducted.[1] Lord Burghley was supported by Lord Hunsdon, Lord Cobham and the Earl of Leicester. His patent was read by John Wooley, the Latin secretary, and the queen then vested him in his robe. After a brief (and no doubt appropriate) word of thanks from the new peer, his title was proclaimed and the company moved off to dinner.

Just why Elizabeth chose to ennoble him at this point is not certain. There was a rumour that he was to be created lord privy seal, but that never happened. It may be that a recent and very severe visitation of the gout had persuaded her that she had better recognize his services appropriately before he became totally incapacitated. It was also significant that one of his supporters was the Earl of Leicester, because it was customary for new barons to be supported by others of the same rank. It seems that Lord Burghley was highly gratified, although he insisted in describing himself (mendaciously) as 'the poorest Lord in England'. Quite apart from the emoluments, official and unofficial, of the secretaryship, he held numerous other offices of profit, including the immensely lucrative mastership of the Court of Wards, which he had taken over after the death of Sir Thomas Parry.[2] For the time being he remained secretary, and the main difference that his peerage made to his conduct of affairs was that when parliament reconvened on 2 April, he sat in the Lords rather than in the Commons. It was apparently intended to appoint Sir Thomas Smith to assist him but, although Smith was sworn of the council, he did not become secretary

until Burghley succeeded the Marquis of Winchester as lord treasurer
in July 1572.

How much difference did it make when Lord Burghley became
lord treasurer? In principle he became more of a statesman and less of
an administrator—but in practice, he had always been a special councillor, and that did not change. He had more formal duties to perform,
such as presiding in the Exchequer Court, and heading commissions
for the taking of accounts. He also continued to be master of the
Court of Wards and that, as well as being very lucrative, carried a host
of duties. Above all, perhaps, it gave him access to the privileged net-
works of peerage families which, as a knight or a new baron, he would
not otherwise have had.

Lord Burghley's attitude to his own status is a matter of some interest. He was not a courtier in the same sense as, say, the Earl of Leicester. Even before the gout incapacitated him there is no record of his
having danced or taken part in any of the festivities of the court,
except as a spectator. He was also keenly aware that his father had been
a mere gentleman and that he had none of the bloodlines of most of his
fellow councillors. It may have been for that reason, rather than
alleged poverty, that he is supposed to have turned down the offer of
an earldom. On the other hand, he was what the modern observer
would describe as a 'snob', and very proud of his friendships with his
aristocratic colleagues.

Pride in such associations, rather than economic acumen, may have
prompted Cecil to join with the earls of Leicester and Pembroke in the
1560s to invest in an Anglo-German metallurgical company. In 1568,
along with Leicester, Pembroke and Mountjoy, he held four and a
quarter of the 24 shares in the Mines Royal Company. Shortly after,
with Leicester, Pembroke and the Duke of Norfolk, he held eight out
of 36 shares in the Mineral and Battery Company.[3] Similarly he was
one of the court-connected investors in the Muscovy Company, and
dabbled in alchemical experiments. None of these ventures (so far as
we know) brought him any financial profits, and both Leicester and
Pembroke are known to have lost heavily on their investments. The
point was that such activity registered his membership of a club of
noble speculators, who were somewhat ostentatiously following the
queen's lead in encouraging entrepreneurial activity. This, and his
conversion of the manor of Theobalds in Hertfordshire, which he

bought in 1564, into a palace fit for a queen, were Burghley's ways of demonstrating his status when he could not rely on noble ancestors or gain reflected glory from their heroic deeds. His strenuous efforts to be a successful patron have to be seen in the same light. It was for him, no less than for the Earl of Leicester or the Earl of Essex, a reflection on his honour if his candidates failed to secure promotion. It was later alleged against him that he became bitterly jealous if any of his clients deserted him for another patron. That might, of course, have been a reflection upon his perceived power—but it was also an implied criticism of his credit. Lord Burghley was a service peer and could not pretend to be anything else. Not for him the military trappings of an Essex or a Cumberland. But in council he was supreme, and that was his real claim to nobility.

For the time being, William Cecil's responsibilities continued unchanged, and the top of his agenda was the position of Mary Queen of Scots. Mary was by now both a domestic and a foreign problem. It appears that French suggestions that Elizabeth might be interested in a marriage with Charles IX's younger brother, the Duke of Anjou, originated from those in France (mainly Huguenots and *politiques*) who were still concerned to countermine the Guises and particularly their alleged plans for a match between the duke and Mary.[4] Early in January 1571 Mary's party in Scotland sent emissaries to England with a view to negotiating her liberty and restoration—a course to which Cecil was vehemently opposed. There was a vigorous debate in the council, and Cecil wrote one of his longer and more emphatic memoranda in preparation for it. Mary, he argued, was a menace. She had refused to ratify the Treaty of Edinburgh, she had encouraged treason in England and she faced serious charges from her own subjects.

IF THE QUEEN'S *Majesty shall put her to liberty, whereby she must needs come to government, she shall then, by implication, discharge her of her heinous crime whereof she was accused before her Majesty and to the which she never did make any clear answer for her acquittal …*[5]

The council recommended procrastination along those lines, and such advice suited the queen very well. James also appointed commissioners to carry his case against his mother into England, but they did not arrive until February. They then protested that they were come only to accuse, and not to negotiate any terms for Mary's restoration; when they discovered that such a proposal might be made, they decided to go home for fresh instructions. Elizabeth, whose main purpose was to avoid making any decision, was happy to see them go. The French ambassador rightly concluded that no agreement was in prospect.

At the same time, the Queen of Scots was playing a double game. Ostensibly she was a monarch in exile, and a petitioner for the good offices of her sister queen to restore her to her rightful dominion. However, she was also the centre of a ramifying network of intrigue, which extended from Florence and Madrid to Edinburgh and London, the object of which was the deposition of Elizabeth and her replacement with her Catholic rival. Exactly how much Mary herself knew of the detail is uncertain, but it is clear that she approved at least the outlines of what was intended.[6] Her official representative in England, the Bishop of Ross, was in it up to his neck, and it was from his confession that the whole tangled web was finally unravelled.

In April 1571, one of Ross's messengers named Charles Bailly was intercepted at Dover and relieved of some illicit publications and a bundle of letters. Thanks to some constructive negligence by Lord Cobham, the lord warden, the letters were returned to him. However, by some means unknown, but probably via an agent planted in Cobham's office, Burghley found out about them and Bailly was consigned to the Marshalsea prison.

With some psychological pressure and the deployment of a further agent, Cecil managed to elicit the existence of a plot that was being engineered by the Florentine banker Roberto Ridolfi and involved the pope, the king of Spain and Mary.[7] Ridolfi had until recently been in England and was well known to the Spanish ambassador—and to Burghley. However, just who was involved and what was intended by the conspiracy remained unclear, although an invasion from the Low Countries was suspected.

These discoveries came against a background of other, somewhat ineffectual plotting in which two junior members of the Stanley family and Sir Henry Percy, the brother of the exiled Earl of Northumberland, were involved. These schemes involved ciphered letters and other fascinating mysteries, but their aims were confused and it is not clear that Mary herself knew anything about them. There was talk of spiriting her out of the country via the Isle of Man, and of proclaiming her in England, but nothing came of any of them—less because of the authorities' vigilance than because of their own self-defeating complexity. De Spes knew about them, and inflated the Stanley plot out of all recognition, but their main result was to create that climate of alarm and suspicion in which the Ridolfi plot was gradually unravelled.[8]

The council, deeply worried and even more deeply mystified, tried to persuade the queen to forgo her summer progress, but she was undeterred by the threat and even visited the Duke of Norfolk at Walden. Norfolk was still under loose restraint following his indiscretions of two years earlier, but there was open talk of freeing him entirely, which would probably have happened had it not been for another apparently fortuitous discovery. 'By good hap', as Burghley somewhat disingenuously put it, it was discovered that the duke was sending money into Scotland. It was not his own money—he was acting as a post-box between Mary's ambassador in France and her friends in Scotland—but it was a highly improper activity for a loyal subject.[9] Norfolk's secretary, one Higford, was taken to the Tower and interrogated. Under pressure Higford revealed that, in spite of all professions to the contrary, the duke had remained in touch with Mary and her friends since the summer of 1569—hence his willingness to act as an intermediary. He also professed his devotion to her, suggesting that the marriage plan was not dead either, but he refused at first to have any dealings with Ridolfi.

By January 1571 Ridolfi, from relative safety in Florence, had set up a support network not only for Mary but for English Catholics in general, and had persuaded both the pope and the Bishop of Ross of the need for military intervention if the negotiations still in train with Elizabeth failed. Of course they did fail, and Mary changed her tactics. Instead of relying on Charles IX and the hope of destabilizing the Morton regency in Scotland, she began to turn to Spain and to the Duke of Alba, making Ridolfi's task easier.[10] At this stage he managed to elicit from Norfolk an undertaking to mobilize the Catholic party in England in support of any invasion from the Low Countries, although whether the English Catholics would have had enough confidence in Norfolk to respond is (and was) another matter.

So much had been achieved when Bailly's letters were detected, and Higford interrogated. At this stage the inconsequential Ridolfi disappeared (he went back to his banking business), leaving his contacts and associates to pick up the tabs. Of these the most vulnerable was

John Leslie, the Bishop of Ross. Kept in relatively comfortable confinement during the summer of 1571, he allowed himself to be convinced that the game was up, and that Burghley knew everything
anyway—which was not true. In consequence, when he was interrogated formally by a council committee at the end of October, he told
them everything that he knew—his own involvement, his mistress's,
the Spanish ambassador's and the Duke of Norfolk's. He even went so
far as to explain (quite unnecessarily) that in his view Mary was not fit
for any husband, because she had been implicated in the deaths of both
the king of France and Lord Darnley. 'What a Queen! What an ambassador!' observed one of Burghley's correspondents.[11]

There were three principal victims of this tangled affair, apart from
servants and agents tortured to produce the initial testimonies. The
Duke of Norfolk lost his head, Guerau de Spes lost his position and
Mary Queen of Scots lost her credit. In the very long term this last was
the most important, because it was to be Mary's transformation from
(possibly) legitimate pretender to client of the king of Spain that convinced both parliament and council—although not the queen—that
she was a menace who would have to be removed. This set the agenda
for much domestic politics over the next 15 years. By comparison, the
expulsion of de Spes was a mere blip. Neither side intended a rupture
of diplomatic relations, and Philip was familiar with the concept of *persona non grata*, because he had done the same with John Man. Elizabeth
had demonstrated that she was aware of the extent of Philip's hostility
and would not tolerate it within her realm.[12] Both of them understood
the nature of the message and its limitations. Bernardino de Mendoza
was to arrive as de Spes's replacement in 1574.

The most obvious casualty was England's premier peer, and only
duke. The case against him was completed in early December 1571,
and he was brought to trial on 16 January following. Whether Norfolk's treason was deliberate, and if so, to what it tended, looks uncertain to modern eyes. He was not a Catholic, at least not the kind of
resolute one who might have earned respect, and his offer to raise support for a rebellion looks extremely implausible. The truth seems to
have been that he never really gave up his hope of marrying Mary,
would have been quite prepared to become a Catholic as the price of
such a deal, and had never really thought through the political implications of such an action. In short, he was muddled and stupid rather

than an enemy of the queen. He was tried by his peers, one of whom was Burghley, and the latter is known to have intervened directly in the proceedings, although only on a point of detail. The verdict was a foregone conclusion, but execution did not immediately follow, and Burghley became frustrated. On 23 January he wrote to Francis Walsingham, at that time his servant and on mission in France, 'The queen's Majesty hath always been a merciful lady and by mercy she hath taken more herein than by justice, and yet she thinks that she is more beloved in doing herself harm ...'[13]

After a number of delays and uncertainties, Norfolk eventually went to the block on 2 June, professing his orthodox Protestantism and attended by John Foxe, his former tutor—his end as problematic as most of his life had been.

Lord Burghley wrote an extended memorandum upon the unfolding of the Ridolfi plot, upon which we are dependent for our knowledge of much of its early development. He may have intended this for publication, but it was never finished, let alone printed, and comes to an end with the interrogation of Higford.[14] What is clear, however, is that Burghley was the 'security chief' who was primarily responsible for unravelling the plot—or plots. It was his agents, strategically placed, who extracted vital information from suspects, and who eventually convinced the Bishop of Ross that he had no option but to disclose the whole sorry tale. Norfolk, meanwhile, had done himself no favours by first denying all the charges against him upon oath and then admitting that some of them were true. According to his own account, Burghley played no part in the interrogations, although he was requested more than once to do so. However de Spes, licking his wounds at home after his summary dismissal, was in no doubt who to blame. 'The principal person in the council at the moment', he wrote, 'is William Cecil, now Lord Burghley, a Knight of the Garter. He is a man of mean sort but very astute, false, lying and full of all artifice. He is a great heretic ... [and] manages the bulk of the business by means of his vigilance and craftiness ...'[15]

Allowing for the ambassador's jaundiced point of view, this is probably a fair assessment of the situation. De Spes was not the only person who thought so, and in the course of 1571 there was a plot against Burghley's life. This was apparently detected by his ubiquitous agent William Herle, and again involved him in worming his way into the confidence of one of the conspirators, a certain Edward Mather. Mather was arrested, interrogated, tried and executed, all before the end of February, but not before he had implicated de Spes, his secretary Borghese and several others.[16] It was, apparently, a hare-brained business, but since one of its objectives had been to free the Duke of Norfolk, its discovery may well have had the opposite effect.

The parliaments that met in April 1571 and May 1572 were both difficult—or rather, the House of Commons was. The members not only wanted to discuss the succession and the queen's marriage—both forbidden topics—but also the further reform of the Church and the future of Mary Queen of Scots. In the last case deep suspicion was converted into open hostility between sessions. 'Cut her head off,' as one member put it, 'and make no more ado about it'. However, the House of Commons could achieve nothing on its own, apart from being obstructive. Only in agreement with the House of Lords could it bring any real pressure to bear upon the executive, and that may well explain de Spes' curious observation that one reason for the ennobling of William Cecil had been to make him more useful in parliament.[17]

At first sight it appears obvious that Cecil's skilful and concilliatory interventions were most needed in the Commons, but if we assume that the queen was taking the intractability of the Lower House for granted, concentrating on keeping the more amenable Lords in line made good sense. We must also remember that, whatever was to happen in the 17th century, in the 1570s the Lords was the more important (and powerful) of the two Houses. It may therefore be significant that it was over the fate of the Scots queen, where Burghley failed to see eye to eye with his mistress, that the most concerted pressure was applied. A joint committee of the two Houses agreed on a formal *consulta* about the matter, offering two alternative courses of action: either Mary should be executed out of hand as a traitor or she should be definitively barred from the succession.[18] As Mary was not a subject of the queen of England by any recognized standards, the former suggestion was a non-starter; and Elizabeth brushed the other aside. On 21 May, halfway through the 1572 session, Burghley lamented the queen's unwillingness to perceive her own danger, but his gout was so bad at that point that he felt incapable of doing anything about it. A bill was actually prepared barring Mary from the succession, and it passed both Houses, but the queen refused her assent. Just after the parliament rose at the end of June, Burghley lamented to Walsingham:

A<small>LL THAT WE</small> *laboured for and had with full consent brought to fashion, I mean a law to make the Scottish Queen unable and unworthy to wear the Crown was by her Majesty neither assented nor rejected, but deferred ... some here have, as it seemeth, abused their favour about her Majesty to make herself her worst enemy. God amend them ...*[19]

Who he had in mind is not clear, but it was certainly not Leicester, who was at one with him on this issue, and the obvious suspect, Winchester, had died a few weeks earlier. What is clear is that Cecil had now identified a mission that was to preoccupy him for more than half of the rest of his life, and set up a subtle duel with his mistress which, over the years, was to tax his famous patience to its ultimate limits—not once but several times.

On 27 April 1572 Lord Burghley was installed as a Knight of the Garter. He had briefly served as chancellor of the order in Edward's reign, but had not been a knight. Now he was elected with full ceremonial, and all of it was lovingly recorded.[20] His sponsors were the Earl of Bedford and Sir Henry Sidney, and the honour probably cost him about £40 in fees and equipment. Shortly afterwards, in early July, Elizabeth elevated him to the vacant lord treasurership, and he was succeeded as secretary by his own nominee, Sir Thomas Smith. This may have been out of recognition for his outstanding services, because the treasurer was one of the great offices of state, or it may have been out of compassion for his declining health and a desire to shift him into a less onerous position. If the latter was intended, it did not really work, because although Smith took over all the formal responsibilities of the office, he was unable to assume the unique mantle of competence and confidence that Lord Burghley continued to wear—or his unique relationship with the queen, which enabled them to disagree so profoundly and yet to work so constructively together. On 27 July Burghley wrote to Walsingham, 'now that I am out of office of the Secretary, you shall do best to write to Sir Thomas Smith'; 'and yet,' he added truthfully, 'I am not discharged from my ordinary care.'[21]

Of course, Roberto Ridolfi and his antics were not the only political preoccupation of these years. An alternative way to solve the succession crisis, and one that had a particular appeal to Cecil, was for Elizabeth herself to marry, and once the Habsburg negotiations had hit the buffers, there was a vacancy for a candidate. Unfortunately, the man proposed was in most respects unsuitable. He was Henry, Duke of Anjou, the younger brother of Charles IX. The idea appears to have originated with the Cardinal of Chatillon who (in spite of his title) was a Huguenot and the brother of the soon-to-be-murdered Huguenot leader Gaspard de Coligny, Admiral of France. Rather reluctantly Catherine de Medici, who wanted an English alliance for other reasons, took up the idea and started to make informal overtures.[22]

She could hardly have chosen a less promising candidate. Not only was he French, which would inevitably involve further disruption to the delicately restored relations with the Low Countries, he was also an ardent Catholic and even younger than Charles, who had been rejected on that ground several years before. He was, in fact, 18 years younger than Elizabeth—almost young enough to be her son, as she pointed out. Nevertheless there were other factors to be considered and the English council (including Cecil) took the proposal seriously. At first, the most positive consideration was that it would cut off French support for Mary, and when Mary made it clear that she would in any case prefer to rely on Philip, the case for a French alliance was doubly strengthened. The one thing that Elizabeth could not afford was to be at odds with both her Catholic neighbours at the same time. Sir Nicholas Bacon seems to have been the most enthusiastic for the marriage, declaring that by it:

THE QUEEN *shall be delivered of the continual fear of the practices with the Queen of Scots, on whom dependeth almost the only prosperity of the queen's whole life and reign, so as her majesty may deliver if she please and permit her* [Mary] *to marry whom she list; and indeed it were convenient she were also married after that the Queen shall be married* ...[23]

Burghley was also supportive, although less enthusiastic. Of Elizabeth's closest advisers, only Leicester seems to have been opposed—perhaps more out of concern for Elizabeth's happiness than for any more political reason. The main obstacle, it quickly transpired, was again religion. Elizabeth started, as she had in the negotiations with Charles, by suggesting the terms of the Philip and Mary treaty as a basis, but of course religion had not been an issue in that case. The fact that the negotiations were conducted in France by Walsingham and in England primarily by Burghley, both of them strong Protestants, may have been relevant, but they do not seem to have differed in any way from the queen in what they were prepared to offer. In England, the duke would have to conform to the established church, and that he absolutely refused to countenance.[24] The negotiators danced around in circles, trying to find a way out of this impasse, but by May 1571 they had failed and the talks were in effect stalled.

However, Charles saw his brother's marriage as a possible way of obtaining military help for a campaign in the Low Countries, and for that reason another attempt was made. Burghley and Leicester now combined forces to suggest that religion should be omitted from the treaty altogether, and dealt with *ad hoc* as it arose. This, however, was acceptable to neither of the protagonists. As the attempts to find some compromise continued, many of Elizabeth's councillors went off the idea of a marriage altogether. Leicester reverted to his earlier opposition, and was joined by Mildmay, Knollys and Clinton. Outside the council, Walsingham was also now advising against. Only Burghley seem to have stuck to his guns, largely because neither he nor Elizabeth could see any future in an alliance without a marriage.[25]

By December 1571, however, the queen had changed her mind. By then it was clear that a marriage on any acceptable terms was out of the question, and she instructed her envoys to cut their losses and change tack. Philip had long since concluded that there was nothing in the talk of marriage, but that a treaty aimed against himself was feasible, which is why he gave guarded support to the Ridolfi plot in its final stages. In a sense he was right, but Elizabeth had more than one purpose in mind in seeking a deal with Charles IX. Sending a message to Philip was intended, and resulted in an agreement with Alba over trade with the Netherlands, but she was also seeking to isolate Mary's party in Scotland from French help, to strengthen the Huguenot party at the French court and to curtail possible French ambitions in the Low Countries.

Early in 1572, Burghley was again ill—so ill, some reports said, that his life was despaired of. However, this seems to have been diplomatic exaggeration as he was back at his desk about a week later. How far this indisposition affected his control of the negotiations with France is not clear, but probably not much, as other councillors were paying him

regular visits. The Anglo-French Treaty of Blois was finally signed on
19 April 1572, promising an anti-Spanish alliance. It was, as events
were to demonstrate, a limited and pragmatic agreement, and the only
problem it really solved was that of possible French intervention in
Scotland. It may have encouraged the Huguenots, but it did not weaken
the Guises, and within four months the whole diplomatic realignment
that it represented was thrown into doubt by the St Bartholomew's
Day massacre of Huguenots in August and all that stemmed from it.[26]

Reaction to the news of that event was almost as worrying to
Burghley as the events themselves. There were demands in London for
revenge attacks upon English Catholics and the Bishop of London (no
less) sent him a list of suggested responses headed, 'Forthwith to cut
off the Scottish Queen's head'.[27] No doubt the lord treasurer would
privately have agreed, but for the time being his public function was to
steady the boat. On 7 September he wrote to the Earl of Shrewsbury
(Mary's 'host'):

THESE FRENCH TRAGEDIES *and ending of [an] unlucky*
*marriage with blood and vile murders, cannot be expressed with*
*tongue to declare the cruelties ... None of any name of the religion is left*
*living, but such as fled and escaped their pursuers ... These fires may be*
*doubted that their flames may come hither and into Scotland, for such*
*cruelties have large scope ...*[28]

He noted also that the king of France now seemed to repent of his role
in the affair. When she received the French ambassador on 8 September Elizabeth was, according to Burghley, cool and sceptical but not
overtly hostile. She did not believe the excuse of a Huguenot conspiracy, but was inclined to accept that Charles had intended no such outcome. Both sides were anxious to protect the Treaty of Blois, so
although the queen had, for the benefit of her own subjects, to go
through the motions of outrage and distress—and may have genuinely
felt both those emotions—no hostile action resulted.

Cecil may well have felt like knocking a few French heads together,
but he fully supported his mistress's detached response. For one thing,
a new Anglo-French marriage negotiation was under way: another
Valois prince had hoven into sight, Francis, Duke of Alençon, the
youngest of the three brothers. This suggestion had been made by
Catherine almost as soon as the negotiation for his elder brother

Henry had stalled. Admittedly Alençon was even younger than the Duke of Anjou, but Elizabeth had appeared to accept the principle of a much younger husband, so what difference did a year or two make? At first the queen was dismissive. She had had enough of the Valois princes and their eternal religious scruples and 'by God's assistance we shall now determine with advice of our good counsellors to enjoy our own natural desire, that is to live unmarried, and yet provide remedies for the quietness of our realm ...'²⁹ However, Elizabeth's statements can seldom be taken at face value, and this time, with a fresh parliament (and a further agitation) in prospect, by the end of April she was beginning to change her tune.

One big difference between Francis and his brother was that he was not ideological. Although he was a Catholic, he was much more malleable, a *politique*, and he picked up support from most of Henry's Huguenot followers who defected when the latter's extremist credentials became clear. In June Francis sent Elizabeth an assurance that religion would not be an obstacle as far as he was concerned. During the autumn, in the wake of the massacre, the initiatives were coming mostly from France. Polite and inconclusive exchanges continued. Alençon proposed a private visit, and the suggestion was delicately evaded. In September 1573, when the queen had run out of excuses, a visit was actually arranged, but then the French backed out, sending instead a high-ranking envoy who achieved nothing.

Catherine lost interest and on 31 May 1574 Charles IX died. This had the effect of bringing Henry (who had briefly accepted the crown of Poland) hastening home. It also had the effect of reigniting the civil wars and Alençon, who was trusted by neither side, became virtually a prisoner at court.³⁰ Meanwhile Burghley, and indeed most of the council, continued to favour the marriage, and worked towards it, taking what opportunities they could from Elizabeth's changes of mood. The queen was now over 40 and, although there was no indelicate mention of her menopause (or climacteric, as it was called at the time), it is fairly clear that the council regarded this as a last-ditch attempt. Any marriage that was to stand a chance of settling the main issue of the succession would have to happen soon—very soon. After that, marriage, although it was still an option, had far fewer arguments to commend it.

Late in 1573, with the negotiation yet again stalled, Burghley was incapacitated by gout. He was absent from council meetings from 3 December until 24 February. In that time he wrote to a friend:

> I MAKE MY ACCOUNT *now of the rest of my life, to become as one subject to the cross, both of body and mind, for indeed I find no other likelihood here about a court. And yet I see I must abide with patience for I see no ordinary remedy, except I should wilfully leave service and incur indignation ...*[31]

Burghley was to be intermittently out of action for most of 1574, some three and a half months altogether. This was less important than it would have been when he had to carry the day-by-day work of the secretariat. Now he was primarily a counsellor, and there is no suggestion that his influence in that capacity was impaired by his frequent absences. Indeed, his incapacity was such that it affected his going rather than his thinking, and there is some evidence that he was consulted, either by his colleagues or by the queen herself, when he was physically unable to get to the court. His friends, nevertheless, were agitated by his absence, as much, perhaps, for his sake as for their own. 'We have great want of you here for despatching matters', Smith wrote to him on 6 December 1574, referring not to any specific business but to their collective inability to persuade the queen to act in any matter whatsoever without his magic persuasive touch.[32]

Cecil was back at his desk on 21 January 1575, and active through most of that year, but his health was becoming something of an obsession. Just about every letter he wrote for the next 12 months complains about it in one way or another. He was 55, and was to live another 23 years, so rumours of his imminent demise were greatly exaggerated; the natural suspicion now is that much of his illness was psychosomatic. He lived under constant stress, ground between colleagues who were passionate for action and a queen who lived by procrastination. Nevertheless, there was nothing new in that situation, and 1574–5 was no different from any other period. He took the waters at Buxton, Derbyshire from time to time, but the 16th century knew no effective treatment for the gout, other than that which his natural resilience could provide. It must be presumed that at this time his resilience had reached a low ebb.

When Archbishop Parker died on 17 May 1575, Burghley recommended Edmund Grindal of York as his successor. He must have been away from court at the time, because he wrote to Francis Walsingham, who had been appointed second secretary in December 1573 and was increasingly trusted with confidential matters, 'I pray you, if you know not the contrary of her Majesty's determination to take my proxy for my poor voice for the archbishop of York ...'[33] This was an usually diffident approach, which may have been partly due to the fact that Grindal's puritan sympathies were well known, and Cecil may have been expecting a royal rebuff. However, his advice was accepted perhaps because Grindal was known to be a competent administrator. The problems were to come later.

Meanwhile, the accession of Henry III to the throne of France had led to an immediate resumption of civil war, and Alençon, ideologically uncommitted, was caught in limbo. Anxious to get him off their hands, and desiring to tie Elizabeth down, in September 1575 Henry and Catherine revived the marriage proposal—a policy, as Susan Doran has said, 'born of desperation'.[34] Elizabeth was not, apparently, any keener on the marriage than before, but was anxious to deploy the duke for her own purposes. After the Peace of Monsieur in May 1576 the Duke of Alençon became Duke of Anjou, and the proposal lay dormant for two years.

When it was revived, apparently at the suggestion of the Earl of Sussex in May 1578, the circumstances were completely different. The rebellion in the Netherlands had smouldered since 1572, but refused to be doused. At first the Prince of Orange had hoped for English assistance—and indeed, some came in the unofficial guise of volunteers—but Elizabeth settled with Alba in the spring of 1573 and the Prince was compelled to look elsewhere. Alba was withdrawn by Philip later in the same year, and replaced with Don Luis de Requescens, whose aims were the same but whose approach was far more subtle. He entered into negotiations with the rebels, but by the summer of 1575 the talks at Breda had broken down, and in November of the same year the estates of Holland and Zeeland offered the sovereignty of those provinces to Elizabeth in return for English military assistance.[35]

There was no chance that the queen would accept. She had sent Dr Thomas Wilson to Requescens, asking for the expulsion of English Catholic refugees and offering to mediate in the on-going war. Wilson's instructions were drawn up by Burghley, who also handled his reports and almost all his letters.[36] Wilson got Antwerp reopened and some of the fugitives expelled, but he got nowhere with his offer of mediation. Philip, although flexible on some matters, would authorize not the slightest concession on religion.

When Elizabeth refused the estates offer, Orange turned instead to the Duke of Alençon, and in May 1576 the same offer was made to him. Requescens had died unexpectedly in March 1576 and Philip was bankrupt. As a result the government in Brussels began to fall apart, and in November an unpaid and mutinous Spanish army sacked the City of Antwerp. This 'Spanish Fury' had immediate political conse-quences. It was believed that as many as 18,000 people had perished, and within days the Pacification of Ghent had been signed, pledging the Catholic provinces of the south to join with their northern and Protestant neighbours in driving out the Spaniards and finding a reli-gious *modus vivendi* of their own.[37] The newly arrived Spanish gover-nor, Philip's bastard brother Don John, with neither money nor troops at his disposal, had to accept the Pacification and to recognize its pro-visional government, which he did by the Eternal Edict in February 1577. Despite its name, this was a mere holding operation until Philip's embarrassment was overcome and fresh resources arrived.

In the late spring of 1578, in sheer desperation, as it would seem, Elizabeth authorized the Earl of Sussex to re-open the marriage nego-tiation with Anjou. Her council, as was customary by now, was divided. Every step of the tortuous negotiations that went on between England and the Estates General, every aborted idea and failed sugges-tion, can be traced in the memoranda and letters that Lord Burghley wrote for the benefit of the queen, his colleagues and the ambassadors in France and the Netherlands.[38] He was, it is clear, equally worried about the possible victory of Don John and the possible appearance of the Duke of Anjou at the head of a powerful army.

Burghley was by this time firmly on the side of the interventionists and was not, apparently, consulted over the renewal of the marriage offer. Late in July 1578 he confessed to Walsingham that he was not privy to the discussions that the queen had been having with the French ambassador. This was most unusual, and was presumably based on the assumption that, as one who favoured direct intervention, he would be out of sympathy with any such proposal. Only by using Anjou to intervene directly, he urged, could Elizabeth avoid the crippling necessity to be 'the head of the war' herself.[39] Once the duke had responded positively to these renewed matrimonial advances, by August 1578, Burghley was, it would seem, firmly back in the negotiating frame. He responded on the queen's behalf to the French envoys insisting, upon her explicit instructions, that she would not marry sight unseen. Anjou would have to come to England to be inspected. The duke sent a confidential agent, Jean de Simier, to England bearing expensive gifts and prepared for what would soon prove to be the last throw of the matrimonial dice.

The situation in the Netherlands was far more complex than this simple outline would suggest. The rebels were divided into several different groups, particularly after 1576 when several of the southern provinces became involved. Not all accepted William of Orange's leadership, and the English council was often uncertain as to just whom it was dealing with.[40] By January 1579 the dominant rebel provinces of Holland and Zeeland had had enough of the confusion. A clearer sense of rebel identity was needed, and in that month they signed the Union of Utrecht, creating an entity which was clearly Protestant as well as anti-Spanish. In the interim Don John had died at the beginning of October 1578, and been replaced with Alexander Farnese, Duke of Parma. Parma was quick to capitalize upon the uncertain situation in which those rebel provinces that had not accepted the Union of Utrecht now found themselves. Negotiating with the Catholic nobles rather than with the estates, he brought about the so-called 'Union of Arras'. Here there were no intractable religious issues to be resolved, and the southern provinces returned to their allegiance in exchange for a few political concessions. This made it possible for Elizabeth to set a price on her assistance, but it also meant unavoidably that any intervention would be seen as serving the cause of international Protestantism, a position that she was most reluctant to embrace.

Meanwhile Lord Burghley, having been out of action for much of 1574 and part of 1575, was back in the thick of things. One of the reasons for this was the failing health of Sir Thomas Smith. By the end of 1575 he had virtually ceased to function, and he was to die soon after. With Walsingham spending an increasing proportion of his time on foreign missions, this meant that Burghley was virtually acting as secretary again. In December 1576 a crisis broke over the English Church, and he became (inevitably) heavily involved. As we have seen, he had successfully spoken for Edmund Grindal as Parker's replacement at

Canterbury in the previous year, in spite of Grindal's reputation as a somewhat angular reformer. Late in 1576 this issue resurfaced because the queen took exception to the 'prophecyings', or clerical training exercises, that he was particularly keen to encourage. These were really embryonic presbyteries, which Thomas Cartwright, among other notable puritans, supported warmly, so it is not surprising that Elizabeth was hostile.[41]

While Burghley was at court during December, the queen summoned Grindal and peremptorily ordered him to suppress them. The archbishop instead wrote her a long letter, pleading their usefulness and sanction in Holy Writ. His conscience, he declared, would not allow him to accept her edict, the effect of which belonged to his own office. There was talk of bringing the archbishop before the Star Chamber, and in that context Burghley wrote to him on 29 November:

I T WERE GOOD *for the archbishop by way of answer to the first [charge] to allow the Queen's majesty's proceedings, grounded upon such cases as to him it doth now appear did move her majesty thereto. And herein to use good speeches of her Majesty as a prince that in all her public doings hath shown her wisdom …*[42]

When he had refused compliance, Elizabeth had gone over Grindal's head to forbid the prophecyings, and it seems to have been that action which Burghley had in mind here. The archbishop was never tried, and nothing came of Burghley's suggestions. The archbishop's sequestration was renewed, and lasted until he died six years later, but it seems clear that the lord treasurer retained his credit with both sides. Undistracted by these ructions he was to stick to his main agenda resolutely until marriage ceased to be an option and the Queen of Scots had gone to the block.

Burghley and Elizabeth never agreed over Mary, or over those who persisted in defending her. After the queen had sought refuge in England, her party in Scotland remained strong, and continued to encourage themselves with illusory hopes of assistance out of France, but they were never strong enough to challenge the regency of the Earl of Mar. When Mar died on 28 October 1572 he was succeeded by the Earl of Morton, but the balance of power did not significantly change. To Burghley's mind the only sensible policy was to back him, and either to suppress the Catholics or force them to settle on unfavourable terms.

After Mar's death, while he was about his judicial duties as lord treasurer, Burghley received a letter from the Earl of Leicester outlining how the council was endeavouring to persuade the queen to take some decisive action against the 'Castillians', as the Catholics were called from the fact that they were holding Edinburgh Castle. 'There will be little done', Leicester went on, 'while you are away. If I say plainly as I think, your lordship, as the case stands, shall do her Majesty and your country more service here in an hour than in all the courts there will be worth this seven years. Therefore I cannot but wish you here.'[43]

The queen sent Morton financial aid, but by February 1573 it was clear that money alone would not be enough. Arms, powder and even troops would be needed to shift the Castillians. While the queen still hesitated, Burghley began to prepare a suitable force, and on 12 March he succeeded in inducing her to commission Sir William Drury, the Marshal of Berwick, to lead a force to the regent's assistance. On 17 May Drury opened fire on the castle and within days its occupants were suing for terms. This was not the end of Scottish Catholicism, but it was the end of Mary's party as an organized political force, and Lord Burghley deserves most of the credit. Nothing further was, or could be, done about Mary herself once the charges against her had been stalled with a 'non proven' verdict. Cecil led a team in negotiation with her in 1570, but her involvement in the Ridolfi plot put paid to any such hopeful thoughts. It also turned Cecil from a sceptic into an enemy, and as Lord Burghley he never had any direct dealings with the Scottish queen.

In March 1575 Burghley was also appointed royal exchanger.[44] This gave him control over all operations for the conversion of foreign currencies into sterling, and vice versa, and was really complementary to his duties as lord treasurer. He presumably discharged the functions by deputy, so how much of his time was actually taken up in this way, we do not know. Smith, who succeeded him as secretary was highly intelligent and industrious, as well as being an old friend, but he had nothing like Cecil's rapport with the queen, and wore himself out in about three years. As we have seen, in 1574 when Burghley was away from his desk, Smith found himself unable to cope, although by that time he had been reinforced by the talents of Sir Francis Walsingham, appointed in December 1573.

Walsingham was a more substantial political figure than Smith, but he pursued his own agenda, and not infrequently had to call upon Burghley in an effort to make that agenda more acceptable to the queen. He also spent much time on foreign missions, both to France and the Low Countries, missions for which Burghley may have been partly responsible. Walsingham was a more straightforward Protestant than Burghley, and the queen occasionally found his outspokenness unattractive. It is also possible that, in spite of his complaints of overwork and poor health, Burghley did not want anyone else to share his unique relationship with Elizabeth, the main substance of the honour of which he was so sensitive. As we have seen, when that was challenged for a few months by Robert Dudley, he talked seriously of flouncing out in a huff. Thomas Wilson, who became second secretary (to Walsingham) in November 1577 was a hard-working bureaucrat who never challenged either of them for political influence.[45]

Burghley's sense of his status required concrete symbols, and a major manifestation, as it would be of his son Robert, was building and landscaping on a major scale. Elizabeth was a regular visitor to Theobalds, which had been constructed partly with such visits in mind. Burghley House at Stamford (plates 11 and 12), which Cecil had inherited from his father, was the oldest of his residences. He had begun rebuilding it during Mary's reign and it was substantially complete by 1564. Only an unexpected outbreak of smallpox had frustrated a royal visit there in 1566, but Lincolnshire was rather off the beaten track as far as progresses were concerned and more likely to be called at by officials or emissaries on their way to Scotland.

The most accessible of Burghley's residences was Cecil House near the Strand in London, which he had acquired from the crown after the attainder of Sir Thomas Palmer in 1553. This was his normal base when he was working in the capital. John Stow believed that it had been 'beautifully increased' by Cecil in the early 1560s[46] (the queen called in during 1561, as much to view the building progress as to stay), but the owner himself spoke of it rather disparagingly, as a modern official might refer to a 'working pad'. However, with the birth (and more important the survival) of his third son, Robert, in 1563, it became clear that more was needed. Burghley House would go (God willing) to his son Thomas, but Robert would also be a man of substance and would require suitable accommodation. Moreover Cecil, excited by the competitive spirit of the age, also needed a prestigious house. So he bought Theobalds and set to work. The location was a convenient one, close to London and to Elizabeth's old favourite, Hatfield, which was nine and a half miles away. It was also surrounded by the homes of his friends and relations—Sir Thomas Smith at Hills Hall, Sir Anthony Cooke at Gidea Hall and Sir Nicholas Bacon, who was similarly building at Gorhambury, near St Albans.[47] Elizabeth called in during July 1564, but that would have been to the old (and seriously inadequate) manor house, because building on the great new house had only just commenced.

The house was built in stages, and was not completed until 1585. When Elizabeth came again in September 1571 the hall block was probably complete, and the accommodation would have been adequate, but it was undoubtedly still a building site as work on the second court had only just begun. It was probably with royal encouragement that at about this time Cecil's priorities changed. Robert would, in due course, inherit this pile, but Robert was a child and that was (hopefully) several years off. Meanwhile what was needed was not just a prestigious house but a prodigy house, matching the greatest that the major peerage families could produce, and designed to entertain the whole court. In 1571–2 the cost of building operations suddenly shot up from a few hundred to £2700.[48] This must have been connected with a frantic rush to get the middle court and the core of what was now a palace ready to receive another royal visit in July 1572, when the newly ennobled Lord Burghley was finally able to play the host in style. Thereafter the annual cost declined again, but work continued. Elizabeth came again in May 1574, in 1576, 1582, 1587, 1591 and shortly before Burghley's death in 1598—more often than she visited anyone else. The cost was enormous, reputedly between £2000 and £3000 a visit, but Burghley (in spite of his protestations) was a very wealthy man, and the social and political capital that these visits conferred made the expenditure well worth while.

Theobalds was not only prodigious, it was a model. Holdenby, Castle Ashby and Audley End all seem to have been influenced by it, and many others may have been. Cecil seems to have been, partly at least, his own architect, and designing his pet palace seems to have been one of his chief relaxations, when he could afford such luxuries. Unfortunately nothing survives of the house itself, so that it is only by an exercise of the imagination that we can communicate with Lord Burghley through one of his favourite projects.

## LORD BURGHLEY, MAN OF MEANS

NOW I HAVE SPOKEN *of his birth, rising and services in public affairs, yet further to prove he was truly honourable, honest and nobly minded, let me describe unto you his course and condition in his private disposition & domestical life, as truly as I can, though not so truly and exquisitely as he practiced the same: leaving it to the censure of the wise and judicious, not of the partial or passionate, to judge of his virtues, rather by his own deeds than by other men's reports. The latter may err through ignorance or design, or other causes; but the former will speak better to the purpose.*

*And first to begin with his housekeeping. It is to be noted that he kept principally two houses or families, one at London, the other at Theobalds. Though he was also at charge both at Burghley and at court, which made his houses in a manner four.*

*At his house in London he kept ordinarily in household four score persons.*

*Besides his lordship and such as attended him at court.*

*The charge of this housekeeping in London amounted to thirty pounds a week. And the whole sum yearly to one thousand, five hundred and sixty pounds. And this was in his absence.*

*And in the terms times or when his Lordship lay at London, his charge increased ten or twelve pounds a week more.*

*At Theobalds he kept continually (himself and his household lying at London) twenty six or thirty persons.*

*The charge of his housekeeping there being weekly twelve pounds.*

*And also (in his absence) relieved there daily twenty or thirty poor people at the gate. And besides gave weekly in money, by the hands of Mr. Richard Neale, his lordship's chaplain, Vicar of Cheshunt, twenty shillings to the poor there.*

*The weekly charge in setting the poor on work there, as weeders, labourers etc., came to ten pounds.*

*And so his weekly charge at Theobalds (over and above the twenty shillings there given weekly to the poor, his household being at London, was twenty two pounds & the yearly sum one thousand one hundred and forty four pounds.*

*His whole household expenses, both at Theobalds and London, being both summed together, his yearly charge was two thousand, seven hundred and four pounds, when his lordship was continually at court.*

*But his charge, you may imagine, much increased at his Lordship's coming home. For I have heard his officers affirm, that, at his Lordship's being at Theobalds, it hath cost him fourscore pounds in a week. That is fifty and eight pounds a week more, over and above the former two and twenty.*

*The charge of his stable ( not here mentioned) was yearly a thousand marks at the least.*

*Besides which certain charge, he bought great quantities of corn in time of dearth, to furnish markets about his house at under prices, to pull down the market, to relieve the poor.*

*He gave also, for releasing of prisoners, in many of his latter years, forty & fifty pounds in a term.*

*And for twenty years together, he gave yearly in beef, bread and money at Christmas, to the poor of Westminster, St. Martins, St. Clements & Theobalds, thirty five and sometimes forty pounds per annum.*

*He gave also yearly to twenty poor men lodging in the Savoy, twenty suits of apparel.*

*He gave also for three years before he died, to poor persons and to poor parishes, in money, weekly, forty and five shillings.*

*So as his certain alms, besides extraordinary, was cast up to be five hundred pounds yearly, one year with another.*

[Francis Peck, *Desiderata Curiosa*, 1779 edition, pp. 22–3.]

As well as being a builder, Cecil was also a gardener. His anonymous biographer tells us that he 'also greatly delighted in making gardens, fountains and walks, which at Theobalds were perfected most costly, beautifully and pleasantly, where one might walk two miles.'[49] There were in fact four gardens at Theobalds; the great garden to the south, the maze garden to the west, the cook's (kitchen) garden to the north-west, and the old privy garden to the north. The east was the main entrance, lined with trees. Not very much is known about the configuration of these gardens, which have long since vanished, but we do know that they were looked after by John Gerard, who cared for all Burghley's gardens, and who dedicated his well-known herbal to his employer in the year before his death.[50]

To Cecil the family man we will return in due course, but of the creator of homes we can only say that, as well as providing some relaxation from his intensely busy work schedules, there was also method in his madness. His delicate and immensely important relationship with his sovereign did not depend upon his being able to entertain her in style, but it was obviously what she expected. Theobalds was a necessary creation—an aspect and a symbol of Cecil's place in the political and administrative hierarchy. It was as important to its builder as were his offices, his armorial bearings and his (largely fictitious) pedigree tracing his descent from the princes of Wales. The political landscape of Elizabethan England was as much about symbolism as it was about function.

# CHAPTER 7

# The Elder Statesman

IT WOULD NOT be quite true to claim that Elizabeth and Burghley grew old together. There were 13 years between them and, while the queen was in robust health (most of the time), her lord treasurer was a martyr to gout and suffered from fits of depression. Nevertheless, he presided over one of her more important rites of passage. Between 1579 and 1581 she conducted her final matrimonial negotiation, and (apparently) underwent her last emotional crisis.[1] After 1581, with Elizabeth in her 49th year, everyone acknowledged that there was no longer any point in pretending. For reasons of his own, unconnected with romantic dalliance, the Duke of Anjou had proposed to Elizabeth in the summer of 1578; she, for equally unromantic reasons, had responded positively. She had also indicated that she would need to see Anjou first, which he had found acceptable, and in January 1579 had sent Jean de Simier, 'a most choice courtier', to England to make the necessary arrangements. As Francis Walsingham observed, 'The negotiation of Monsieur here taketh greater foot than was at first looked for', a reaction that he rightly ascribed to 'the decayed state of things in the Low Countries' and to the fact that Elizabeth still viewed a French marriage as the best security against the Spaniards.[2]

Simier made a most favourable impression, but he was referred for the political aspect of his negotiation to a committee consisting of Burghley, Leicester, Sussex and Walsingham. Of these, Burghley and Sussex supported the proposal, while Leicester and Walsingham (for different reasons) were hostile. The fact that Anjou was making no headway in the Netherlands, and had actually retreated into France, encouraged both the queen and the pro-marriage politicians; it seemed clear that he could only succeed with English backing, and that fear of an overwhelming French presence was totally unrealistic. Burghley, as was his wont, set out the pros and cons in two lengthy memoranda at the end of March.[3] These were agenda for council discussions, but it is equally likely that they were intended for the queen's eyes. In the first of these he effectively put the case against the marriage, based partly upon the queen's age and the unlikeliness of children and partly on the ancient hatred of the English for the French. In the second memorandum, he proposed to answer the objections, and his answers appear lame enough to modern eyes although they clearly had force for him. If there were no children of the marriage, no great harm would be done. Her Majesty would have done her best, and the Lord would no doubt provide for the succession. At the same time Anjou was the best of the French princes and sympathetic to true religion.

It seems that Burghley was persuading himself against his own better judgement. Other contemporary notes (although not in Burghley's hand) make the same points. A French alliance was desirable for a number of reasons, and an alliance with Anjou would protect the Huguenots. Cecil came out in favour of the match, for two reasons: first, he was desperately worried about the threat from Spain, and saw this as the only possible safeguard; and second, he was close enough to the queen to have divined that that was what she really wanted.[4] The arguments went backwards and forwards. In addition to worrying about Spain, Burghley was deeply concerned about Mary Stuart and about the threat from the English Catholics, both of which he thought that the alliance would remedy. Simier wanted to begin negotiations straight away, Elizabeth wanted to see the duke first.

By the end of March, Elizabeth had decided to concede, and Leicester wrote, 'I newly hear and find her in deep consideration of her estate, and that she is persuaded nothing can more assure it than marriage. I may be of a mind that she will marry if the party like her'[5], which was more or less the conclusion that Burghley had come to, although Leicester remained opposed to the union. However, he had compromised his influence by his own secret marriage (to Lettice, Countess of Essex) and the opposition to the match in council was thereafter led by Francis Walsingham—to whom all papists (and especially French ones) were bastards. It is also worth noticing that Burghley had been losing ground in council over the previous few years, especially in relation to Walsingham and especially over foreign policy, and that it was his positive role in these negotiations that restored his influence. It may be too cynical to suggest that that was part of his purpose, but that was certainly the effect.[6] By the middle of June he and Sussex had sufficiently prevailed in council for a safe conduct to be issued for Anjou to come to England and, after some intense negotiation on the French side, he reached Greenwich on 17 August.

The duke's visit was brief and uneventful, but its effect upon the relationship was positive. Elizabeth nicknamed him her 'frog', carried his picture and entertained him lavishly. Whether she was genuinely attracted to him, or merely on the rebound after the news of Leicester's marriage we do not know—but she gave the impression of being a woman in love. However, her subjects were not amused, and in August 1579 *The Discoverie of a Gaping Gulf* by John Stubbs hit the streets of London. This suspiciously echoed all the arguments that had been used against the marriage in the council earlier in the summer, only with a much sharper and more puritanical edge. The queen would put her life at risk; and like any weak woman, she was vulnerable to the wiles of Satan—and so on.[7] Elizabeth, understandably, was furious, not only at the attack on her intentions but at the unsubtle echo of John Knox's *First Blast of the Trumpet.* Stubbs and his printer were both judicially mutilated, and if it had not been for their support in high places would probably have lost their lives.

Burghley tried to refute the arguments of *The Gaping Gulf,* but outside the court the opposition was thoroughly stimulated. Sermons were preached against it, agitators ranted and the more subtle published allegorical stories like *The Moste Strange Wedding of the Frogge and the Mouse,* and *Mother Hubbard's Tale.*[8] The fury of this opposition seems to have taken both the queen and the council by surprise. Elizabeth called upon the latter again, and in early October they began to backtrack. Burghley continued to argue positively, but he was losing ground and on the 7th they simply handed the decision back to Elizabeth, who reacted by 'shedding many tears'—as much of rage as of real sorrow.

After dithering for over a month, the queen decided to exercise her prerogative and to proceed regardless. She authorized a committee of the council (on which both Burghley and Sussex served) to draw up a treaty based on that between Philip and Mary, which was done within a few days, and Simier took it back to France, where it was swiftly signed. Elizabeth then appears to have changed her mind. In January

1580 she announced that she would have to obtain the consent of her subjects—presumably by recalling parliament—and until then the treaty could not be ratified. Anjou did not want to withdraw, but could make no progress on his own, and through most of 1580 the negotiation remained in limbo.

Meanwhile, threats grew on all sides. Pope Gregory XIII renewed his predecessor's excommunication of the queen; Philip II occupied Portugal; in September Spanish troops occupied Smerwick in the west of Ireland; and the Catholic Duke of Lennox appeared to have gained a complete ascendancy over the young James of Scotland.[9] At the same time, the first Jesuit missionaries arrived in England. These tidings shifted Elizabeth far enough to encourage her to admit French commissioners in August, much to Anjou's delight, but no further progress was made. Finally, in July 1581, Elizabeth informed the French ambassador that marriage was out of the question, and suggested some other form of 'amity'. She would prefer to run the risk of a war with the marriage rather than without it, but since it was now out of the question because of the opposition of her subjects, it was necessary to find another way.[10] By this time, however, the duke was not disposed to take no for an answer—not least because he was again in desperate financial straits—and he returned to London on 1 November 1581 in a last-ditch attempt to rescue the marriage negotiations. It seems that he almost succeeded. On 22 November Elizabeth suddenly announced that she would marry him after all, kissed him passionately and gave him a ring. If this had not been done in public, with many witnesses, such behaviour might well seem incredible—but the news spread like wildfire and bonfires were lit in Antwerp.[11]

The celebrations were premature. Not only did the queen's ladies express genuine horror at such a dangerous commitment, but the opposition in council was immediately resurrected. Elizabeth summoned Anjou and withdrew her pledge. He was furious, 'taxing the lightness of women, and the inconstancy of islanders, with two or three biting and smart scoffs', but there was nothing that he could do. With this somewhat bizarre episode Elizabeth's protracted and inconclusive courtships finally came to an end. Whether Burghley was as upset as logically he should have been is uncertain. He had restored his credit as a councillor and, at the end of the day, that may have been the most important consideration to him.

Of course, this drama was not played out in a vacuum. In the summer of 1581 there was a plan afoot to send Sir Francis Drake to the Azores, partly in support of Don Antonio, the pretender to the Portuguese throne, and partly to form a base from which to raid Spain's transatlantic shipping. Drake's reputation was at its height following his circumnavigation of the previous year, and Philip was already seriously annoyed, so this would be a risk too far unless an alliance was concluded with France. The council discussed the plan at length, and Burghley pointed out that since the Azores had not actually been taken over by Spain, such an expedition could be represented as support for the legitimate ruler, Don Antonio—an intervention that no treaty between England and Spain forbade.[12]

Meanwhile the Duke of Anjou got his intervention in the Netherlands into a terminal mess. After making an abortive attempt to seize Antwerp in January 1583 he withdrew in disgrace, while the Duke of Parma continued his advances in the south. In August 1583 the estates general moved its base from Antwerp to the Hague and the whole of Brabant was lost to the rebels.[13] In June 1584 the duke died, still unmarried, and the possibility of French intervention effectively died with him. The heir to the childless Henry III was now the Huguenot leader Henry of Navarre, and that fact alone was sufficient to destabilize the fragile French regime.

Then came a much more serious blow. In July 1584 Catholic attempts to assassinate William of Orange were at last successful and the Dutch rebels were deprived at once of their military leader, chief negotiator and inspiration. The English council was now faced with a stark choice. The queen called it together on 10 October and Burghley, as usual, drew up the position papers.[14] He reminded his colleagues of the likely fate of England should the Dutch be overcome. Philip would have been encouraged by the death of Anjou, and even more by that of William, 'who of all men living hath been the greatest stay of his conquest'. The queen, he wrote, had no choice but to intervene, although this would mean an unsupported war against the only great power of the era. 'Finally,' he concluded, 'it ought to be Alpha and Omega to cause the people to be better taught to serve God, and to see justice daily administered unto them.'[15]

It was a gloomy picture, but, of course, resort to prayer was not seen as a last desperate gamble at that time; rather, it was a proper and sensible precaution in any kind of danger. Although he concluded in favour of intervention, Burghley's conduct of the council discussion was hardly a clarion call to arms. He knew, better than those who issued such calls —notably Walsingham—that Elizabeth would be extremely reluctant to act, no matter how great the danger, and would have to be persuaded. The council ended by advising intervention, which was probably what Burghley intended, although he did not want to appear as the protagonist.

Meanwhile, the situation in France took a turn for the worse with the signature at the end of December 1584 of an agreement between the Duke of Guise and the King of Spain. This was aimed at the exclusion of Henry of Navarre from the succession and the extirpation of heresy wherever it might be found. The threat to England was direct and manifest. When the council discussed the situation again on 18 March 1585 at his own house, Burghley changed sides. He was now convinced that a purely defensive option was the best.[16]

However, with the Dutch situation becoming more desperate by the day, the interventionists became increasingly persuasive, and at the end of June Elizabeth allowed Sir John Norris to lead 3000 foot and 200 horse in an emergency rescue attempt. Philip promptly seized all English ships in Spanish ports, and Drake was allowed to set forth on a mission for their recovery. Perhaps bowing to the logic of events, Burghley even urged him to set off at once—before the queen changed her mind!

Finally, on 10 August 1585, the Treaty of Nonsuch with the Dutch was signed, and Elizabeth was committed to military intervention. It is possible that Burghley's conversion to the anti-interventionists held up this treaty, and there was a campaign of vilification against him.[17] Suddenly, all the errors and delays of English policy became his fault. 'They say,' he wrote in a bitter letter of self-defence, 'in a rash and malicious mockery, that England is become a *regnum Cecilianum* ... if there be any cause given by me of such a nickname there may be found in many others juster causes to attribute other names than mine.'[18] The Treaty of Nonsuch was a messy compromise, but that was not Cecil's fault and, in a perverse way, the vilification was a compliment. Not willing to blame the queen, the disgruntled turned on Burghley. He did not relish being Elizabeth's whipping boy, but that was the position to which his success had brought him. Leicester and Burghley had, as we have seen, a complex relationship, which varied with mood and circumstances. In the summer of 1585 Leicester was inclined to blame the lord treasurer for the delays and uncertainties, but it was Elizabeth, not Burghley, who was dithering during the autumn.

When the earl eventually departed to lead the Dutch campaign Cecil was again laid up with the gout, but in a friendly exchange of letters he assured Leicester of his support, and seems to have been as good as his word. 'Truly,' one of Leicester's henchmen wrote to him in February 1586, 'I do know by very good means that my Lord Treasurer dealt most honourably and friendly for your Lordship to her majesty.'[19]

It was not Burghley's fault that Robert Dudley made a mess of his mission. On the field of battle he was no match for the Duke of Parma, and in politics he was no match for the Dutch. A few days later the same man wrote, 'Truly, my good Lord, I am now persuaded that this strange proceeding growth from her Majesty's self ...'[20], in which he was undoubtedly correct. Burghley gave the earl consistent support, both in general and over particular points, and did his level best to persuade Elizabeth to commit sufficient money to the operations. The annual budget for the Netherlands was £126,000, which was supposedly despatched in instalments, but there were constant quarrels over exactly how much had been received. Leicester claimed a shortfall, and was compelled on one occasion to borrow from the merchant adventurers; the queen blamed irresponsible extravagance, and both seem to have had a case. The well informed perceived that without Burghley's constant pressure no decisions would be made. 'I perceive', as one correspondent wrote, 'the Queen will conclude nothing.'[21] It has been unkindly suggested that Burghley was giving the earl enough rope to hang himself, but it is more likely that he regarded the Netherlands campaign as the earl's show, and simply acted as a facilitator.

The prestige that a great English lord was supposed to bring to the Dutch cause had quickly turned sour, and the purposes of the Treaty of Nonsuch were never properly fulfilled. Relations between the two parties were at a low ebb by the time that Leicester was eventually recalled in December 1587, but in one crucial respect the treaty had succeeded. In spite of his gains and general superiority, the Duke of Parma had not overrun the rebels, and in Maurice of Nassau, William's son, they had discovered their own commander of genius. In one sense, Leicester had ruined his standing with the queen. When he accepted the governor generalship, shortly after his arrival, she had written in a fury,

> H OW CONTEMPTUOUSLY *we conceive ourselves to have been used by you, you shall by this bearer (Sir Thomas Heneage) understand ... We could never have imagined (had we not seen it fallen out in experience) that a man raised up by ourself and extraordinarily favoured by us ... would have in so contemptible a sort broken our commandment ...*[22]

Following this stinging rebuke, confidence was never fully restored, but the sexual chemistry between them survived, as it had survived the advent of Lettice, whose visit to her husband abroad was bitterly resented. Consistently unable to live up to expectations, Leicester nevertheless remained the queen's unique favourite, and she was shattered by his death in the following year.

By the time that Leicester came back with his tail between his legs, Burghley had secured one of the great coups of his political life—the execution of Mary Queen of Scots. The lord treasurer had spent endless time and energy stabilizing the Protestant regime in Scotland, and with the demise of the Duke of Lennox in 1583 he finally seemed to have secured the good will of the 16-year-old James.[23] Meanwhile, the discovery of the Throgmorton plot to assassinate the queen and stimulate Catholic rebellion had raised domestic anxiety to fever pitch.

The unravelling of that plot was Walsingham's work, not Cecil's, but the consequences affected the whole council. The plan had involved an invasion by Guisard forces from France rather than Parma's veterans, but Mendoza the Spanish ambassador was heavily implicated, because that was where the money was to come from. The papacy, inevitably, was a party to the proposals. Throgmorton paid for his treason at Tyburn, and on 9 January 1584 Mendoza was summarily expelled. He was not replaced, so that diplomatic relations with Spain had effectively broken down over a year before the Treaty of Nonsuch, which partly explains Philip's somewhat confused reaction to that event. The other thing that Throgmorton's confessions had clearly revealed was the involvement of Mary. Her role was passive, but she knew and sanctioned the intentions, which left Elizabeth with the problem of what to do about it.

Burghley set off in the certain knowledge that Elizabeth would do nothing if she could avoid it, so he started with a private initiative. Working closely with Walsingham, but not through official channels, he produced a document known as 'The Bond of Association'—basically an undertaking on the signatories' part to revenge the queen in the event of her murder, and to exclude from the succession anyone suspected of having a part in it.[24] Mary was not named, but the implication was clear. The bond began to circulate in October 1584 and quickly attracted thousands of signatures. His second initiative was to draw up a paper 'On the dangerous Estate of the realm'. This, probably another council position paper, was almost entirely concerned with the recusant problem—the progress of the Jesuits, the sinister influence of the Catholic nobility and the incompetence of the Church in dealing with such challenges.[25] The council endorsed his concern, but the new Archbishop of Canterbury, John Whitgift, would not be dictated to; strained relations followed.

Basically, the lord treasurer could see only one menace at this stage —the Catholics. To him puritan agitators were a mere marginal nuisance, while to Whitgift, and the queen, both were equally threatening. The parliament, or rather the House of Commons, which assembled in November 1584, agreed with Burghley, but because it had been 12 years since the last elections only about 25 per cent of the members were 'old parliament men'. The lord treasurer's friends in the House had great difficulty in persuading them not beat their heads up against the wall of royal disapproval.[26] Nevertheless Elizabeth was induced to approve a modified version of the Bond of Association and an act virtually outlawing all Catholic priests.

The Act for the Security of the Queen's Person received the royal assent on 25 March 1585. It authorized the Bond and laid down detailed procedures for dealing with those suspected of procuring the queen's death. It reaffirmed that any such suspect person was debarred from succession, and set up an augmented council for emergency government, but stopped short of declaring how to determine the succession thereafter.[27] Burghley seems to have envisaged this emergency council as being vested with that right, but no such provision ever made it to the Act. He seems to have been quite happy with the prospect of a 'monarchical republic', in which the occupancy of the throne would be determined by a combination of the existing council and the last parliament, but he failed to get that past the queen, whose commitment to hereditary right was far more implacable than it was entitled to be. She chose to ignore the fact that her own title to the crown depended upon her father's last succession act. But Burghley did not forget, and he also knew perfectly well that a similar sensibility governed Elizabeth's attitude to Mary.

In this connection, the queen's determined efforts to sweep the implications of the Throgmorton plot under the carpet were frustrated by the discovery of the insubstantial but (in the circumstances) worrying Parry plot in the spring of 1585, as we shall see.[28] Meanwhile the Queen of Scots had been removed from the custody of the Earl of Shrewbury to that of Sir Amyas Paulet at Tutbury. This probably had more to do with the fuss that the countess was kicking up than with any desire for extra security, but it had the effect of placing her under distinctly unsympathetic surveillance. It was because of Paulet's vigilance, allied to the ingenuity and excellent contacts of Walsingham, that the Queen of Scots was tempted into her final and fatal indiscretion.

Anthony Babington, a young Catholic gentleman from Derbyshire, had, thanks to his contacts in that part of the world, served as a page in the Earl of Shrewsbury's household. There he had met Mary, and become a passionate admirer. Later he had travelled to London, and hovered on the fringes of the court. By 1580 he had become a recognized leader of the Catholic 'young Turks' and an ardent supporter of the Jesuit mission. During a trip to France he had met Thomas Morgan, one of Mary's supporters in Paris, and when he returned he bore letters of commendation from Morgan to Mary.[29] In May 1586 he was approached by John Ballard, a missionary priest, who suggested that he might lead a conspiracy for Elizabeth's assassination and her replacement with the Scottish queen. By early July he had embraced this idea with his habitual enthusiasm, and set out a plan that he communicated to Mary. On 17 July she replied, urging that the assassins should strike before any attempt was made to free herself. 'The affair being thus prepared,' she wrote, 'and forces being in readiness both within and without the realm, then shall it be the time to set the six gentlemen to work, taking order, upon the accomplishment of their design, I may be suddenly transported out of this place ...'[30]

From this it is clear that an immediate strike was not intended, and as far as we know no plans had been made for foreign intervention; but time was not on the conspirators' side. Walsingham's agents intercepted the letter, and he was able to read it before sending it on to Babington. The latter appears to have become suspicious, and attempted to escape, but he was arrested in London on 14 August. So far Walsingham had been entirely responsible for this sting, but Elizabeth knew about it by the 18th, and informed Burghley. The same day he, Hatton and Sir Thomas Bromley examined the prisoner. Babington seems to have confessed the whole plot with a kind of insouciance that has aroused the suspicions of historians. Was the whole plot an invention of Walsingham's designed to entrap the Queen of Scots? If so, Babington was doubly deceived because on 13 September he was tried, along with several accomplices whom he had named and who had been swiftly rounded up, and he and Ballard, the originator of the whole affair, were executed on the 20th.[31] Mary's complicity had now been proved beyond all reasonable doubt, her papers had been seized and she herself put in close confinement at Chartley. Burghley was now left with the unenviable task of trying to persuade Elizabeth to do something about her.

At first, progress seemed promising. On 8 September he wrote to Walsingham that the queen had flatly refused to send Mary to the Tower, suggesting far-off Fotheringhay in Northamptonshire instead, but she had agreed in principle to put her on trial, and had even named a panel of peers to serve as commissioners. 'We are with many offers to and fro in words, but I cannot certify you what shall be determined … Nevertheless I hope it will be concluded this day'.[32] On the same day he drew up a memorandum for the council, detailing the arrangements for Mary's removal to Fotheringhay, and for a parliament to meet on 14 November. At this stage the intention seems to have been to try her by special commission, under the provisions of the Act of the previous year, and to have the sentence ratified by parliament. The fact that she was not a subject of the English crown removed her from the jurisdiction of the normal courts—even that of the Earl Marshall —but the statute had been drafted precisely with her in mind, and placed no limitations upon who could be tried under its terms. However, two days later Burghley wrote again, 'We are still in long arguments, but no conclusions do last, being as variable as the weather.' The issue was whether to send Mary to Fotheringhay (as Elizabeth seemed to want) or to Hertford (which the council would have preferred). 'Until the Scottish Queen be removed, there can be no hearing', Burghley concluded—not without irritation. Walsingham was laid up at this point with a sore leg, which is why so many letters passed between them, and Burghley found himself once again by way of being secretary. 'Having my hands fuller than I can deliver by Mr. Secretary's infirmity, I am constrained to scribble here ...'[33] He was himself a man of 65 or 66, and not in the best of health, but at this point he was driven. Mary reached Fotheringhay on 25 September, and Burghley followed a couple of weeks later, deeply engrossed in preparing evidence for her trial. On 2 October he wrote to Sir Edward Stafford in France, giving him a blow-by-blow account of developments so far. 'I was never more toiled', he concluded, 'than I have been of late and yet am, with services that daily multiply ...'

However, progress was being made. In spite of some last-minute doubts on the queen's part over the composition of the commission, its members met in the Star Chamber on 27 September and were briefed.[34] Preliminary drafts of the evidence were shown to them and they were despatched to Fotheringhay on 11 October. Meanwhile, Elizabeth had notified Mary of her impending trial.

Burghley reached Fotheringhay on the 12th, and proceedings commenced on the 14th. Mary, as was expected, pleaded her status and refused to accept the jurisdiction of the court. The trial proceeded none the less. Burghley appears to have worn two hats, because although he was a member of the commission, he was also presenting evidence for the prosecution. 'Ah,' Mary is alleged to have said, 'you are my adversary.' 'Yes,' said he, 'I am adversary to Queen Elizabeth's adversaries.' She tried to demand a trial by parliament (perhaps unaware that it would have been the last body to favour her), a private session with the council and a personal interview with Elizabeth.

On 15 October, the trial was suspended on the queen's orders and the commissioners headed back to London. On 25 October they reconvened in the Star Chamber and on the 31st, as Elizabeth made no further intervention, proceeded to find the Scots Queen guilty and to sentence her to death.[35] That, it soon transpired, was the easy bit. Parliament had been called in September specifically for the purpose of deciding Mary's fate, but the date of its assembly was changed several times and it did not finally convene until 29 October, by which time the sentence against Mary was a foregone conclusion. For several weeks the two Houses did little but listen to denunciations of Mary, and before they adjourned in December presented a joint petition to the queen, requesting that 'declaration of the said sentence and judgement be made and published by proclamation, and thereupon that direction be given for further proceeding against the said Scottish Queen according to the effect and true meaning of the statute'.[36]

Everybody was in an agony of indecision. Elizabeth did not know what to do, and Burghley and his colleagues did not know what to do about that. Left to herself, the queen would probably have pardoned her cousin, but the pressure on her to carry out the death sentence was remorseless, as every letter in the lord treasurer's substantial correspondence testifies. In her desperation, Elizabeth even hinted at the need for a privy assassination (about which she would, of course, have known nothing), but to his credit Paulet would have nothing to do with such an evasion of responsibility. It seems that it was not Mary's death that troubled the queen, but her own unavoidable responsibility for it. The sentiment—while understandable—does her little credit.

Burghley's position, in contrast, was straightforward. Sentence had been passed, and should be carried out. If it were not, Elizabeth's chronic insecurity would continue. Eventually, on 1 February 1587, the queen sent for the warrant and signed it. William Davidson, upon whom we depend for the account of what then happened, whisked the warrant away to Burghley and told him how he came by it. Elizabeth, he said, wanted to hear no more about it until the deed was done.[37] That did not prevent her from sending after him to withhold the warrant on the grounds that it had not been sealed. However, the messenger came too late, as he may have been intended to do, and the warrant was immediately despatched to Fotheringhay.

Burghley and Walsingham had already choreographed the ritual of the execution, but at the end of the day it was a drawn match. On the one hand the power of the state was upheld, but on the other Mary conducted herself with skill and dignity, sufficient at a later date to elevate her cause into one of Catholic martyrdom. On 11 February, two days after the execution, Elizabeth threw a defensive tantrum and committed Davidson to the Tower. Burghley might have joined him if he had not, by sheer good fortune, been laid up at home after a fall from his horse. He made several attempts to recover his position, or at least to gain a hearing, but it was the end of February before Elizabeth would so much as receive a letter from him.[38] Burghley seems to have feared that the queen's irrational anger would take some arbitrary form, either against Davidson or himself, but in that he did her an injustice. By the middle of March he was back at court, apparently none the worse, and could console himself for his temporary rustication with the thought that he had masterminded the demise of the woman whom he had regarded for nearly 20 years as the greatest single menace to Elizabeth and her crown. Perhaps the queen, in the calm of later recollection, agreed with him.

Elizabeth's mood fluctuated. In the middle of March Burghley was being consulted as though nothing had happened, but a month later he was out of favour again, and there was talk of his being sent to prison. The Earl of Leicester was still in the Low Countries, but it has been suggested that some of his associates were endeavouring to divert the queen's dissatisfaction with him onto Burghley. It is possible, but the earl's moods were also erratic. Burghley and Walsingham were both strongly in favour of maintaining support for the Dutch after Leicester's recall; indeed, they were in favour of sending him back. This had nothing to do with any perceived effectiveness, and everything to do with a desire to get him out of Elizabeth's hair She was always moody and unpredictable, but the earl's presence made her worse. Burghley also suspected, not without reason, that Leicester was undermining him, and although their direct correspondence continued to be friendly, his erratic favour at this time was probably due to the earl's influence.[39]

It was not until March 1588 that Leicester formally resigned his connection with the Low Countries, and he continued to support the ultra-Calvinists there against Maurice of Nassau, a policy analogous to that of supporting the Presbyterians in England and one that Burghley regarded as counter-productive. At the same time, England was at war with Spain, and the English council was pursuing two complementary but separate policies. On the queen's insistence they were seeking for a negotiated peace, and out of sheer necessity they were building up the country's military capacity.

The only member of the council unequivocally in favour of peace was the elderly Sir James Croft. Burghley, on Elizabeth's insistence, handled most of the negotiation through intermediaries, but he was unconvinced of their wisdom. At the same time mutual hostility to any such negotiation brought Walsingham and Leicester back together

[18] WILLIAM AND ROBERT Cecil (*above*), father and son, or—to their opponents—the so-called *regnum Cecilianum*, as imagined in a Hatfield House portrait from after 1606. Both men wear robes of the Garter.

[19] THOMAS CECIL (1542–1623), the 'unsatisfactory son' who would later inherit Lord Burghley's title. The unattributed painting, *c.*1605, is from Burghley House and shows him after his elevation as Earl of Exeter.

[20, 21] ROBERT DEVEREUX, the colourful 2nd Earl of Essex, one-time queen's toy-boy and later self-destructive plotter. The portrait (*right*) by Gheeraerts the Younger, *c.*1596, and cameo (*below*), *c.*1660, attributed to Isaac Oliver, both suggest the dashing courtier.

[22] SIR WALTER RALEIGH (1552–1618) (*right*), courtier, poet, explorer and adventurer, in an anonymous contemporary painting. His eventual fall from grace was ensured by his former friend Robert Cecil.

[23] ROBERT CECIL (1563–1612) (*below*), his father's protégé, as depicted in a contemporary painted panel from New College, Oxford.

[24] THIS MAGNIFICENT
portrait of Elizabeth I, ageing
but still resplendent (*above*),
is attributed to Marcus
Gheeraerts the Younger and
hangs at Burghley House. The
queen relied on Burghley to
the end of his life, visiting her
loyal servant on his deathbed
and allegedly feeding him
with her own hands.

[25] WILLIAM CECIL's effigy
(*right*), surmounting his
tomb in St Martin's Church,
Stamford, Lincolnshire. The
great statesman wears armour
and the robes of the Garter.

[26] JAMES I OF ENGLAND (1565–1625), after a portrait by John de Critz (*c.*1555–1641). Robert Cecil did much to ease the Scottish king's accession to the English throne, but the challenges of James's finances made for a difficult relationship later on.

the more... 
and knoo a knaue lyttel fellowe that well
...ule themselves as well myghe. I see
that he deunhely that bet... and that he
would proue to be... and to do
... rates hepuo... 
     Guido fauke

X...ngham suffolke    Fr: won...

Deuonshyre   H Northampton   Salisbuey

---

...my lord out of the loue I beare vnto to some of youre frends
I haue a caer of youre preseruacion therefor I would
aduyse yowe as yowe tender youer lyf to deuise some
exscuse to shift of youer attendance at this parleament
for god and man hathe concurred to punishe the wickednes
of this tyme and thinke not slightlye of this aduertisment
but retyre youre self into youre cuntri wheare yowe
maye expect the euent in safti for thowghe theare be no
apparance of anni stir yet I saye they shall receyue a terrible
blowe this parleament and yet they shall not seie who
hurts them this councel is not to be contemned because
it maye do yowe good and can do yowe no harme for the
dangere is passed as soon as yowe haue burnt the letter
and I hope god will giue yowe the grace to mak good
vse of it to whose holy proteccion I commend yowe

11A

[27] ROBERT CECIL'S COUNTER-SIGNATURE (*opposite top*), as 'Salisbury', accompanying others on Guy ('Guido') Fawkes's second and final confession, 8 November 1605, following the débâcle of the Gunpowder Plot [TNA SP14/216 F.112V].

[28] THE CONTROVERSIAL 'Monteagle letter' (*opposite bottom*) warning the Catholic lord not to attend parliament on the designated day of the Gunpowder Plot explosion, which he passed to Robert Cecil on 1–2 November 1605 [TNA SP14/216 F.11A].

[29] HATFIELD HOUSE, Hertfordshire (*bottom*), as depicted in an 1812 watercolour. Robert Cecil pulled down most of the existing old royal palace to replace it with this much grander replacement, at immense expense.

[30] A PROPOSED addition to the gardens at Hatfield House (*below*), which were originally planted by the renowned and globetrotting horticulturist John Tradescant, gardener to Robert Cecil (and later Charles I) [TNA SP14/67].

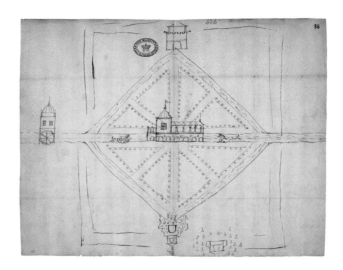

SERO. SED SERIO.

[31] ROBERT CECIL, 1st Earl of Salisbury, a copy of a contemporary portrait by John de Critz. His immense power, appetite for work and wealth rendered him a fitting son to his father, but he had no offspring to maintain the Cecil pre-eminence in the years that followed.

again. It is fairly clear that Parma had no real desire for peace, but he hoped to inhibit English preparations to fight by spinning out talks through hints of compromise. As early as August 1587 Elizabeth was delighted to hear that Parma was expecting her commissioners, but a few days later Burghley deliberately threw a spanner in the works by enquiring whether Parma had commission from Philip to negotiate, probably knowing well that he did not. The talks about talks went slowly on, because the one thing that neither side wanted was expedition. Parma's military build-up continued, and of that Elizabeth was well aware; she was doing the same thing herself.[40]

In December the return of the Earl of Leicester from the Low Countries concentrated minds, and the council formally debated the issue. On 14 December, Burghley drew up a memorandum for the discussion that probably reflects his position. Peace, he argued, was desirable, but only by treaty and upon the right terms; the Dutch would need to be parties to any agreement, and their minimal demands would have to be met.[41] The upshot of this discussion was that Burghley was instructed to draw up instructions for the English commissioners, which he did, and they set off in February 1588. Whether anyone, except Elizabeth, had any expectation of success is uncertain. For two months they then wrangled about procedures without getting anywhere near the issues in hand, and frustration then prompted Sir James Croft to strike out on his own by seeking a personal interview with Parma. Extraordinarily enough, he was successful, but since he understood no language other than English, he allowed himself to be completely misled about the duke's position. The result was a blind alley which cost Croft his favour with the queen, and eventually consigned him to the Tower. However, proper negotiations did then commence, and were still going on when the Armada appeared in the Channel. There was never any real chance of success, and a further papal bull against Elizabeth at the end of June thoroughly soured the atmosphere.[42] On 24 July the queen called her commissioners home, having antagonized the Dutch and done nothing to improve Anglo-Spanish relations.

It is unlikely that Burghley was disappointed. He seems to have believed throughout that, although peace was desirable (and worth some effort to achieve), it must be on the right terms and that these were never likely to be conceded. In one respect he agreed with the

war party; maximum efforts must be made, irrespective of negotiations, to mobilize the country for its own defence. Although he had
recovered his favour with the queen, 1588 was in many ways a difficult
year for William Cecil. He was getting old, and his health was increasingly uncertain. On 10 April he wrote typically to Walsingham, 'I cannot express my pain newly increased in my left arm. My spirits are
even now so attenuated as I have no mind towards anything but to
groan with my pain ...'[43]

In March he had lost his mother. Jane had been 87 and he might
have taken her longevity as a good omen, but he clearly felt the loss
keenly. Elizabeth, who did not remember her mother, thought his
grief somewhat self-indulgent, but it was an emotional outlet that he
probably needed at the time. By contrast, he was stoical when his
favourite daughter, Anne, also died in June. Her marriage to the Earl
of Oxford had been something of a disaster, as we shall see, but reconciliation of a kind had brought Burghley grandchildren—two surviving daughters were living under his care when their mother died and
doubtless formed some kind of a memorial that their grandfather
cherished. More positively his second son, Robert, was turning out
exceptionally well, and during this year proved a major prop to his
father, not only emotionally but also in the conduct of business. For a
man who was clearly beginning to fail, this was an asset beyond price.

Meanwhile money had to be raised, musters held and the navy put
in a fit state to face what was likely to be its sternest test. Burghley had
had *de facto* oversight of the navy since the beginning of the reign, and
the 'Book of Sea Causes' of 1559 had been drawn up for his enlighten-
ment.[44] It was, however, the lord admiral and the Council for Marine
Causes who determined policy, building and deploying ships, in consultation with experienced sea captains such as John Hawkins and
Francis Drake. When Hawkins took over as treasurer of the navy from
the long-serving Benjamin Gonson in 1577, Burghley supported his
plans for reform and economy, although these were controversial
among his colleagues.[45] He was not wildly enthusiastic about the
adventures of the so-called 'sea dogs', believing that they were unnecessarily provocative and refusing to accept that they in any way promoted Protestantism. The queen was keen however, and neither as
secretary nor as lord treasurer did he attempt to stand in the way.

There is no evidence to substantiate the story that Burghley opposed Drake's voyage of 1577–80, although he did believe that the booty should be restored—advice that Elizabeth ignored. As we have seen, in 1585 he urged Drake to sail immediately upon his mission against Spain; but when the crisis came in 1587–8 it was Hawkins, rather than Burghley, who successfully put the fleet on a war footing, and he should be given most of the credit for the ship design and gunnery skills that were to be decisive in the great Battle of Gravelines. Musters were called in June 1588 as the news of Spanish invasion preparations became increasingly pressing, and Lord Burghley provided fifty lancers and fifty light horse—not the largest contingent, but one commensurate with his real wealth rather than with what he declared for tax purposes![46] He was not a soldier any more than he was an admiral, and he did not bother to provide himself with armour.

Lieutenants had already been appointed, and on 22 May 1587 Cecil had written to Walsingham, who clearly was seen to have some control over such matters, asking that he be considered for Lincolnshire. This is interesting in two respects: first that Burghley, who had no intention of leading any men in person, should have sought such a position, which clearly owed more to his desire for local prestige and recognition than to any service which he hoped to give; and second that the queen's most senior statesman and councillor should have felt obliged to apply to another rather than directly to Elizabeth. Eventually he was appointed, not only for Lincolnshire but also for Essex and Hertfordshire as well.[47] Like other councillors who were similarly placed, he discharged his duties on the ground by deputy. As with just about everything else, Burghley had in the past come up with ideas for improving the army, particularly that part of it which was sent abroad to the Netherlands, but there is little evidence that his ideas were ever implemented. When Leicester came back from the Low Countries, questions immediately began to be asked about the state of military preparedness, and on 2 December Walsingham, who was on his sick bed at the time, pointed out that, thanks to the council's efforts, two armies of 26,000 and 24,000 men had been raised and equipped—'a thing never put in execution in any of her majesty's predecessors' times'.

His figures were wildly inflated. When the actual musters were held in July, one army of about 12,000 men could be deployed to Tilbury and a bodyguard of about one tenth that size provided for the queen's personal security.[48] This did not mean, of course, that no more men were available, but they were suitable only as local-defence forces. These 13,000 or so were all the force that was sufficiently weaponed and trained to stand any chance against the likely invaders. It was not a hopeful prospect. Soon after Walsingham made his estimate, the council also took stock of the situation, and for that meeting we have again one of Burghley's memoranda. England's first trust, he began piously, must be in God, but thereafter, 'Her majesty's special and most proper defence must be by ships … for her majesty is of her own proper ships so strong as the enemy shall not be able to land any power where her majesty's navy shall be near …'[49]

The navy, he went on, should be divided into two fleets, one to guard the narrow seas and the other westward, towards Ireland and Spain. He advocated an immediate raid upon the Azores. All ships in English ports should be stayed and musters of mariners held as a matter of urgency. All naval stores on their way to Spain should be intercepted. Not forgetting the forces already in the Netherlands, and the armies to be deployed within England, he estimated the cost to be £250,000. Although this would be his main responsibility, he did not say how it was to be achieved. In the event he negotiated about £26,000 worth of loans from the London livery companies, and found the rest out of the exchequer. There was no parliament in 1588, but the lord treasurer knew perfectly well that most of the burden would ultimately have to be met out of taxation, and he did not relish the prospect of having to ask for it. In July he was to write apprehensively to Walsingham:

> THE REPORTS *which I hear out of sundry counties of the reiteration of unsupportable charges towards musters do trouble me as much as the expenses of the Queen's treasure. I assure you I know that whole towns pay as much as four subsidies, so it will be very unreasonable to demand new subsidies …*[50]

However, when the time came necessity knew no limitation and the House of Commons (which thoroughly approved of the war) was more amenable than he had hoped.

Between 20 July and 10 August 1588, the council met daily, either at Richmond or at St James's, and Burghley attended every session. During the actual fighting and its aftermath, and down to the somewhat desperate demobilization, there was little he could do, except to try unsuccessfully to ensure that money was where it was needed. More significantly, he contributed to the propaganda that followed the naval defeat and (thanks to bad weather) dispersal of the Spanish Armada with two pamphlets, *The copy of a letter sent out of England to Don Bernardino de Mendoza* (by this time ambassador in France), and *A pack of Spanish lies sent abroad into the world*, both designed to milk the extraordinary victory at sea, which had so devastated Philip and terminally discredited the Catholic cause in England.[51] Burghley was not the most felicitous or effective of writers, but with this sort of material he could hardly go wrong.

In spite of her remarkable victory, however, the year ended as it had begun, with the queen apparently in two minds about everything, and (according to his own account) heavily dependent upon William Cecil. This dependence now had an emotional element to it that it had earlier lacked, because the queen's old servants were dying—notably the Earl of Leicester in September 1588. For all his inadequacies, Robert Dudley had been the one love of Elizabeth's life and she felt his loss keenly. She was getting old herself, and in need of props that she would not willingly have acknowledged. One such was now Lord Burghley. In January 1589 she wanted to promote him to the earldom of Northampton, but he declined on the grounds of poverty. This need not be taken too seriously, because he was still a very rich man, but he had a family to provide for and there is evidence that he was restricting his expenditure in the later years of his life. As we have seen, it probably had more to do with his sensitive awareness of status. Conyers Read observed that between 1592 and 1595 Burghley's household expenses were not much more than a third of what they had been in the early 1570s.[52] Several other promotions were also proposed early in 1589, but none of them took effect. In this respect, at any rate, Elizabeth was not determined to have her own way.

The big adventure of 1589 was the Lisbon expedition, designed to put Don Antonio on the throne of Portugal. Burghley was not enthusiastic, because he would have preferred that such resources as were available should be devoted to preserving a presence in the Low Countries. He spent much of the year in fruitless bids to raise loans abroad, and was desperately anxious about the state of the treasury. However, Lisbon was supposed to be a joint stock venture in which the queen was merely a shareholder, so the risks were limited, and if it had been even partly successful, it would have been another heavy blow against Philip. Burghley drew up the instructions for Drake and Norris which, if they had been followed, would have guaranteed at least some return. He even urged Elizabeth to accelerate her payments so that the voyage could get away.[53] The instructions were ignored, and the result was a notable fiasco that wasted men and money and ruined the careers of both commanders. The only benefit of this, from Burghley's point of view, was that it removed another source of maverick advice. With Leicester dead and Drake in disgrace, the queen might be more inclined to listen to the sort of cautious advice that he was now increasingly disposed to offer.

Two other events of this year affected him profoundly, although in quite different ways. At the beginning of April, his wife Mildred died. They had been married for more than 40 years and had enjoyed the kind of harmonious relationship that was as rare then as it is now. Mildred was angular in every sense of the word. Not a social butterfly, she did not relish attendance at court even in her younger days, and went less and less as she grew older. She found no favour with Elizabeth, and her rugged puritanism was a liability rather than an asset to her husband's career. Whether she ever commented upon his involvement in public affairs, we do not know. Scarcely any letters passed between them because they were so frequently in each other's company. What we do know is that their intellectual tastes were very similar, and that Mildred was never one to suffer fools gladly. Fortunately, William's own robust faith enabled him to take this blow philosophically. 'There is', he wrote, 'no cogitation to be used ... to have my dear wife to live again in her mortal body ... whose soul [is] taken up into heaven there to remain in the fruition of blessedness ... Therefore my cogitation ought to be ... to thank Almighty God for his favour in permitting her to live so many years with me ...'[54]

It was a long, pious and affectionate meditation, but it tells us far more about Mildred's good qualities and numerous charities than it does about their conjugal relationship. Lord Burghley may have worn his theology on his sleeve, but he did not wear his heart there.

The second event, or rather series of events, was the appearance of the so-called 'Marprelate Tracts'. These were puritan attacks upon the established church, which appeared between October 1588 and the spring of 1589. They were scurrilous, witty and (even to modern eyes) very funny. Martin Marprelate's early efforts provoked ponderous responses from the bishops, which drove him to fresh heights of exuberance. The court was highly amused, and the Earl of Essex is alleged to have carried copies around in his pocket.[55] Elizabeth's sense of humour deserted her. She was furious, realizing perfectly well that the real object of the attack was her own use of her ecclesiastical supremacy. Whitgift was very much her man, and it was his severe attitude towards puritan dissent that had provoked the attacks.

Burghley disliked Whitgift, and his methods, and it might be supposed that he would have sympathized with Marprelate, but nothing could be further from the truth: this was a destructive assault upon authority as such. In this context the bishops were the queen's agents —and however much one might disagree with their policies, to treat them with such ridicule and contempt was quite unacceptable. Moreover, if the bishops were to be lampooned in this fashion today, tomorrow it might be the nobility and the whole social hierarchy. In other words, Martin Marprelate was subversive in the most comprehensive sense. It was this that finally convinced Burghley that, for all its worthy and godly associations, puritanism was a corrosive force in both the church and the commonwealth, and that its more radical manifestations would have to be resisted. Marprelate was running riot during the session of parliament that ended on 29 March, and perhaps for that reason only one mild demand for church reform surfaced as a bill. Both Burghley and Whitgift spoke to it in the Lords, but Elizabeth would have none of it. Not even the most moderate and sensible changes would be tolerated as long as Marprelate was on the loose.

Walsingham was out of action throughout the early summer of 1589 and, there being no other secretary after Davidson's dismissal, much of the burden again fell on Burghley, although his own health was soon troubling him again. In France Catherine de Medici died and Henry III was assassinated, triggering a long struggle for the succession in which both Spain and England dabbled.[56] In Ireland the deputy and council frankly admitted that they had no power in Ulster, which represented a constant pressure point.[57] Only in the Low Countries did the situation ease as the wealth of Holland and the military talents of Maurice of Nassau slowly began to turn the tide. English forces continued to be deployed there, but they were more a symbol of the alliance than a strict necessity. Then in April 1590 Francis Walsingham died, and was not replaced. Burghley's first reaction was to try and spread the work around, but the council was dwindling and experienced men were hard to find. Leicester had gone in 1588, Mildmay in 1589, Walsingham in 1590. Hatton was in poor health and was to die in 1591. Burghley drew up a memorandum of suggestions, but the chief of them was to appoint a new secretary, and that was not heeded. Nor was Burghley a war minister. Along with most of his surviving colleagues he was a civil administrator, adept at finding ways and means but not fit to determine military strategy. Only two councillors could be counted as military men, Lord Hunsdon and Lord Charles Howard, and neither of them had a tithe of the lord treasurer's political skills.[58]

Fortunately help was at hand in the person of Burghley's second son, Robert Cecil. Robert was 27 by this time; trained like his father at Cambridge and the Inns of Court, he had sat in parliament since 1581 and had been carefully groomed for a prominent role in public life. As soon as Walsingham died (and perhaps before), he began unofficially carrying much of the routine work. He did this in his father's name, and remained in the background, but the evidence is clear and Elizabeth knew perfectly well what was going on. In May 1591 she spent ten days at Theobalds, and took the opportunity to get to know the young man. She knighted him during the visit, and three months later appointed him to the privy council.[59] From then until 1596, when he secured the appointment officially, Robert Cecil acted as principal secretary and, as we shall see, did almost all the work.

It was not glamorous, and Robert was not a glamorous man, but like his father he was exceptionally diligent and efficient. Glamour at this time was virtually monopolized by the Earl of Essex. Robert Devereux had succeeded his father at the age of ten in 1576, and as a ward of the crown had grown up in the household of the master of the wards, Lord Burghley. He was three years younger than Robert Cecil, but handsome and athletic where Robert was frail and partly deformed by a childhood accident. They would have known each other well, but the nature of their relationship is not recorded. To judge from what happened later the young earl probably relished his physical superiority and developed all the 'blood's' contempt for the 'swot'.

If so, it was a serious mistake. Essex was sent off to Cambridge where he seems, unusually for a nobleman, to have taken a degree, but his fortune was made at court when his widowed mother married the Earl of Leicester. In 1584, when he was 18, Leicester introduced him there and Elizabeth, who could not stand the sight of his mother, took to him immediately.[60] In 1585 he accompanied his stepfather to the Low Countries, and in December 1587 succeeded to his position as master of the horse, which Leicester resigned specifically for that purpose. After Leicester's death, Essex was his heir as much, it would seem, in the queen's affections as in anything else. Essex saw himself as a soldier and in July 1591 was given command of an expedition sent to Normandy to relieve pressure on Henry IV, whose authority was not acknowledged by the Spanish-backed Catholic League. He made a mess of his commission. Burghley was constrained to write several letters of rebuke on the queen's behalf and a year later he was recalled in disfavour. Once back at court, however, he quickly recovered his position, and in 1593 was appointed to the privy council. He was never Elizabeth's lover in the sense that his stepfather had been, but rather what would nowadays be called a 'toy boy'. Essex began to see himself as a statesman, controlling the careers of numerous clients, but he overestimated his powers again, and while he collected a substantial affinity, he was able to do disappointingly little for them — a situation that he attributed to the machinations of Robert Cecil.[61]

After 1591 Lord Burghley's now flagging energies were directed to two main ends. The first was combating religious dissent at home, and the second supporting Henry IV abroad. In October 1591 a comprehensive and lengthy proclamation established special commissions to deal with seminary priests and Jesuits:

> FOR THE AVOIDING WHEREOF, *and either to discover these venomous vipers or to chase them away out of the realm ... we do order and straightly charge and command all manner of persons of what degree soever ... to make a present due and particular inquisition of all manner of persons that have been admitted or suffered to have usual resort, diet, lodging, residence in their houses or in any other place of their appointment ...*[62]

This was immediately followed with another proclamation detailing the questions that were to be asked of such suspect persons. Burghley is plausibly credited with the authorship of both these proclamations, and is known to have been pressing for further parliamentary sanctions.

These were partly achieved in the Act against Popish Recusants, which received the royal assent on 10 April 1593 and restricted the movement of known Catholics. They were also to be disarmed, but a proposal to make conforming husbands responsible for their wives' recusancy was not included. Catholic publicists spoke of a 'Cecilian Inquisition' and the leading Jesuit Robert Persons particularly blamed Burghley for this new round of severity, but in truth it was a reaction to the election of the bellicose Gregory XIV, and William Cecil would have been only too pleased to accept the credit.

At the same time Cecil wrote, 'Care is to be taken to suppress all the turbulent Precisians who do violently seek to change the external government of the church', a sentiment that found embodiment in the Act against Seditious Sectaries in the same parliament.[63] By the last years of his life Cecil had become convinced that these perpetual campaigns for further reformation—of which he continued to approve in principle—were seriously damaging the structure of the royal authority. Rightly or wrongly, the queen had assumed responsibility for the government of the church and all radical assaults upon her chosen agents—such as those of Martin Marprelate—were subversive in a realm that was locked in a life-and-death struggle with the Popish Antichrist. It was the duty of all such persons to complain only to the queen, and then, 'If it please her to reform it, it was well; if not [they] were to pray to God to move her heart thereunto, and so to leave the matter to God and her Majesty...'[64] This was not quite the archbishop's way of looking at it, but for all their differences they were effectively allies after 1590.

Nevertheless, 1592 was heavily interrupted by illness. In June Lord Burghley took the waters at Bath, but was apparently despatching business all the time, and shortly after that he accompanied the queen on progress. When his health permitted, he continued to sit in the council, in the Court of the Exchequer and in the Court of Wards, but went relatively little to court, relying on Robert to keep his seat there warm. Towards the end of the year he was so ill that his life was despaired of, but by January 1593 he was back at his desk, 'well recovered, thanks be to God,' as one correspondent reported, 'for the whole state of the realm depends upon him. If he goes, there is not one about the Queen able to wield this state as it now stands ...'

However, the time was coming when Lord Burghley would not be there—whether to pick up the pieces of other people's mistakes or to sooth and cajole his erratic mistress into taking some desired action. In 1596, while Essex was away at Cadiz, Robert was at last formally appointed to the secretaryship. Burghley thanked the queen, and she replied 'with many gracious words'. Burghley also made strenuous, and superficially successful, attempts to reconcile the animosity between Essex and Robert.

## QUEEN ELIZABETH'S GRATITUDE FOR A LIFETIME OF SERVICE, 1597

HER MAJESTY *commanded me* [*Lord Admiral Howard*] *to write this to your Lordship, that you do not give her so many thanks for that she did to your son, as she giveth herself for the doing that which may any way comfort you. And also to give your Lordship thanks from her for your kind and most dutiful letter—and saying although you have brought up your son as near as may be like unto yourself for her service, yet are you to her in all things and shall be Alpha and Omega. Her Majesty also prayeth your Lordship that you will forbear the travail of your hand, though she is sure you will not of your head for her service.*

*Her Majesty giveth your son great thanks that he was the cause of your stay, for, she saith, wheresoever your Lordship is, your service to her giveth hourly thanks, and prayeth your Lordship to use all the rest possible you may, that you may be able to serve her at the time that cometh.*

*My honourable lord, let me crave pardon that for want of memory cannot so fully write her Majesty's gracious words ... It sufficeth that your Lordship knoweth her excellency and my weakness to express it: but I protest my heart was so filled with her kind speeches as I watered my eyes ...*

[Lord Admiral (Charles) Howard to Lord Burghley, 10 October 1597. Taken from BL Lansdowne MS 94, no. 65.]

In January 1597 Lord Burghley's long-running diary came to an end. Although there were determined efforts to maintain an impression of business as usual, and he continued to attend council meetings whenever he could, he was clearly failing by the end of 1597—not surprisingly, as he was 77 years old and had lived a life of constant activity. As late as July 1598 he was still sitting in council and busied with discussions about the possibility of peace negotiations with Spain, but before the end of the month he had taken to his bed, not so much in pain with gout as debilitated with general exhaustion. 'His mind was troubled', his biographer wrote, 'that he could not work on peace for his country which he earnestly laboured and most desired of anything, seeking to leave it as he had long kept it.'[65]

Elizabeth visited him *in extremis* and allegedly fed him with her own hands. It was the end of a remarkable partnership, because on 3 August, surrounded by his children and grandchildren, William Cecil recited the Lord's Prayer, and died in the small hours of the following morning. His friend William Camden wrote of him, 'Certainly he was a most excellent man who ... [with] wisdom strengthened with experience and seasoned with exceeding moderation, and most approved fidelity' served God and his queen, who 'was most happy in so great a councillor'.

The *regnum Cecilianum* was now in the hands of a new generation, more specifically Robert. He had already demonstrated his ability to carry the burden effectively, and the queen's last years were to benefit from his wise guidance, even as most of her reign had benefited from that of his father.

# CHAPTER 8

# Prodigals and Prodigies

ROBERT CECIL MAY have been the white sheep of the family, who would fulfil his father's legacy, but of course he was not Burghley's first-born son. That was Thomas Cecil (plate 19), and for a while it seemed that the family prospects rested on this distinctly blackish-looking sheep.

Beyond the fact that Thomas was born in 1542, the product of William's first marriage, we know very little about his upbringing. From the fact that Cecil had a schoolmaster on his staff at Wimbledon in 1550 we can gather that the boy was taught at home, perhaps sharing his lessons with Cecil's ward Arthur Hall, who was also resident at Wimbledon at the same time.[1] Thomas does not seem to have been a good pupil, or particularly amenable to discipline. He was sent to Trinity College, Cambridge, in 1558, and to Gray's Inn in the following year, but his career at both seems to have been brief and shadowy. As a youth, Thomas probably lacked for nothing, except the kind of affectionate understanding that might have made him a rather different man. As William later admitted, 'I never showed any fatherly fancy to him but in teaching and correcting.' Since his own mother had died shortly after his birth and his stepmother Mildred, for all her undoubted virtues, is not known to have been a warm personality, it looks as though the unfortunate Thomas had rather a bleak childhood and adolescence.[2] In 1553, when William was contemplating fleeing after the death of Edward VI, he thought of settling all his lands on Thomas as a means of saving the family estates. At this stage Thomas may have been an unsatisfactory boy, but he was the only heir William had.

We next hear of Thomas in 1561, when his father decided that, at the age of 19, he would have to set about making something of himself.

On 8 May William wrote to Sir Nicholas Throgmorton, 'I am disposed to send him abroad.'[3]

## THOMAS GOES ABROAD, 1561

I HAVE FOREBORNE *to send my son Thomas Cecil out of the realm*
*for that I had no more* [*sons*], *and now that God hath given me*
*another* [ *William, who died a year later*], *I am disposed to send him*
*abroad, meaning only to have him absent one year, so as, on his return,*
*if God so grant, to see him married, for that he shall then be full 20.*
*I mean not to have him scholarly learned but civilly trained, and to have*
*either the French or the Italian tongue, in which I know he can have*
*no perfection without greater time, and yet, so he can entertain one in*
*common speech of salutation, it shall suffice. Now resteth for me whither*
*to send him and how, and being inclined to send him into France, the*
*rather because religion is in some good state, I will only rest upon your*
[ *Throgmorton's*] *advice ... If he might without corruption of life have*
*been in that court three months I think he should thereby learn more*
*both in tongue and knowledge than otherwhere in double space ...*
   *... The boy is hard enough, and so his mind might be kept from hurt*
*I would take small care of his body for I would it were hardened, and not*
*made subject, as mine hath been, by study to sickness ... Blame me not*
*though I be long herein, for indeed to this hour I never showed any*
*fatherly fancy to him but in teaching and correcting. Yet would I fain now*
*towards my age receive some comfort of his well being ...*

[Sir William Cecil to Sir Nicholas Throgmorton, 8 May 1561. Taken from
TNA SP70/26.]

Protestant influence was strong in William's favoured destination,
France, at that point, so he had no particular anxiety about Thomas's
faith being corrupted, but his morals were another matter. William
seems to have reckoned that his son was physically tough but vulnerable in other ways, and in that he was to be proved right. His first
thought seems to have been to commend him to Admiral Coligny, a
senior Huguenot leader, but he revised that opinion within a matter of
days and eventually accepted Throgmorton's offer to find the young
man suitable accommodation, within reach of the court but not in the
court.[4] So on 29 May Thomas set out, armed with sufficient money to

meet the ten crowns a month that he was expected to pay for himself, his servant and three horses, and an onerous set of parental admonitions entitled 'A memorial for Thomas my son to peruse and put in use …'[5] Ahead of him lay a steep learning curve, ostensibly of courtly accomplishments such as French conversation, riding, dancing and music; in reality, what he learned was of a more earthy nature. In spite of being under the 'conduct' of Thomas Windebank, Cecil's secretary and a man of proven probity, young Thomas soon began to go off the rails. The pious exhortation he bore with him tells us more about William's own priorities and humourless puritanical attitudes than they do about Thomas, who ignored them.

In July he was presented at court, and met Mary Queen of Scots, who received him graciously for his father's sake. Thomas seems to have been behaving himself reasonably well at that point. However, the costs of his trip began to soar, and were soon running at 300 crowns a year instead of the 120 that had been budgeted for.[6] Windebank excused this by the cost of living, but it seems that Thomas was extravagant. According to his father he was 'negligent and rash in expenses', largely because he was gambling. This would have been difficult to avoid, even if Thomas had been made of sterner stuff than he was. Courtiers, especially those on the fringes of the court, had a great deal of time on their hands, and games of cards or dice were the normal way of passing the hours. Windebank did not think him particularly culpable, but his father was a strict abstainer.

In September 1561 Thomas was sufficiently unwell for Throgmorton to take him into his own house to recuperate. We do not know the nature of his illness, but from the fact that it was followed by a fit of penitence and of application to study, some overindulgence may be suspected.[7] By the end of the year his self-indulgence — whatever it was — seems to have resumed. His father wrote stern admonitions and cut his allowance. Unfortunately, we do not have any direct evidence of what these misdemeanours may have been. The surviving letters of Throgmorton and of Windebank are discreet, and Cecil's responses contain more fulmination than facts. Faced with the reduction of his resources, Thomas seems to have taken to borrowing on his father's credit from other English residents in Paris, and on two occasions broke into Windebank's strong box in search of cash.[8] He was also pursuing a young lady. We do not know much about her, but she seems to have been of a respectable kindred, and both Throgmorton and Windebank feared the worst. They remonstrated with him in vain, and the former wrote apprehensively to William that 'she is a maid, and her friends will hardly bear the violating of her'.[9] Either Thomas never went that far, or he was lucky, for we hear of no pregnancy nor other dire consequences, and it may well be that his anxious mentors took some adolescent high jinks too seriously.

On 24 March 1562 William sent yet another remonstrance to Thomas, accusing him of doing nothing but bringing grief to his father and disgrace to himself. He did not call Thomas home, partly because he continued to hope for some improvement and partly, it would seem, because he did not want him spreading alarm and despondency in England, where his father's career was at a delicate stage. Bringing the errant Thomas home, he told Windebank, would be a last resort. It would be hard to say which of them was getting more grief out of the situation as it was. 'I could be best content', William wrote, 'that he [Throgmorton] would commit him secretly to some sharp prison.'[10] Needless to say, that did not happen.

Further travel might provide an answer, and the deteriorating security situation in France, particularly around Paris, made that a desirable option in any case. Early in August 1562 Thomas and Windebank left France for Antwerp, and then into Germany, in company with Henry Knollys, who was on a diplomatic mission. Apparently the German air suited Thomas, or else the opportunities were fewer, because for the first time his conduct earned the commendation of his chaperone. In October and November the plan was that he should move on to Italy, to see the sights, but when Cecil consulted Knollys (who had been in Italy during Mary's reign), he advised against. For 'delightful instruction in virtue and religion' the place above all others was—Geneva.[11]

No doubt the young man would have found his wild ways suitably restrained there. However, it was not to be, because early in December the younger William Cecil died, and his father faced the unpalatable necessity of bringing Thomas home. He had been intending to leave him in Italy (or Geneva) until the end of the summer, 'at which time I am resolved to procure him to marry', but the younger William's death altered the schedule, and in January 1563 Thomas and Windebank were on their way home. 'You shall see him amended,' the latter wrote optimistically, 'and well enabled to serve his country in many things.'[12]

In spite of the low opinion that his father had conceived of Thomas, Windebank was not far from the mark. Although Thomas's career was to be nothing like as distinguished as those of his father and half-brother, he was not the nonentity that he has sometimes been represented as. He married in the summer of 1564, his bride being Dorothy Neville, the daughter of Lord Latimer. The match was apparently brokered by Sir Henry Percy, whose praise of Dorothy in a letter to William was lavish:

I ASSURE YOU ... [*her conversation*] *is so good and virtuous as hard it is to find such a spark of youth in this kingdom. For both she is very wise, sober of behaviour, womanly, and in her doings so temperate as if she bore the age double her years ...* [13]

This was obviously aimed at the prospective father-in-law rather than the bridegroom, and we do not have any idea what Thomas thought about her. However, since they had a numerous brood of children over the next 15 years, it can be assumed that he found her pleasing enough. Thomas and his new wife took up residence at Burghley House, which William had taken to visiting only infrequently. As the son and heir of Sir William, he was granted the revenues of various lands in nearby Northamptonshire in November 1569.[14] Perhaps this was in reward for his service against the northern rebels, although this was not stated. Thomas had commanded a force of 300 horsemen under the leadership of the Earl of Sussex and, although it is not recorded that he saw any action, such a position was commensurate with his status in the community and must also have reflected some confidence in his capability. He was on the commission of the peace for Lincolnshire by June 1570, and was granted the office of bailiff of the lordship of Collyweston, and the keepership of the park there in August 1571.[15] He sat in parliament for Stamford in 1563, 1571 and 1572, and for Lincolnshire in 1584 and 1586, and served against the Castillians at Edinburgh Castle in 1573.

By the time that the Treaty of Nonsuch was signed in 1585, Thomas had been knighted. He also seems to have risen somewhat in his father's estimation, because although the Earl of Leicester was nominated to head the English forces, the governorships of the four Dutch 'cautionary towns' given over to English authority seem to have been in the hands of Lord Burghley, and he decided that Sir Philip Sidney was to have Flushing and Sir Thomas was to have Brill. He then drew up the instructions for them both, although they were sent in the name of the whole council.[16] Thomas served at Brill from January to September 1586, when he resigned after falling out with the Earl of Leicester, a service alleged to have cost him £5000 because it was not properly funded. Two years later, Sir Thomas was named as deputy lieutenant for Lincolnshire, his father being lord lieutenant, and he served as a volunteer captain in the fleet that set out against the Armada.

In the year of his father's death, when Robert was controlling the privy council, the new Lord Burghley (as Thomas had become) was appointed president of the council in the north, in succession to Lord Hunsdon. He supported Robert, as we shall see, against the Earl of Essex's 'rebellion' in February 1601.[17] Finally, on 4 May 1605, Thomas was created Earl of Exeter.

Thomas lived until 1623, dying eventually at the age of 81; of the whole family only his grandmother Jane lived longer. He seems to have been a modest man, diligent and anxious to please (as a child he was described as 'soft and gentle'), but by no means devoid of either courage or competence. He suffered, both at the time and since, by comparison with both his father and his half-brother, but such criticism does him less than justice. No doubt he owed his promotions to the influence of his family, but that was perfectly normal, and no one complained that he was the kind of bungling idiot that his father's strictures on his youthful indiscretions had suggested. In fact, once he had returned from Europe in 1563, and particularly after he had married, we hear no more of that kind of criticism. Perhaps Dorothy made a new man of him, or perhaps he was never as bad as his censorious sire, who had once complained that he would sooner have lost him to an 'honest death' than endure the disgrace that he was bringing on the family name, made out.

Thomas Cecil was no disgrace in later life. He was a competent military commander and a more than adequate administrator. Perhaps an earldom was an over-enthusiastic reward, but James was anxious to seal the loyalty of the whole Cecil family, and we do not know the extent to which Thomas may have helped his brother during those difficult years when the succession was at the head of the political agenda. In fact, Thomas's reputation has depended far too much on the evidence deriving from his stay in France in 1561–2 when he was 19 years old.

That he did misbehave, both over money and over his girlfriend, is undeniable, but his father's reaction was excessive and Windebank was nearer the truth.

Why William became so angry about behaviour that he had clearly anticipated, we do not know. Thomas had probably been a troublesome adolescent, reacting against the oppressive strictures of his home life. He had no aptitude for study and would probably have been better off placed in the household of one of William's military friends. It may also have been that he was a troublesome reminder of the only rash and impulsive action of which we know Cecil was guilty—his marriage to Mary Cheke. It looks as though William had been even less able to control himself with Mary than Thomas was with his unnamed French paramour—and that may well have been an uncomfortable thought for the pillar of Protestant rectitude that Elizabeth's secretary had now become.[18]

By contrast Robert was, from the very beginning, the apple of his father's eye. Born in 1563, he was the third of the four children that Mildred is known to have born to her husband, and was the product of a mature marriage. William and Mildred had been married for 18 years, and their children had come late. Anne, the eldest, was not born until 1556, and William, who lived less than a year, in 1561. Elizabeth, their youngest, was born in 1564, when Mildred was close to 40. It may be that Cecil's persistent optimism about the fertility of a mature queen was based on his experience with Mildred. By 1563 he was the master of a large establishment, so it is highly unlikely that Mildred nursed the child herself. It might have been better if she had, because the deformity of the spine from which Robert later suffered is attributed to his nurse having dropped him in early childhood.

Robert was born on 1 June, probably at Cecil House in the Strand, and baptized on 6 June at St Clement Danes.[19] He was to spend most of his childhood at the same address. We do not know the name of his nurse—who may well have been dismissed for incompetence—or anything else very much about his nursery years. We do not even know whether his general health created any anxiety, but probably not or it would have been commented upon. Thomas had already left home, and was married when Robert was little more than a year old, so the latter would have had no childhood memories of his company. As he grew up his most consistent companions were his sisters Anne and Elizabeth. It seems that some of Cecil's numerous wards were also living in his household at that time, but the only boy we know to have shared his lessons for a while was Richard Neile, a protégé of Mildred's who was later sent on to Westminster School.[20]

Robert himself was taught at home by tutors specially employed by his father. The first of these was Michael Hicks, a cheerful young man just down from Trinity College, Cambridge, who later became William's secretary and a great friend of the family; the second, who may have taken over from Hicks, was Richard Howland, who also served as a chaplain to the household. Howland was similarly a Cambridge man, who drew attention to himself by petitioning Lord Burghley, the Chancellor of the University, on behalf of the radical Calvinist Thomas Cartwright in 1571, who was deprived of his university chair under a new decree.[21] His defence of Cartwright seems to have been on academic principle rather than because he agreed with him, because two years later he is noted as having preached a remarkable sermon in defence of the establishment. At about the same time (and perhaps in consequence) he entered Burghley's service as chaplain and tutor. In the latter capacity he presided over Robert's precocious progress in both Latin and Greek between 1573 and 1577. These were subjects much cherished by his father who, it seems, also insisted on instruction in cosmography, French, Italian and the rudiments of protestant theology.[22] Whether Howland was expected to teach all these subjects himself or was allowed to call on specialist assistance is not clear.

After his disappointing struggle with the unresponsive Thomas 15 years earlier, Burghley was overjoyed by his younger son's progress, and above all by the enthusiasm with which he tackled his studies. Here was a boy after his father's heart. The fact that Robert was somewhat deformed meant that he was physically unable to pursue any of the more robust pastimes of the Tudor gentry—even dancing was apparently beyond him—and this undoubtedly heightened the delight that he took in pursuits of the mind.

However, there are signs that even this admirably amenable child underwent periods of loneliness, and when his books were no consolation he would take refuge in one of the crowded offices of the large household and talk to anyone who happened to be willing to converse. 'Cherishing', as the contemporary saying ran, 'marreth sons but utterly ruineth daughters.' So cherished, in the sense of being cosseted, he was certainly not. His father was far too busy and his mother too austere to indulge him in any such fashion.

Growing up also had its compensations, however. In 1577, when he was 14, his father secured for Richard Howland the mastership of St John's College, Cambridge, and it is practically certain that Robert followed his tutor back to Cambridge.[23] The chronology of what followed is somewhat obscure, although it seems likely that he resided at St John's until about 1581. At some point the Protestant activist Walter Travers is known to have been his tutor, and it is likely that this was at Cambridge. Travers was appointed on Burghley's insistence, but of course Howland would have been in no position to refuse such a request from his patron.

Robert took no degree, but that was quite normal, and he seems to have applied himself to his studies as he had done at home. Again, his physical limitations would have made any normal student life difficult, but he had long since learned to accommodate himself to such circumstances and companionship in the ordinary sense he would have found in plenty. Like his father, he made at Cambridge friendships that would remain with him for the rest of his life. Following the usual career ladder, in 1580 he enrolled at Gray's Inn shortly before he finally left Cambridge, where he stayed for a few terms and acquired enough familiarity with the law for his purposes.[24] Again he took no formal qualification. It seems that by this time, when he was about 18 years old, Robert was already marked out for a career in government service, and since his father was the most powerful provider of such careers, it could be said that the wind was in his sails. For such a career a knowledge of the common law was useful, but he was not planning to enter the judiciary, so a formal qualification would have been an irrelevance.

Much more importantly, when parliament in January 1581 reassembled his father seems to have secured a seat for him. This must have been the result of a by-election, because it was not a new parliament, and it is not known which seat he secured. The chances are that it was one of the boroughs under Cecil's influence, probably Westminster, but we have only his own word for it, delivered in 1593.[25] Like his days in Cambridge, Robert's first appearance in parliament is not precisely recorded, but it would have been exactly the next step that an aspiring royal servant, just emerging from the university, would have sought; and when you were Robert Cecil, whatever you sought, you were well on the way to attaining. The session was short, and mainly concerned with a subsidy. Robert is not known to have spoken, or taken any noticeable part in the business of the House, but he would have been given a unique opportunity to see how his father's friends, notably Sir Walter Mildmay and Sir Francis Knollys, conducted the queen's business.

Whether he made any particular friends during this session we do not know. Unlike his father, it is difficult to trace the contacts that he made at this stage in his later career. He is supposed to have been close to Thomas Howard at Cambridge, and to have renewed acquaintance with Richard Neile and with the young Earl of Essex, but all this is conjecture based upon coincidence of residence. For about two years, from 1580 to 1582, Robert seems to have been juggling his time between St John's, Gray's Inn and the House of Commons. His reputation as a debater and as a good companion and conversationalist comes from the university, but could be equally relevant to either of his other two roles.

At some point in 1582 William drew up a set of instructions for his son, as he had once done for Thomas. They bear so close a resemblance to Polonius's words to his son Laertes in Hamlet that it is tempting to suppose that Shakespeare must have seen them. However, by the time the play was written, Burghley's reputation was legendary, and it is possible that Robert himself had disclosed some of the contents in one of his lighter moments.[26]

### POLONIUS ADVISES LAERTES

*Be thou familiar, but by no means vulgar.*
*The friends thou hast, and their adoption tried,*
*Grapple them to thy soul, with hoops of steel.*
*But do not dull thy palm, with entertainment*
*Of each unhatch'd, unfledg'd comrade. Beware*
*Of entrance to a quarrel; but being in*
*Bear't that th' opposed may beware of thee.*
*Give every man thine ear, but few thy voice;*
*Take each man's censure, but reserve thy judgement.*

*Costly thy habit as thy purse can buy,*
*But not express'd in fancy; rich, not gaudy,*
*For the apparel oft proclaims the man.*
*And they in France of the best rank and station,*
*Are of a most select and generous chief in that.*
*Neither a borrower nor a lender be;*
*For loan oft loses both itself and friend;*
*And borrowing dulls the edge of husbandry.*
*This above all: to thine own self be true;*
*And it must follow, as the night the day,*
*Thou canst not then be false to any man.*
*Farewell: my blessing season this in thee.*

[William Shakespeare, *Hamlet*, ACT I SC. iii, first performed *c*.1601–2]

William did not, of course, intend his own homily to be taken lightly. His injunctions were presented under ten headings and, unlike those for Thomas, were entirely practical and secular. He was confident, he wrote, that his son sufficiently understood his duty to his Maker. Instead, he started with the choice of a wife and the education of children; point four reminded him of the duties of kinship, and point five dealt with the lending and borrowing of money. Point seven covered patronage, and may be summed up as, 'be sure to keep some great man thy friend', while point eight dealt with due social decorum and warned against the cultivation of 'popularity'—a vice of which William apparently suspected the young Earl of Essex, although he was scarcely fledged from the university. Point nine warned Robert about being over trusting with 'life, credit or estate', while number ten, perhaps realizing that Robert possessed a sense of humour that he lacked, solemnly admonished him not to take any of these prescriptions lightly. A joke, he solemnly declared, was not like a child which must by course of nature see the light of day.[27]

These admonitions were only the tip of a veritable iceberg of instruction that the lord treasurer issued, so it is to be hoped that Robert's sense of humour remained in good working order. A royal servant should not be swayed by emotion or 'affection', but rather base his judgement upon facts, which he should be diligent to acquire. He should be systematic, and keep proper records of his correspondence, and of decisions that affected him. He should never endorse any project over which he had been consulted without finding out how much it would cost—and so on. All this sounds a little like a self-portrait of Burghley, and so it was in a way. Additionally, no one should enter the queen's service simply (or mainly) for the money. He should not be greedy, or thought to be greedy, and he should handle all financial transactions with scrupulous and transparent integrity.[28]

It seems fairly obvious that Burghley had his eye on the office of secretary for Robert, having himself held and developed the position for 14 years to 1572. Thomas Wilson had died on 20 May 1581, and in 1582 there was only one secretary, Sir Francis Walsingham. Elizabeth showed no sign of wanting to replace Wilson, and it may well be that Burghley was advising against an immediate appointment in the hope that his son (who was showing immense promise, but was only 19) would grow into the job over the next two or three years. 'It is convenient', Robert Beale was later to write, 'for a secretary to understand the state of the whole realm.'[29] He should be familiar with the justices of the peace for each county, know who the leading recusants were, and the state of the musters. He also needed to understand the London and Antwerp money markets, the overall state of the country's trade and the operation of the exchanges. This was a formidable agenda, even for the most teachable of young men; but Robert was ambitious and he had the best possible support. His Cambridge years had also taught him, in addition to some tricks of oratory and the ability to spice his conversation with classical references, how to learn and how to commit complicated facts to memory. It might be thought that three or four years spent on Seneca and Tertullian would be a poor preparation for the affairs of a complex modern state—but that was not how the 16th century saw it.

However, a worthy secretary could not be created overnight. Some experience of Europe and its foibles was eminently desirable (a dimension that William Cecil himself had lacked), and at some time during 1583 he found it possible to send Robert to France.[30] Not very much is known about these trips, neither the reason, nor the duration, nor even where he was sent. In October the newly appointed ambassador, Sir Edward Stafford, wrote to Burghley about some incident in Paris that had been 'but to keep Mr. Cecil aloof from me, which of his good nature he hath not done ...' This suggests that Robert was not part of the ambassadorial entourage, but was nevertheless in Paris.[31]

The same letter suggests that he had also been there earlier in the year, but not why. Probably some study at the Sorbonne was the pretext, but the real reason would have been to keep an eye on the Duke of Anjou after his enforced retreat from the Netherlands. In February 1584 Robert was back in England, apparently acting as his father's amenuensis, but he returned to Paris in August of that year. By that time Anjou was dead, and Robert's ostensible purpose was to immerse himself in the social life of Paris in order to perfect his French—away from the contaminating context of the English embassy. By the middle of August he had managed to attach himself to the household of the Seigneur de Marchemont, who had been Anjou's last representative in England, and who was an expert on Anglo-French relations. Marchemont also knew a great deal about the troubled state of France, which he was only too happy to communicate to his visitor.[32] He was a highly intelligent and sophisticated nobleman, and seems to have found a kindred spirit in his young English guest—which was no mean tribute to the latter's qualities and upbringing.

From an English point of view, however, the situation in France was not promising. The death of Anjou had created a potentially danger-ous instability, because the heir to the childless Henry III was now the Huguenot leader, Henry of Navarre. The prospect of such a succes-sion was anathema to the ultra-Catholics, and before the end of the year a political league had been formed to prevent it. Moreover, the assassination of William of Orange in July made it imperative to dis-cover what French policy in the Low Countries was likely to be. At the same time English Catholic exiles were lurking in Paris, ever will-ing, or so it appeared, to give heed and support to plots against Eliza-beth. Robert was reasonably successful at penetrating that somewhat porous community, and by the end of September was sending lengthy and systematic reports to Walsingham of all that he had managed to learn. By that time he had joined Stafford, and had dutifully tracked the court as far as Orléans, but he failed to secure the promised audi-ence with the king and returned to Paris in early October.

By then he had drained himself of information, and his reports to Walsingham contain many pages on the detailed affiliations, marriage connections and likely political allegiances of everyone he had come into contact with—and quite a few others for good measure.[33] Robert's health was never robust, and the effort seems to have exhausted him.

In England, the writs were issued for a new parliament on 12 October, and Robert had every intention of representing Westminster, so within couple of weeks of sending his last despatch, he was on his way home—'run out of money', as his father put it with unexpected humour. It seems that he was glad to have his son's company again, and even more pleased to have retrieved him in one piece from what was becoming an increasingly dangerous country.

The talk of parliament was of the Bond of Association, of the consequent Bill for the Queen's Safety, which Elizabeth checked before the Christmas recess, and of a bill against Catholic priests, which was also stymied in debate. During the holidays it emerged that one William Parry, who had spoken against the priests' bill but whom Burghley thought he had befriended, was in fact a double agent, and was deeply implicated in yet another plot to assassinate the queen. Robert had corresponded with Parry several times in the most amicable terms, and seems to have trusted him completely. It was not a very threatening plot, and Parry's role had been an ambiguous one, but he was tried and convicted in February 1585, leaving the Cecils, both father and son, with a good deal of egg on their faces.[34] Aware of the Cecil connection, Walsingham at first handled Parry with kid gloves, but decided eventually that he had a mind 'full of treason and disloyalty'. The fact that he had actually lived for a while at Theobalds only made the situation worse. For Robert Cecil, William Parry's treason was a timely warning never to trust anyone whose antecedents were not completely known. In the extremely slippery world of Elizabethan espionage, there were many plausible rogues, and Parry was a salutary example.

By the end of 1585 Robert seems to have been working as his father's confidential secretary. There was no official name for what he did, and certainly no official reward, but his name appears upon a number of sensitive papers composed by or for Burghley, particularly in relation to the Earl of Leicester's expedition to the Low Countries and the growing crisis over the fate of Mary Queen of Scots.[35] When parliament reassembled on 29 October 1586, the latter was at the front of everyone's mind. The Babington plot had not long been exposed, and the House of Commons was baying for Mary's blood. 'Filthy and detestable ... grounded in Papistry' was Hatton's (comparatively mild) description of her behaviour. Elizabeth saw two delegations from the

House of Commons, on 12 and 24 November, but sent both away answerless.[36] Mary had been duly condemned by the commissioners appointed to try her, but the execution of the sentence was at the queen's discretion, and that was the point of the audiences. By the time of the second audience, Robert Cecil was a member of the Grand Committee of the House, but he seems to have attended both sessions as his father's representative rather than as a member. Not long after he wrote, and published at the queen's behest, a tract entitled *A Copy of a Letter to the Right Honourable the Earl of Leicester* ..., which set out not only the parliamentary petition, but also the reasons for the queen's refusal, under the guise of informing the earl of something he would have known perfectly well by other means.[37] It seems likely that it was Walsingham, rather than Burghley, who suggested Robert for this task, which constituted his first emergence into the public arena. His careful and elaborate reports of intelligences from France had not only impressed the secretary, they had earned his good will.

As we have seen, once Elizabeth had signed Mary's death warrant, and execution had been carried out, Davidson went to the Tower and Burghley was 'rusticated' to the country from the court. He did not even sit in the House of Lords for the remainder of the session, which came to an end on 23 March 1587. Robert, however, was not involved in his father's 'disgrace' and became increasingly prominent during his exile. It is even possible that Burghley exaggerated his own disfavour in order to give the young man a better chance. At one level this tactic (if that is what it was) worked very well. Under Walsingham's sympathetic eye he carried out quite a lot of routine work and, because Sir Francis's health was visibly declining by the summer of 1587, the thought may have been in both their minds that he was being groomed for the succession. In another sense, however, he was completely eclipsed by the dramatic rise of the young Earl of Essex (plates 20 and 21).[38]

By 1585 Essex was, as we have seen, the Earl of Leicester's stepson, and Leicester introduced him at court. His impact had been immediate, and not at all benign. As early as July 1585 Burghley had heard that he 'bore malice' to the younger Cecil, and although this seems to have been a spat that was quickly appeased, it was a sign of things to come. For the time being the issue was postponed because Essex went with his stepfather to the Low Countries in the autumn and there, although he scarcely covered himself in glory, he blooded his sword, earned a knighthood and reinforced his self-esteem.[39] It was the summer of 1587, when he was back at court and Elizabeth was recovering from the trauma of having executed her cousin, that he really came into his own. The queen, it appeared, had eyes for no one else. 'When she is abroad, nobody near her but my Lord of Essex … he cometh not to his lodging until birds sing in the morning …'[40] Once she had forgiven Burghley over Mary's despatch, in July 1587, Elizabeth visited Theobalds, but this made no difference at all to their behaviour pattern.

Essex got into a series of childish quarrels with Sir Walter Raleigh, and was appointed to his stepfather's office of master of the horse. All this was no doubt somewhat galling to both Burghley and his son, although the former had seen it all 25 years earlier with Robert Dudley. In political terms at this stage they were not even rivals, let alone enemies. When Elizabeth insisted upon appointing commissioners to treat with the Duke of Parma early in 1588, Burghley somewhat reluctantly went along with the initiative, and after a good deal of heart searching secured a place for Robert to go to the negotiations, not as a commissioner, but as an observer.[41] No doubt he wanted to know what transpired from someone whom he could trust absolutely. He could not, however, resist the temptation to admonish his son to keep his religion pure in the popish environment into which he would soon be travelling.

Once these negotiations had failed, and the Spanish Armada had been and gone, it was in Burghley's mind to upgrade his son's presence in the House of Commons. At the beginning of September a new parliament was in the offing. It was summoned originally for 12 November 1588, but did not eventually convene until February 1589, and at some time between 18 September and 14 October, the lord treasurer wrote to the sheriff of Hertfordshire (Robert being normally resident at Theobalds):

CONSIDERING *the parliament is summoned to begin about 13th November next, for the which purpose there is election to be made of two knights of the shire, and therefore I know that you, being of credit with the freeholders of that shire, to whom the election belongeth, shall have opportunity to further any of your friends to those places, if so it be that you have not made any earnest determination to grant your good will to some others, then I would be content to have your favourable to*

*frame my son Robert Cecil, being already a justice of the peace in that*
*shire ... to be one of the said two knights ...*[42]

Needless to say, Robert was duly returned, and continued to represent Hertfordshire until his elevation to the Lords. In terms of Robert's career this was a rite of passage, and shortly after he underwent another, albeit of a more private nature. In June 1589 he married Elizabeth, the daughter of Burghley's old (if occasionally indiscreet) friend, William Brooke, Lord Cobham. At the same time Burghley created a trust, of which Cobham and Sir Thomas Cecil were both members, to ensure that Theobalds and various other properties in Hertfordshire would descend to Robert after his death.

Walsingham was sick again in the spring of 1589, and the work of secretary descended once again on Lord Burghley—or more accurately on his son. Walsingham was back at his desk by July, and Burghley was not in the best of health himself, but his involvement in affairs apparently continued unabated. It is very difficult to judge from the records how much of this burden was actually being carried by Robert, but common sense would suggest a lot. Sir Francis died early in April 1590, and Burghley seems to have hoped that, after a decent interval, the place would go to Robert.[43] That, however, was not the queen's way, and the Earl of Essex was soon fishing in the same pool, urging the reinstatement of Davidson. Essex probably shot himself in the foot by promoting a candidate who remained so far out of favour, but he did succeed in blocking the Cecils' ambitions—and that may have been his main objective. Essex, however, was a soldier, and while he was in Normandy making a hash of an expeditionary force to assist the French king Henry IV, Elizabeth knighted Robert and appointed him to the privy council. This served to confirm what everyone in the government already knew, that Sir Robert Cecil was the acting (or *de facto*) secretary, but would not be formally confirmed in post as long as the Earl of Essex continued to call the shots at court.

In comparison with Robert's businesslike rise and Thomas's rather less businesslike, but still satisfactory, establishment among the county elite of Lincolnshire, the life of Burghley's elder daughter, Anne, was troubled and eventually tragic. Anne was born in December 1556, and although it is not certain that she was William and Mildred's first-born child, she was certainly the first to survive infancy. As a baby she was known as 'Tannykin', but virtually nothing else is known about her childhood and upbringing.[44] By the time that she was old enough to be educated Thomas had left home, and if she had any companions of her own age they would have been the children of neighbouring gentry who had been drafted in for the purpose. Given her mother's formidable intellectual reputation, it is difficult to imagine her schooling being neglected, but it has left no traces. She was four when William, her short-lived brother, put in his brief appearance, and whether she became attached to him we do not know. She was certainly fond of Robert, and he of her, but the age difference of seven years would have made sharing lessons difficult. There was, of course, no question of her going away to study, and the chances are that she learned the arts of being a Tudor gentlewoman at home, perhaps from her mother's ladies rather than from Mildred herself.

The first talk of her marriage arose in 1570, when she was 13, her prospective groom being the young Philip Sidney, son of William's long-time friend, Sir Henry Sidney.[45] Also living at Theobalds were some of the crown's noble wards, thanks to Cecil's position as master of the court, but again age differences make it unlikely that any of them were companions for the young Anne. The nearest in age would have been Edward de Vere, Earl of Oxford, but he was 12 when he entered Cecil's household in 1562, at which point Anne would have been five. An 'Order for the Earl of Oxford's exercises' has survived, which show him learning French and Latin, dancing, calligraphy and cosmography; so it is likely that Anne followed a similar regimen, with perhaps needlework in place of cosmography.[46] Two years later the earl went off to Cambridge, at the same age at which Robert was to follow him a decade later.

Although he was by all accounts a good scholar, Oxford was rather a wild young man, and in 1567 he actually killed one of the servants during a fracas at Cecil's London house. The circumstances are unclear, but thanks to Cecil's position and influence the verdict was returned as *felo de se*, i.e. suicide, a dubious process of which Sir William later repented.[47] When the northern earls rose in rebellion in 1569, Cecil planned that his ward should work off some bellicose energy in active service, but he fell sick, and by the time he recovered the rising was over.

Early in 1571, when he had just come of age, Oxford made his debut at court. He was a young man of parts, a good dancer and a competent

musician, just the kind of man to catch the queen's eye. Above all, he
was a first-rate jouster. As a martial art, jousting was somewhat irrelevant by this time, but as a form of courtly athleticism it was at its
zenith, and in a great tilt before the queen at Westminster Oxford took
'the chief honour'. It was a worthy achievement 'far above the expectation of the world', as John Stow commented.[48] Because he was
hereditary lord great chamberlain, the earl had a warm seat in the court
at any time when he chose to use it, but it was obviously more satisfactory to him to make an impression by what he did rather than by who
he was. Whether the queen could ever have been persuaded to take a
matrimonial interest in this promising young man (only 17 years her
junior) we do not know, nor whether the thought ever crossed his
mind. Probably not, because by July 1571, he had already committed
himself to marry the 14-year-old Anne.

How this came about is something of a mystery. Fourteen was
young for marriage, but not exceptionally so—the minimum age for
cohabitation according to the old canon law had been 14 for boys, but
only 12 for girls, so no eyebrows would have been raised on that score.
Anne was much commended for her modesty, grace and virtue (particularly piety), but not for her beauty, wit or learning. The natural
suspicion is that William arranged the whole thing himself, venturing
his much-treasured daughter in a plan to form an alliance with one of
the oldest noble families in England. However, his own words do not
confirm that. In August he wrote almost apologetically to the Earl of
Rutland (no longer his ward, but a friend):

I THINK *it doeth seems strange to your Lordship to hear of the*
*purposed determination of my Lord of Oxford to marry with my*
*daughter. And so, before his Lordship moved it to me, I might have*
*thought it if any other had moved it to me but himself ...*[49]

So the initiative came from the earl, and great was the lamentation
among the aspiring brides of the court when they heard the news.
Cecil made no secret of his pleasure. It was as good a marriage for
Anne as he could have hoped by long scheming to have brought about,
and if he had any doubts about the young man's character, he gallantly
thrust them aside: 'I do honour him [Oxford] so dearly from my heart
as I do mine own son, and in any case that may touch him for his honour and weal, I shall think him mine own interest therein ...'[50]

They were married on 19 December 1571 (by which time Anne was 15) at Westminster Abbey in the presence of the queen, and a great feast followed at Cecil House in Covent Garden. What the bride thought of her fate, as usual we do not know, but the chances are that having been very strictly brought up, and not being particularly clever, she was by turns overwhelmed and terrified by the thought of the married life that lay ahead.

The general atmosphere of good will that immediately followed the wedding did not, however, endure for long, and the cause seems to have been the demise of the Duke of Norfolk. Although they were very different in age, Oxford and Norfolk were cousins, and the former seems to have done his level best to get his kinsman off the charges of treason against him.[51] There were rumours that he was trying to bribe the gaolers to bring about his escape, that he had fallen out disastrously with his father-in-law about the matter and even, within a few months of his wedding, that 'he had put away from him the countess his wife'. Such reports cannot be substantiated, and the latter appears to have been unfounded, but there were tensions between the two men and somewhat contradictory letters passed between them in the autumn of 1572.

For a time thereafter, Oxford seems to have sailed dangerously close to the wind. Early in 1573 he was reported to be much in favour at court, but then he got himself entangled with the English Catholic refugees in the Low Countries, and was apparently restored to favour only on Burghley's intercession.[52] In January 1574, with his credit running low in every sense, he eventually got leave to travel abroad, and Burghley, with considerable difficulty, got him to put his finances in order before he went, an order which included 1000 marks for his wife's jointure and £300 a year for her living expenses.[53] Both of them seem to have anticipated a long absence. Such evidence as we have of Oxford's relations with his wife do not, however, suggest estrangement. She was pregnant when he left, and bore a daughter in July, while he was in Italy. He received the news happily enough, but showed no sign of wanting to return. Instead he asked Burghley to get the queen to extend his licence, and to provide him with money by selling lands. This Burghley was extremely reluctant to do, because of the risk to his patrimony and to the future of his daughter and granddaughter. By this time Oxford's letters reveal an extraordinary degree of self-absorption, which left him quite careless of his responsibilities. He had, he wrote, given up all hope of advancement in the queen's service, and as for money, 'I have no help but of mine own, and mine is made to serve me and myself, not mine ...' This letter was written from Sienna in January 1576, by which time he had been away for two years.[54] What Lord Burghley made of it, we do not know.

Oxford's time, however, was running out. In March 1576, when he was back in Paris, he learned that the queen would not extend his licence further and had summoned him home. He came with the worst possible grace, refused to meet his father-in-law when he landed and immediately accused his wife of infidelity. For the latter accusation there seems to have been no evidence whatsoever, beyond the fact that it was natural to suspect that a sexually active girl of 17 might wish to find some consolation in the absence of her regular partner. The earl had no doubt indulged himself in the same way, but that, of course, was different. Nothing that we know about Anne gives the slightest substance to such charges, but Oxford seems to have become quite paranoid on the subject. He would, he declared, have nothing more to do with her, and the sooner she returned to her father's house the better 'for there, as your daughter, or her mother's more than my wife, you may take comfort of her, and I, rid of the cumber thereby, shall remain well eased of many griefs'.[55]

We are entitled to wonder about the earl's state of mind, because he would make no specific accusation against his wife, but eventually repudiated the child she had borne during his absence, on the grounds that he had not slept with her for more than a year before its birth. Why this had not occurred to him at the time, and why he had changed his mind having shown every sign of pleasure at the news, we shall never know. Burghley was both wounded and outraged by this assault. He sought the queen's mediation, and was promptly accused by the earl of poisoning his monarch's mind against him. Having insisted that Anne return to her father's house, and that he would be well rid of her, he then accused Mildred of alienating her affections from him![56] Nowadays the divorce courts would give short shrift to such ramblings, but Burghley had no such option. The best that he could suggest was that Oxford and his wife should appear before what would effectively have been a tribunal, at which the queen would be present. Meanwhile the debilitating quarrel ground on. Oxford could not prevent his wife from going to court if she were summoned, but he declined to be present at the same time, or to speak to her, 'for always I have and I will still prefer mine own content before other'. Consumed with self-pity, he wrote poems about his own grief, 'My spirits, my heart, my wit and force, in deep distress are drowned.'[57] What (if anything) Anne had ever done to deserve this treatment is a mystery. No case was ever heard, and no charges brought. Even Burghley's old friend Catherine, Duchess of Suffolk, interested herself in the case and tried to bring about at least a meeting, but without the smallest success. Meanwhile, in 1581, the earl conducted a passionate affair with Anne Vavasor, a lady of the court, and earned himself a bastard child and another dose of royal disfavour.

Then, rather surprisingly, and perhaps as a result of this experience, Oxford's mood seems to have changed. In 1582 he was reconciled to his wife, and the couple began to live together again. Over the next five years, Anne became pregnant four times. A son and a daughter died in infancy, but two other daughters survived. Burghley continued to be unhappy about the relationship, and we know nothing about the state of mind of either of the protagonists, but formally at least, their marriage was back on course.

Once the quarrel was appeased, the lord treasurer had no incentive to pursue his son-in-law with reproaches, and occasional letters were exchanged which profess a conventional affection, but it is unlikely that the wound ever healed. Then in June 1588, at the age of 32, Anne died. Both her father and her brother Robert, who knew her best, were grief stricken. She seems to have been a gentle, submissive creature, battered by the storms of an unhappy marriage that she had done nothing to provoke. It may have been some consolation to her family that she was interred in Westminster Abbey with the full honours due to the Countess of Oxford. We do not even know whether her husband was present.

Oxford married again, had a son who was born in 1593, and died himself at the age of 54 in 1604. He had no public career to speak of, although he did recover a measure of favour at court, and his quarrel with Burghley went on at a low level as long as the latter was alive. But he did achieve note as a poet, and years afterwards, in the eyes of some literary conspiracy theorists, he was championed as the 'real' author of Shakespeare's works.

The Cecils' second daughter, Elizabeth, was born in 1564. What little we know about the circumstances is derived from William's diary. She was born on 1 July at Cecil House, and baptized six days later at a grand ceremony in which the queen herself and Lady Margaret Douglas were the godmothers.[58] The child was named for the queen, who dined at Cecil House the same night. All this, of course, had much more to do with William's importance as a councillor than it has with the child. We know no more of her childhood and upbringing that we do of Anne's, but she would have been twelve when the ten-year-old Robert Devereux joined the household, so it is tempting to think that they shared their lessons, at least for a while. Shortly before this, in the summer of 1575, the Earl of Shrewsbury apparently proposed to Burghley a marriage between Elizabeth and his own fourth son, Edward. Burghley was too polite to say so, but his experience with the Earl of Oxford was proving extremely trying at that very time, and he had no desire to inflict a similar fate upon his younger daughter, so he professed himself gratified by the earl's interest, but replied 'I have determined ... not to treat of marrying her, if I may live so long, until she be above fifteen or sixteen ...'[59] He had, he declared, received other similar offers, but his mind in this respect was made up. There is no clue as to what (if any) other offers he may have received. The letter to Shrewsbury is mainly concerned with his responsibility for Mary Queen of Scots, and the possibility of their meeting at Buxton in Derbyshire when both took the waters, so it may be that the marriage proposal was a fairly casual afterthought on the earl's part. In any case, we hear no more of it.

We know very little of Elizabeth's appearance or temperament, but in 1581, when she was just turned 18, she caught the eye of Lord Thomas Wentworth's son, William. Rather unusually, the young man himself seems to have taken the initiative. When writing to Burghley on 8 July, Wentworth was suitably diffident: 'Truly my Lord, for this liking of my son of your daughter, I never thought of it, nor knew anything of it till himself opened the matter with me ...'[60]

This may have been disingenuous, but there is no reason to suppose that it was. Wentworth was a baron, and a man with a good record of service, but neither in wealth nor in influence could he compare with the lord treasurer. He was keenly aware that Burghley could have had the pick of the heirs of the higher peerage for his daughter, if he had so desired. However, Burghley had been once bitten in that respect, and seems to have determined that parental ambition should not be the determining factor here. What prompted William Wentworth to raise the matter with his father we do not know, but it would be pleasant to think that it was the qualities of the young lady herself, rather than the status of her family, that attracted him. Although he was not a ward of the crown, it is possible that William had spent some time in Burghley's household as a youth. That would have been an old-fashioned but still acceptable aristocratic alternative to a spell at university, and he would have been of an age to have shared Robert's schooling. There is no firm evidence that he was ever so placed, but it might account for the fancy that he had taken to Elizabeth. Unfortunately, as usual we know nothing about her reaction to the proposal, but she seems to have raised no objection. Perhaps like her sister, she was rather submissive and put upon; with so dominant a mother that would not have been surprising.

It seems likely that Burghley already thought well of the young man, because he accepted the suggestion at once, and negotiations for a settlement began. Burghley accepted that he would have to bear most of the cost. Thomas Wentworth was not a rich man, but William Wentworth would in due course inherit lands to the value of £800 a year.[61] Perhaps because he had no suitable secondary residence to offer, Wentworth suggested that the newly weds should live at Theobalds: 'For my son, I think it much better that he should remain with you, both that you may see his usage and behaviour towards your daughter, and also that he may learn of you to become a meet and serviceable man towards her Majesty and the Commonwealth.'[62]

This suggests not only a proper appreciation of Burghley's position, but also an understanding of the unhappy lot of Anne de Vere, which was presumably common knowledge. The final details were agreed by the end of June, and the wedding duly took place on 26 February 1582 at Theobalds, the festivities lasting several days. The queen did not attend, but sent a gracious message that gladdened the heart of the bride's father who was (very inappropriately) laid up with gout at the time. The festivities cost over £600—including 57 shillings for broken glasses![63] The couple duly settled at Theobalds, and became apparently very happy, both in each other's company and in their hosts. Alas for high hope! In November of the same year William Wentworth caught the plague and died. Elizabeth was a widow at the age of 18, and her father was left to lament the loss, not only of a good son-in-law, but also of 'a virtuous gentleman in whom I took so great delight'. It was an inscrutable deity that took his worthy son-in-law and left the unworthy one to plague him. Elizabeth survived her husband by less than a year. Nothing is known of her death, except that it occurred in April 1583. Whether grief had weakened her immune system, or whether William had left her pregnant and she miscarried or died in childbirth, we do not know. Her father, and no doubt her mother and sister, mourned her deeply, and she left them no child to remember her by. She was not quite 20. So it came about that when Lord Burghley himself died in 1598, all the women in his life had gone before.

# CHAPTER 9

# Robert Cecil, Secretary and Heir

ALTHOUGH ROBERT had been undertaking most of the secretary's work since Sir Francis Walsingham died in April 1590, it was not until Elizabeth visited Theobalds in May 1591 that the issue of his official appointment to the position came to the fore. Although he had no intention of resigning his posts, it seems clear that Burghley wished to go into semi-retirement, and allowed one of the entertainments put on for the queen's benefit to spell that out.[1] He also wanted the secretaryship for his son. Elizabeth, however, much as she valued his father's unique services, was also aware that the Cecils were perceived in some quarters to be running the country, and was in no hurry to advance Robert. The Earl of Essex was notoriously opposed to his appointment, but he was not the only one. So Robert was knighted, but for the time being not further advanced.

Then, on 2 August, while the court was at Nonsuch Palace, Sir Robert was summoned and admitted to the privy council.[2] By this time the council was a small and intimate body of advisers, and since Sir Robert held no other office and was not a great nobleman, this summons was in effect an admission of his *de facto* position. It was said by one well-informed adviser that no other secretary could now be appointed 'during the life of his father'. For now Essex did not need to expend either time or energy frustrating Sir Robert's ambitions, since the queen was obviously quite satisfied with things as they were, but they sparred over other matters. The attorney generalship was vacant, and the earl made no secret of the fact that he favoured Francis Bacon for the place. Burghley opposed him, and Essex suspected (probably rightly) that he was using Sir Robert to further his case.[3]

There was further conflict over the so-called Lopez plot, but there the honours were more even. Rodrigo Lopez was a Portuguese Jew who had sought refuge in England in 1559. He was a skilled physician who had been several times consulted by the queen, although he did not have an official position in the household. Probably for financial reasons he had been recruited by Walsingham as a secret agent, and had taken the dangerous course of posing as an enemy agent in order to secure his cover. The Earl of Essex had just been appointed to the privy council in 1593, and was anxious to demonstrate his zeal in the queen's service. Above all, he was concerned at this stage to demonstrate the ineffectiveness of the official secret service, run (of course) by Robert Cecil.[4] He therefore employed his own agents who, towards the end of 1593, denounced Lopez for treason. Put on his mettle, Sir Robert hastened to assure the queen that there was no substance in the charges, but Essex and Anthony Bacon, who was running his service, persisted. The supposed conspirators were arrested and an enquiry instituted. Lopez naturally protested his innocence vigorously, and the evidence discovered was ambiguous. However, the unfortunate doctor was tried and convicted, both Essex and Robert apparently concurring in finding him guilty.[5]

Although the queen remained sceptical, it seems that Lopez was as much a victim of the paranoia of the time as he was of the Earl of Essex, and that Robert escaped a political defeat by recognizing that fact. With the benefit of hindsight they were almost certainly mistaken, because there is nothing in the Spanish, or any other foreign archive, to confirm that there was any such plot. Lopez was executed on 7 June 1584, and Lord Burghley iced the cake by writing and publishing *A True Report of Sundry Horrible Conspiracies.* This covered two other minor, and equally dubious, plots and was rather a piece of war propaganda than a collection of news stories.[6] Indeed, the focus was less on the guilt of the conspirators than on the murderous intentions of the king of Spain. About Lopez, Elizabeth seems to have retained her doubts, and subsequently compensated his widow, but about the need to stir up anti-Spanish feeling, there was no disagreement.

Although it started out as another round in the Essex–Cecil rivalry, the Lopez plot ended by easing tensions between the two parties, and the appointment of Sir Edward Cooke as attorney general in April 1584 contributed to the same cause, in spite of the disappointment that it represented to the earl. Although this was a defeat for Essex, the effect was mitigated by the fact that both Burghley and his son strongly endorsed Francis Bacon's bid for the solicitor generalship, which now became the earl's main concern.[7] At some point, probably in May, the feud was reconciled, at least for the time being, and a friendly exchange of letters ensued between Essex and Robert Cecil.

Another outcome of the Lopez affair was the apparent confirmation of the value of the earl's intelligence network, and an encouragement to him to persist with exotic and dubious agents. One of the most dubious was Sir Anthony Standen, formerly an agent of Mary Queen of Scots, and latterly in receipt of a pension from Philip of Spain. He was drawing money from both sides and his true allegiance was (and remains) uncertain. In 1594 he returned to England after a prolonged absence, professing his loyalty to the queen. Robert Cecil kept him at arm's length, but Anthony Bacon welcomed him on Essex's behalf, and placed him on the payroll.[8] The most exotic recruit, however, was Antonio Perez, sometime secretary to Philip II, whose imprisonment and escape to France had made him famous. Perez arrived in England in 1593 in the suite of the French ambassador, and took up residence at Essex House early in 1594. He stayed in England until 1595, and was paid by the earl at the rate of £20 a month. He moved freely in court circles and was generally welcomed, although what he may have done for his £240 a year remains obscure.[9] He was probably most valuable as a symbol of Philip's limitations. Essex was by this time a councillor of substance, exercising significant patronage both within the court and in parliament, where he is alleged to have had 30 MPs 'at his devotion', but he could not resist the maverick. Standen and Perez are good examples, but so also was Anthony Bacon, a depressive invalid who could never face an appearance at court and whose waspish tongue was a major factor in frustrating all attempts at a permanent reconciliation with the Cecils.

Sir Robert, meanwhile, had been steadily establishing himself. His failure to halt the trial of the former lord deputy of Ireland, Sir John Perrot, for treason (over which he seems to have made common cause with Essex), while demonstrating that England was not a *regnum Cecilianum,* proved no check to his career. Then in September 1592 the *Madre de Dios* arrived at Dartmouth. This enormous Portuguese carrack had been captured off the Azores by a syndicate of English ships, some royal, some privateers, and the division of her immensely rich cargo became both a challenge and a vexation. On 15 September Sir

Robert was given the queen's commission to divide the spoils, but he had no standing in the maritime community, and arrangements for the security of the cargo pending the allocation were imperfect. Quite a lot simply disappeared. With great acuity, Robert secured the release of Sir Walter Raleigh (who was in the Tower of London for having married without the queen's consent), and took him along as a support. Raleigh (plate 22) had been one of the investors and was not therefore impartial, but he did have immense prestige, and that he placed at Sir Robert's disposal.[10] The latter's first task was to round up the looters, many of whom were strongly protected by local interests. This he confronted rigorously; 'by my rough dealing,' he admitted, 'I have left an impression'. The local authorities were bludgeoned into action, and Raleigh (with every incentive to recover the queen's favour), mobilized his mariners, who were so pleased to see him that they almost forgot their plunder.

Within a week much of the missing cargo had been recovered—an almost incredible achievement in the circumstances. Sir Robert then had to check the cargo lists, both against what had been recovered and what remained in the carrack. It was an immense labour, and he had to undertake it himself, because the local officials could not be trusted and Raleigh's men were not sufficiently literate. Raleigh estimated that he saved the queen at least £10,000 in recovered goods, and the royal share eventually amounted to some £80,000.[11] Raleigh got £24,000 (which did not cover his outlay) and the City of London about £30,000, but Raleigh's real reward was that he recovered his liberty and a measure of royal favour.

Robert returned to London while the loading was still in progress to bring the cargo round to the Thames and, as soon as his back was turned, the pilfering began again, although not on the same scale. Back in the capital, he was expected to check the whole cargo over again as it came off the hoys that had brought it from Devon. His struggle with the cargo of the *Madre de Dios* proved two things. The first was that, if it was properly handled, the authority of central government could overcome the most determined local resistance, not by violence, but by its sheer presence. The second was that Robert Cecil was the most diligent, determined and honest of agents. No part of this wealth stuck to his fingers, and his devotion to the queen's service could not have been more perfectly expressed.

The parliament that met in February 1593 contained, as we have seen, a rather large number of Essex clients, but this did not matter as they had no particular policy to put forward or obvious interest to support.[12] The main issue was over the subsidies, of which the Commons offered two, but the Lords opted for three. Francis Bacon used the Commons' alleged privilege of free speech to object to Lords' interference, earning him Elizabeth's lasting disfavour and undermining all Essex's subsequent efforts on his behalf. The third subsidy was eventually accepted, although some compromise was obtained over the period of collection. By the time that the session ended in April Sir Robert Cecil had gained further ground, and had now emerged as the council's most articulate and persuasive orator, as well as its most skilled manipulator. It was this advance of confidence and authority for which the queen (with her usual sense of balance) was seeking to compensate when she made Essex a member of the council.

Essex's private secret service, and his willingness to entertain some very dubious agents, was not simply a species of 'one-upmanship' against the Cecils. It was designed to fuel and support his anti-Spanish policies. These were visceral rather than rational, and were part of the same worldview that promoted his own self-image as a soldier. They were, at the same time, very popular, and Essex gained a great deal of what we might now call 'street cred' by posing as the uncomplicated antagonist of all things Catholic and Spanish. The appearance of Robert Persons' *Conference on the Next Succession to the Crown of England* in 1594, which argued in favour of the deeply unpopular Spanish Infanta, put wings on his heels in this respect.[13]

The only person in England who knew that James of Scotland was himself soliciting Spanish aid in his bid for the same succession was Robert Cecil and he was not telling anyone—least of all Essex. He knew this because his namesake, John Cecil, was a priest in James's service who was canvassing his claims in Madrid, and informing Robert of every step in that complex dance.[14] On this, as on so many other matters, Robert Cecil kept his counsel. He was not a soldier, and war had no attractions for him. It was vastly expensive, disruptive and wasteful. At times it was unavoidable, and 1595 was such a time; but given peaceful options, he would always have taken them.

Apart from anything else, Robert was keenly aware of the value of trade. The future wealth of England lay not in its limited resources of corn, cattle and minerals, but in the almost unlimited possibilities of international trade. The Dutch, with almost nothing by way of natural resources, were making themselves immensely rich by carrying other people's goods. Once England ceased to be a customer and became a provider, that way was open. But unlike the Dutch the English did not seem to be capable of fighting a life-and-death war and exploiting her trade at the same time.

By 1595 Robert Cecil was hankering after peace, and the queen was of the same mind, but there was no realistic chance and the continued fighting played into the hands of Essex and his friends in the council. One of the main obstacles to any peace settlement, as Sir Robert knew perfectly well, was that the Dutch would have to be included, and consequently at least some of their demands would have to be met. As freedom of worship was for them non-negotiable and Philip had sworn that he would never be a king over heretics, there was no prospect of progress as long as he was alive.[15]

So while Sir Robert busied himself with endless matters, and passed through the presence chamber 'like a blind man, without a glance' for those in attendance, the soldiers prepared to take the war to Spain. That there would be a summer expedition of some kind in 1596 had been decided before the end of the previous year. English forces had been withdrawn from France because Elizabeth judged (rightly as it turned out) that with some help from the Dutch, Henry was now able to hold his own. He had solved his main problem by converting to Catholicism in 1593, which had taken most of the wind out of the sails of those who could not contemplate a Protestant king. The Catholic League, increasingly and visibly dependent upon Spain, continued its opposition, but began to look more like a fifth column in a conventional war. Elizabeth (who had been shocked by Henry's conversion) nevertheless continued to need him as an ally, just as he needed the distraction of the Anglo-Spanish war to protect himself, so at a diplomatic level the alliance held, although no English army was now directly deployed in France. In the Netherlands the Duke of Parma had died, depriving Philip of his ablest general. Nevertheless one of the first things that the Archduke Albert, his replacement, did was to launch a surprise attack across the border and capture Calais.[16] Strategically the town was of little importance, but it still had an iconic significance for the English as the French toehold lost in 1558, and the thought of it in Spanish hands rang alarm bells all over the south of England. There was talk of launching an expedition to rescue it, but the place fell before anything could be done, and attention reverted to plans for the summer. The lord admiral, Charles Howard, and the Earl of Essex were named as joint commanders and the preparations were marred and delayed by their constant bickering, which at time verged on the childish.[17] The queen was well aware of this, but unable, or unwilling to change the arrangement. Instead she unburdened herself to the French ambassador on the subject of the earl's wilfulness and ungovernable behaviour, no doubt intending this to get back to Essex, as indeed it did. Unfortunately the Frenchman added a gloss of his own, naming Robert Cecil and his brother-in-law Henry Brooke as the men who were 'stirring [Elizabeth's] passion' against the earl—an unfounded charge that he was nevertheless predisposed to believe.[18] For the time being, however, rancour was set aside, and even the lords general managed to agree (more or less)—sufficiently at any rate for the most outstanding achievement of the war, the capture of the Spanish port of Cadiz on 30 June.

This remarkable and celebrated victory was secured by an Anglo-Dutch force in which the English commanders could scarcely agree on anything for five minutes at a time. Essex was the hero of the hour, and he returned to a rapturous welcome from the citizens of London and anyone else who was within reach of the fulsome ballads, broadsheets and sermons that greeted him. It was, he was told, the greatest achievement of the age.[19] Beneath this glittering surface, however, was an angry and disappointed man.

On 5 July, while Essex was still on his way home, Robert Cecil had been formally (and finally) appointed to the office of secretary. He now kept the queen's signet and was free to act without commission in any matter that she might refer to him. For a man who had already borne the burden and suffered the heat of the day, this recognition was extremely gratifying. Lady Bacon wrote to her son, Anthony, 'Sir Robert is now fully stalled in his long longed for Secretary's place. You had more need now to be more circumspect ... walk more warily ... The father and son are affectionate, joined in power and policy.'[20]

## ROBERT, THE QUEEN'S SECRETARY, 1596

I [LORD NORTH] *heartily thank God, good Mr. Secretary, that Her Majesty hath graced you with this title, which your painful service hath long since deserved, and which will encourage you to undergo the great burden you are charged withal. The Lord God bless you in all your counsels and actions, and assist you with his Holy Spirit. I would sooner have congratulated this your dignity, if sooner I had known of it. Harrow Hill hath late news or none at all.*

*At Harrow Hill, 9th July 1596*

[Lord North to Sir Robert Cecil, 9 July 1596. Taken from HMC Salisbury MSS, VI, p. 248.]

Robert Cecil was not a man to bear grudges, but he knew who his friends were. For the moment, Essex shrugged off the setback, but he was less tolerant of the criticisms that soon began to be voiced in council about his dealings in Cadiz. He advised that the city should be held and garrisoned, and his advice was rejected for the perfectly good reason that the expense would be prohibitive. Neither he nor anyone else in England was probably aware that the Duke of Medina Sidonia had already reoccupied the town. He advised that the English fleet should be immediately redeployed to the Azores to intercept the *flota*, the Spanish transatlantic commercial ships, and that suggestion was also rejected, although for less obvious reasons. Finally, he wanted to use the army to retake Calais, an unrealistic ambition given the strength of its defences.

These were council decisions and may well have been prompted by the lord admiral, who felt (with some justice) that he had been given far less than his share of the credit for the great victory and may well have been only too willing to take his fellow commander down a peg or two. However, Essex chose instead to blame Sir Robert and his supporters. In one respect he was right: Sir Robert instructed that a pinnace loaded with goods for one of Essex's agents be stopped and searched at Plymouth. On board was an assortment of plunder from Cadiz, clearly intended for Essex's private profit.[21] Since the public purse had gained almost nothing from the seizure of this very rich city, this would have been a major embarrassment for the earl—if he had been in a mood to notice.

Instead of being a period of relaxation, or indeed of self-congratulation, the aftermath of the Cadiz expedition was fraught and stressful. Sir Robert was entrusted with the unenviable task of clearing up the accounts, and that would have been tricky even if the earl had been more responsible and less prickly than he actually was. The lords general, it transpired, had given away over £12,000 from the plunder of the city, and had neglected to seize another £11,000 that had lain in the city treasury. Only about £8000 actually reached the exchequer as a return on an investment of some £56,000. Thanks to Sir Robert's tireless exertions another £20,000 was recovered, but that was due to the other investors and did not represent a profit for any of them.[22]

Of course, it could be argued that this had been an act of war and the crown should have been expected to pick up the whole bill, but that was not the way in which the expedition had been set up. Instead it had reflected the delusion that war could be expected to pay for itself, a delusion based upon the profitability of some privateering, particularly the very rich pickings from the *Madre de Dios*. As it was the accounts were chaotic, and even Robert Cecil's orderly mind could not make them appear anything else. Essex waved the whole problem away as being beneath his notice — he was a soldier, not an accountant, and it was not his job to see that money reached the exchequer.

It was, however, Sir Robert's job, and he would have been less than human if he had not derived a certain satisfaction from the earl's confusion. In return he earned the venemous hatred of some of Essex's following, notably Anthony Bacon, and their contemptuous abuse followed him onto the streets of London. For them, Essex was a great and high-spirited nobleman who had bearded the greatest king on earth, and in return was being baited by a pack of contemptible curs.[23] Essex himself affected a pious indifference to this campaign of vilification, but Lady Bacon warned him that rumours of his 'carnal concupiscence' were serving to undermine his efforts.[24] Elizabeth was so disillusioned with her victorious captain that she considered withholding the ransoms of the Spanish prisoners. But as Lord Burghley pointed out, Essex was entitled to these by the rules of war, and he was by no means anxious to give him a genuine grievance to add to his imagined ones — so the ransoms were duly paid.

Although buoyed up by popular and international support, Essex's influence at court was in temporary eclipse, and he began to occupy himself with schemes for rescuing the situation in Ireland, which was getting dangerously out of hand. By Christmas, Sir Robert Cecil had come to the conclusion that the court had become dysfunctional and, prompted by Elizabeth, 'professed very seriously an absolute amnesty and oblivion of all miscontents passed'.[25] He was in a position of strength, because the queen had demonstrated her favour by visiting him at his house in the Strand on 23 December and had been lavishly entertained along with most of the court. Essex was theoretically sick, but probably sulking. For whatever reason he was not present and the proposed reconciliation was apparently one sided.

In the midst of all these preoccupations, Robert suffered a great personal loss. His wife Elizabeth had struggled with the duties of hospitality just before Christmas, and being nearly eight months pregnant, the effort had exhausted her. When she was brought to bed around 20 January, her physical resources were drained and the exertions of labour killed her. She seems to have been a gentle, inconspicuous creature, 'silent, true and chaste' as she was described, and they had been married less than ten years. She left behind her a son and a daughter. The latter, Frances, was fragile and somewhat deformed like her father, while the former, William, turned out in time to be slow and rather docile, like his mother.[26] Robert had loved his wife greatly, but his choice had been less effective dynastically than those of either his father or grandfather.

His friends rallied round, rather ineffectively, it would appear, but Robert found the best antidote to grief was work and, having laid her suitably to rest in Westminster Abbey beside his own mother, he returned to the turmoil of business. He was just 33 and at the height of his powers, which was just as well because the death of his father-in-law Lord Cobham, the virtual incapacity of his own father and the withdrawal of the Earl of Essex left him in splendid isolation in the council. At the same time, the death of his wife eased the tensions. She had been in no way responsible for those tensions, but sympathy for her bereaved husband took some of the edge off the campaign of vilification against him; even Anthony Bacon fell silent.

Sir Walter Raleigh mediated a truce and the queen sensibly appointed Essex as master of the ordnance, a position that fitted excellently with his self-image.[27] He returned to court immediately after his appointment on 12 March. He did not apparently notice (and it may even have been unintentional) that this essentially military post would be no help in his ambition to establish himself as a statesman. Meanwhile Sir Robert, Essex and Raleigh worked together in apparent amity in the preparation of the summer expedition—to be known later as the Islands Voyage—visiting each other's houses and praising each other's abilities. At the end of May Essex was appointed chief (and sole) commander of the fleet against Spain, and in his gratification raised no objection either to the appointment of Robert as chancellor of the duchy of Lancaster, or of Henry Brooke, Lord Cobham, as lord warden of the Cinq Ports. Lancaster was a revenue department of profit and importance, while Brooke was a protégé of Lord Burghley. The earl seems not even to have noticed.

The fleet sailed from Plymouth on 10 July, but this was not to be another Cadiz. The expedition was a complete, and expensive, failure. This was not entirely Essex's fault—the weather and other factors contributed—but all the brave words about destroying the Spanish fleet and intercepting the king's silver proved to be just so much hot air.[28] Worse still, when the Islands Voyage returned to Plymouth on 28 October, a Spanish fleet was lurking in the Channel, its destination Ireland. The earl had fallen out with his subordinate commanders, as he had with Howard the previous year, and had even attempted to have Raleigh executed by court martial. The hopeful amity of the spring had completely disappeared, and this time Robert Cecil was neither a party nor an agent.

For the time being the Spanish presence off shore created a sense of emergency, and no one expected Essex to appear either at the parliament or at the court; but storms dispersed the threat, and still he did not come. The fact was that he had been thoroughly humiliated by the multiple failures of the Islands Voyage and lacked the sense of duty necessary to put such personal considerations behind him. In an attempt to mollify him, Elizabeth gave him the vacant office of earl marshall, a position of great precedence and prestige but no political power whatsoever.[29] The parliament, which had been adjourned during the panic over the Spanish fleet, reconvened on 5 November and was once more primarily concerned with subsidies. Again three were accepted, with much grumbling, and a compromise over collection. Sir Robert Cecil again spoke effectively, but this time he did not lead, that role falling to Sir John Fortescue. It was a productive parliament in terms of legislation, but perhaps the most important issue was one that got no further than the appointment of a committee, because it touched the royal prerogative.

For a number of years past—in fact, going back to about 1585—there had been a shift in royal policy over patronage. Less land was granted to the deserving, and fewer leases of crown property. Instead, patents and monopolies on trade and manufactures were granted not in anticipation that the recipients (who were mostly courtiers) were about to transmute into entrepreneurs or merchants, but that they would sell their grants on to the interested parties.[30] No trader or manufacturer could legally pursue his business without a licence from the patent holder, who was thus entitled to charge what he liked for the essential permission. It was a form of taxation—or blackmail—which had the immense advantage from the crown's point of view of not costing a penny. Lord Burghley seems to have been responsible for the origination of this device, although it had the queen's whole-hearted support, and now that Burghley was failing its main protagonist was Robert Cecil. In due course these patents were to become a major grievance, and were to subject Sir Robert to an even fiercer (and much more widely based) barrage of criticism than that which had been directed against him by Essex's following. However, in 1598, when the parliament was dissolved, this was only a cloud on the horizon.

At the beginning of 1598, while the parliament was still in session, Robert Cecil was preparing to return to France, a country that he had not visited for 14 years. This time his mission was to preserve the Anglo-French alliance by dissuading Henry IV from making a separate peace with Spain. The weather was vile (it was February) and a Spanish fleet was off the Britanny coast, but as it happened these two threats cancelled each other out and Sir Robert got safely across to Dieppe. The omens were not auspicious. The Dutch, who were supposed to be taking part in the discussions, were late and Henry was indifferent.[31] But when Robert did succeed in obtaining an audience with the king, he made a most favourable impression. He was intelligent, discreet and, above all, spoke excellent French—the result of his schooling rather than of recent practice. He was also well received at court, but his mission made no progress. In the formal sense, Henry was not yet committed to the Franco-Spanish Treaty of Vervins that would see Spanish recognition of his kingship and end the religious wars, but his mind was made up and he was merely teasing Robert with awkward questions about the queen's intentions.

By the time that Robert left on 15 April, his failure was evident, and in commenting sourly upon the unreliability of the French as allies he was merely expressing his own frustration at having been unable to cajole Henry into changing his mind.[32] He vowed that he would never trust the French in future and, as far as we know, he was as good as his word. He also returned more than ever convinced that the war with Spain must be brought to an end. The French had proved unreliable, and the Dutch were not much better, now that increasing affluence and military success had made them even less biddable than before. The questions were how to engineer such a peace without surrendering the Protestant cause, and how to sell such an unpopular notion, either to the Earl of Essex or to the people at large.

Once the Treaty of Vervins was concluded in 1598, the Dutch followed Robert to England, seeking reassurances. They were greeted warmly by Essex, but made no headway either with the queen or with Robert. Robert was increasingly concerned about his father's health, and the council was preoccupied with the affairs of Ireland, where Tyrone's rebellion in Ulster was in temporary remission but nowhere near a resolution.[33] It was imperative that a major military effort should be made in Ireland, under the leadership of a good soldier. Essex suggested George Carew, but his arguments found no favour, and in a fury of frustration he made a scene in the presence chamber, turning his back on the queen. This was bad enough, but when she boxed his ears for impertinence he went for his sword. Overpowered, he stormed out swearing that he would never endure such indignity. Although his action was technically treason, Elizabeth soon forgave him. As one observer put it, 'I know but one friend and one enemy my Lord hath; and that one friend is the Queen, and that one enemy is himself...'[34]

The whole episode would have created a very bad atmosphere, except that Elizabeth was determined that it should not. Essex was received again at court, and even danced with the queen at the Twelfth Night celebrations in January 1599. The one fatal consequence was not directly intended. By blocking every attempt to appoint an alternative commander for Ireland, the earl had boxed himself into a corner. When he was offered the Irish command himself early in 1599, he could not refuse. If he was England's leading soldier, as he pretended, then let him go to Ireland and prove it. His friends and followers were filled with foreboding, but he had no option but to go.

Robert Cecil had nothing directly to do with all this, and that was just as well, because on 3 August his father, Lord Burghley, died. Burghley had not only been his son's mentor, he had been his example and inspiration. For ten years at least, the two had worked closely together, and such disagreements as had arisen had not affected their relationship. In some ways they had been too close, and coming so soon after the death of his wife, the loss of his father deprived Robert of emotional outlets. He became less open in his friendships, as though there was always a level of commitment that he could no longer give.[35] No doubt there were many who rejoiced that the 'old fox' was gone, but none said so openly — not, at least, to Robert. Neither his power nor his favour at court was adversely affected; indeed in some ways they were augmented, because there could no longer be any doubt about who led the Cecil clan.

Thomas, the new Lord Burghley, inherited Burghley House, where he had lived for years, the Lincolnshire estates and the 'great house' in London but did not attempt to compete with Robert politically. Robert himself received Theobalds and the Hertfordshire estates. He already had his own house in London. He did not become lord treasurer — that dignity went to Lord Buckhurst — but he did receive, after an interval of several months and despite efforts by Essex's supporters to frustrate it, the office of master of the Court of Wards, which his father had held for 35 years.[36] This was important, because of the potential income it offered. Even Burghley, who was comparatively restrained, had accepted over £3000 in 'arrangement fees' for wardships in the last two and a half years of his life. Robert, while not conspicuously corrupt, was less scrupulous about such matters than his father had been; as one observer put it, 'nothing there (the court) is done without a fee'.[37]

For this reason another legacy that Burghley bequeathed to his son was the 'black legend' of the unscrupulous, domineering Cecils; the old lord treasurer's role in the promotion of monopolies was well known, and deeply resented. As one correspondent put it, 'you may boldly write for his [Cecil's] favour — you paid well for it'. There was, of course, an element of truth in all this. Robert built on an even grander scale than his father, and maintained a very large clientage, but for the most part the legend was created by people like the Bacon brothers, who discovered too late that they had hitched their wagon to the wrong star.

In one other respect William Cecil's death altered the political land-scape. Both Buckhurst and Archbishop Whitgift had obtained their initial advancement with Lord Burghley's support, and although Whitgift, in particular, often found himself at odds with the old man after 1590, neither of them quite forgot their original obligation. They had no such obligation to Robert; they were his equals, not his clients, and in religion particularly the Cecil influence was increasingly side-lined.[38] It was perhaps just as well that Robert did not inherit his father's evangelical proclivities.

At the end of March 1599 Essex departed for Ireland, in an atmos-phere of patriotic fervour and acute anxiety. The citizens of London turned out in their thousands and cheered him to the echo. To them, he was still the hero of Cadiz. 'Into Ireland I go,' he wrote to his friend, Lord Willoughby, 'The queen hath irrevocably decreed it, the council do passionately urge it, and I am tied by my own reputation ...'[39] Not the least of his worries was the thought of leaving his back uncovered while he was away from the court. Whatever reconciliations there had been in the past, he did not trust Robert Cecil, and was keenly aware that his favour with the queen hung by a thread. Even if Robert had been disposed to destroy Essex, and there is no evidence that he was, he could hardly have done it more effectively than the earl did it for himself. The English had suffered a disastrous defeat at the Battle of Yellow Ford on 14 August 1598, losing 2000 men, but Essex, at the head of the largest and best-equipped expeditionary force ever to be sent across the Irish Sea, then wasted his resources and exhausted his men while failing to confront Tyrone immediately.[40] Essex was dis-tracted and resentful.

B UT  WHY *do I talk of victory or success? Is it not known that from England I received nothing but discomforts and soul's wounds? Is it not spoken in the army that Your Majesty's favour is diverted from me and that already you do bode ill both to me and it? Is it not believed by the rebels that those whom you favour most do more hate me out of faction than them out of duty or conscience ...*[41]

Suffering a complete breakdown of morale, he signed a six-week truce with Tyrone and against all orders quit Ireland and headed back to London to justify himself to the queen.[42] By this time he had convinced himself that whatever had gone wrong in Ireland was the result of the poisoning of the minds of queen and council against him by his enemies. Those enemies were now firmly identified as Robert Cecil and his friends, partly through his own paranoia and partly through the loaded circumstantial evidence that he was receiving from supporters.

However, Robert Cecil had more important things to occupy his mind than seeking to undermine the Earl of Essex, a feat that he rightly judged the earl could perform much better for himself. He was concerned with trying to set up a peace negotiation with Spain. By June 1599 negotiations of a preliminary nature were taking place using an intermediary called Dr Jerome Comans. Comans went off from London with a series of proposals, but it was 20 August before he returned. The good news was that Philip III had given him authority to 'treat of peace'; the bad news was that the Spaniards were insisting as a precondition that English trade should return from Amsterdam to Antwerp.[43] England's implacable enemy (and one-time king) Philip II, had died in 1598 and his son was not ideologically driven in the same way, but he was nevertheless not prepared to concede any point unnecessarily. Sir Robert, at the same time, was well aware that any revival of Antwerp would pose a threat to the position that London was beginning to acquire as a money market, and so the talks stalled almost as soon as they had begun.

Before Comans had even returned to London, however, there was a panic. The origin of this was never traced, but given the extreme unpopularity of any feelers for peace, it seems that someone had got wind of what Sir Robert was about. A Spanish fleet was assembling off Brest with unknown intent, and then (alarming indeed) a report reached London that Spanish troops had actually landed on the Isle of Wight.[44] Sir Robert's famous intelligence service let him down on this occasion, for he apparently believed this fiction and ordered an emergency mobilization from 11 counties. The panic passed and the dreaded fleet turned out to be a collection of fishing boats, but the atmosphere of apprehension remained for several months, and it was into this nervous climate that the Earl of Essex made his celebrated intrusion on 28 September.

He had apparently toyed with the idea of bringing a part of his army with him, and forcing a showdown with his enemies at the point of his sword. Wiser councils prevailed, but he still had a sizeable company of gentlemen and officers with him when he reached the court, which was at Nonsuch and entirely unprotected. Ostensibly his purpose was to explain and justify his proceedings in Ireland and to convince the queen of his loyalty, but he went a strange way about it, marching unannounced into the queen's bedchamber at an hour when she was still *en déshabillé*.

Completely taken by surprise, but with admirable presence of mind, Elizabeth kept him talking, and even persuaded him to withdraw peacefully.[45] So great was his capacity for self-delusion that he was completely unable to see the enormity of what he had done, and believed that he had earned a favourable hearing. Nothing could have been further from the truth. Once she had reassured herself that she was not about to be the victim of a coup d'état, she collected her thoughts, assembled such of her council as were to hand, which included Cecil and Knollys, and summoned Essex to reappear. He did so, in a slightly more rational state of mind, and justified his actions in a manner that seemed to him to be absolutely convincing. The council did not agree. He had concluded an unlawful truce with the queen's enemy and had deserted his post without permission. The same evening he was committed to the custody of Lord Keeper Thomas Egerton at York House and forbidden to communicate with anyone.[46]

At first, the earl appears to have been determined to outface his critics and to return vindicated to his command. He believed his discomfiture to be temporary and blamed it on Robert Cecil. Some of the wilder members of the following that he had brought from Ireland were even threatening to kill the secretary if they could lay their hands upon him. However, such wild talk led nowhere and on 6 October, after a three-hour session with Egerton, Buckhurst and Cecil, he eventually accepted their suggestion that he withdraw into private life, at least for the time being, and accept the fact that he had failed in Ireland. He was not the first to have failed across the Irish Sea and he would not be the last. Having apparently defused a potentially dangerous situation, Robert Cecil again offered reconciliation with the earl which he, away from the inflammatory urgings of his so-called friends, seems to have taken in good part.

It might have been expected that, after a decent interval, Essex would be quietly released.[47] Unfortunately this was not to be, because he and his supporters were treading a very dangerous path. The earl had been in friendly but surreptitious correspondence for some time with the king of Scots, and there was a wild plot for a Scottish invasion, backed by elements of Essex's command from Ireland, to rescue the earl by force. The whole idea was ridiculous because Lord Mountjoy, who had taken over Essex's deserted command in Ireland, was loyal to the queen and James had not the slightest intention of jeopardizing his chances of the English succession by countenancing such a venture. In fact, it was a good indication of how far out of touch with reality Essex was becoming. It was also highly treasonable.

Robert Cecil knew of this plot, but does not seem to have taken it seriously, because when the council in Star Chamber came to examine the earl's case towards the end of the year, it was not mentioned. Instead, the investigation concentrated upon the earl's dereliction of duty and particularly upon the unacceptable nature of his dealings with Tyrone. Robert Cecil spoke at length on this subject, and carried most of the council with him, a fact of which Essex's friends were soon aware. Inevitably, they represented him as working off a personal grudge: 'men say that they [the council] are either carried away with passion, or yield too much to the passion of others ... His [Essex's] are imputed to proceed from the malice of his adversaries ...'[48]

This was personalized politics with a vengeance and completely unfair to Sir Robert, who seems to have worked very hard to keep the proceedings at an objective level. Meanwhile, Essex became seriously ill. A mixture of depression and chagrin worked upon an infection of some kind to bring him to the point where his life was thought to be in danger, and public prayers were offered for him in the City churches. However, by the end of February 1600 a combination of improved weather and the attentions of his dutiful and misused wife brought about a recovery. Some sort of a trial was clearly in the offing, but Sir Robert managed to get it postponed—not so much out of any solicitousness for the earl as out of the consideration that the public arraignment of anyone who was in any sense incapacitated would directly fuel the venomous propaganda against the secretary that was filling every ballad-monger's stall and appearing as graffiti on the walls of the city.

It was 5 June before Essex was finally arraigned, and then it was not before the Council in Star Chamber, but in front of a special commission held at York House. There were 18 commissioners, including Cecil, and the proceedings were attended by some 200 'men of quality' who had been, presumably, specially invited. The result was an anti-climax, because although there was much emphasis upon the excessive number of knighthoods that he had conferred, and upon his mismanagement of the campaign in Munster, nothing was said about his invasion of the court or about the suggestions of treason, which were plentiful in intercepted correspondence.[49] The commissioners failed to agree and Essex was placed under house arrest in his own residence until the queen's pleasure was known.

It is hard to believe that this outcome was unintended. Cecil had more than enough ammunition to have secured a conviction for high treason, but he chose not to use it. Essex, for all his foolishness, was a great man. He had been the queen's favourite, and might be so again. Moreover, the last thing the secretary needed (or wanted) was to give further occasion to those who were anxious to prove that he was hounding the earl to his doom. Above all, he probably sensed that Elizabeth's anger had passed, and by this somewhat equivocal verdict, he could give her an opportunity to exercise the prerogative of mercy. Some, at least, of the commentators on the drama seem to have understood what he was about. One wrote that his conduct had been 'wise and temperate'. 'By employing his credit with her Majesty in behalf of the Earl, he has gained great credit to himself, both at home and abroad ...'[50] However, if he was looking for gratitude where it mattered most, he was to be disappointed. The queen did indeed release Essex from his house arrest, but he was not restored to favour or allowed to return to court.

Essex also had enemies, notably Lord Cobham and Sir Walter Raleigh, both of whom looked for an increase of favour as a result of his disgrace. Neither was successful. In spite of unofficially attaching themselves to the peace negotiations that were currently going on at Boulogne, neither was called to the council. Cobham got no further than the wardenship of the Cinq Ports, and Raleigh was effectively exiled as governor of Jersey. Robert Cecil, although in most respects the earl's opponent, was not his enemy in that sense, so it cannot be pretended that Essex was eventually ruined by court conspiracy. He was the author of his own downfall. The critical factor was Elizabeth's refusal to renew his sweet wine monopoly. His debts were now running at over £16,000, and without that income, he would be ruined.[51] The monopoly had been granted for ten years in 1590, and came up for renewal in the autumn of 1600. The queen, however, was not in a generous mood; 'an unruly horse must be abated of his provender, that he may be the easier and better managed', she commented.[52]

Management was precisely the point. Essex had been suspended from all his offices, but not deprived of any of them. He discovered that his patronage had almost totally evaporated, but if he had behaved himself circumspectly, there was no reason why he should not be restored. Canny observers expected such a rehabilitation. However, circumspection was not in Essex's nature. He wrote passionate begging letters, full of self-dramatization ('Time itself is a perpetual night, and the whole world but a sepulchre ...'). The queen had heard all this nonsense before. Once she had been moved by it, but not any more. At the beginning of October, the earl returned from the country to his residence at Essex House. This was partly to continue pressing for his sweet wine grant, and partly to be on hand while his friends countermined the conspiracy that he believed to involve Robert Cecil, Cobham and Raleigh (and others) in a plot against him at the court. He also tried, unsuccessfully, to mobilize James on his behalf by claiming that Sir Robert favoured the succession of the Infanta, a claim apparently based on the secretary's involvement in the abortive peace negotiations at Boulogne.[53] At the same time the Earl of Southampton returned from Ireland (where Lord Mountjoy was managing perfectly well without him) and took up residence at Drury House, close to Essex. There were busy comings and goings, Southampton being one of the few peers who was still wholly at Essex's 'devotion'.

It was in these comings and goings that the rebellion of February 1601 was conceived. Essex had by this time lost all confidence in Elizabeth, but was not prepared to go so far as to propose her murder or deposition. The excuse was to be the ancient one of 'evil counsel', the councillors in this case being Robert Cecil and his allies—most of the privy council, in fact. They were to be instantly dismissed and a parliament summoned. On the strength of his 'following' of about 30 MPs last time around, the earl seems to have believed that he could dominate the elections. That was to be the official agenda, but in fact the impatient young men who were gathering at Essex House and Drury House were hardly politicized at all. They were mostly soldiers, many of whom had served in Ireland, and they were impatient. Ill-used and unrewarded as they saw themselves, they wanted Elizabeth out of the way, convincing themselves that by removing her the golden gates of patronage would be opened by their noble leader.

The council was suspicious, but patient. On 7 February they sent the newly appointed second secretary, John Herbert, to Essex House, summoning the earl to appear before them. This precipitated a crisis of guilty conscience. Essex replied that he would not come, because he feared for his life. Specifically, although not to the council, he accused Raleigh of conspiring to murder him.[54] By this time Robert Cecil must have known what was afoot, and the speed of his subsequent reaction indicates no less. Nevertheless, a final attempt at negotiation was attempted. Four senior councillors, led by Sir Thomas Egerton, the lord keeper, waited on the earl at Essex House. After a hasty consultation, they were detained and Essex led his motley collection of some 300 swordsmen out onto the streets of London, crying 'for the Queen, for the Queen' and 'the crown of England is sold to the Spaniard'. The citizens were bemused, but no one was inspired to join him. The earl had totally misjudged the enthusiasm with which his earlier prowess had been received. Then he had been the agent of Elizabeth, now he was her enemy. Hard on his heels came Thomas, Lord Burghley, with a posse of soldiers, proclaiming Essex a traitor.[55] Essex's following melted away, and the earl retreated to Essex House, where he was shortly under siege.

The besiegers could afford to be patient, but they did not have long to wait. After vowing that he would fight to the death, that same evening the earl surrendered. The whole affair had been completely botched. It was later pointed out that had he gone straight to the court 'he would have surprised it unprovided of defence', although that is by no means certain, given that both Thomas Cecil and the Earl of Nottingham were able to deploy significant forces the same day.

The examinations and enquiries began on the morning of 9 February, and the chief burden was inevitably borne by Robert as the secretary.[56] When the council assembled in the Star Chamber to hear the results on the 13th, although Robert Cecil was not the first speaker his was the most critical presentation. Apart from his dealings with Tyrone, the charges that Cecil concentrated upon were not the most obvious. Perhaps appearing in arms against the queen was too obvious to need emphasis, but he concentrated instead upon his ingratitude and upon his affection of 'popularity'. More strangely, he declared that 'He [Essex] had been devising five or six years to be king of England; had wit, and much power put into his hand, and meant thus to slip into Her Majesty's place ...'[57]

Some of the earl's wilder remarks could have been construed in that sense, and perhaps some of his more far-fetched schemes, but real evidence of such an intention is almost entirely lacking and Essex's correspondence with James seems to make it clear that he regarded the king of Scots as the lawful heir. The Court of the Lord High Steward convened for the trial in Westminster Hall on 19 February. Not being a peer, Robert Cecil was not present officially, and the charges against the defendants (the Earl of Southampton was tried as well) were based mainly on the actual rebellion. However, when Essex tried to justify his actions on the grounds that the secretary had supported, and still supported, the Infanta's claim, Sir Robert emerged dramatically from behind a tapestry to challenge the allegation. Put on his mettle, the earl claimed that he had been told no less by Sir William Knollys, but when Knollys was summoned to substantiate the claim, he revealed that the alleged remarks had been made in the context of a discussion of the *Conference on the Next Succession*. 'Hereupon', he concluded, 'was grounded the slanders upon Mr. Secretary, whereof he is as clear as any man present'.[58]

Essex had deluded himself by a piece of hearsay, and seems to have based much of his hatred of Robert (or at least as much as could be admitted in public) upon a misapprehension. The secretary took his opportunity, declaring that all this malice arose from his attempts to find a way to peace, which was so inimical to Essex's interests and instincts. 'I beseech God to forgive you for this open wrong done unto me, as I do openly pronounce and forgive you from the bottom of my heart.'[59] He was in a good position to be magnanimous, because both earls were condemned and, barring the royal prerogative of mercy, were destined for the scaffold. Southampton was eventually pardoned, but Essex was executed on 25 February, quite unable to see, even at the very end, the extent to which he had brought nemesis upon himself.

As we have seen, the royal succession played a leading part in this drama. It was a subject that Elizabeth (naturally) abhorred, and it could not be discussed openly, or in her presence. Nevertheless, it could not be avoided, and as the associates of the Earl of Essex fell over each other in their haste to confess other men's guilt, the extent of the earl's Scottish connections became clear. Sir Robert already knew quite a lot of this through John Cecil, at least in outline, but Henry Cuffe, one of those condemned on 5 March, provided valuable corroboration. It transpired that Essex had been in communication with the Earl of Mar for several years, knowing perfectly well that his communications would be disclosed to James. Far from showing any desire to thwart the Scottish king, he was mainly concerned to secure his own future when (rather than if) James succeeded to the crown of England.[60] His main concern was to establish himself as the heir's great friend among the English nobility, and by extension to present Sir Robert Cecil as his great enemy. This may, or may not, have been done out of malice, as Cecil claimed. It was, after all, a fairly obvious political manoeuvre, because the secretary was clearly Elizabeth's great councillor; no one had more power, or more influence with the queen, but the continuation of that power into the new reign was a different matter entirely.

There was another possible royal candidate in the person of Arabella Stuart, the niece of Lord Darnley and consequently James's cousin, but although her claim was canvassed it found little support. The only serious rival (in a sense) was the Spanish Infanta Isabella, who had been bequeathed her father Philip's claim. It had lain dormant since the 1550s, but she was seriously backed by the extremer sort of English Catholic. The reverse side of Essex's self-promotion in Scotland was, as we have seen, to state categorically that Cecil supported the Infanta. James had toyed with the idea of sending a mission to intercede for Essex, but had delayed, and when his representatives eventually reached London the earl was already dead. His representatives were the Earl of Mar and Edward Bruce, the titular Abbot of Kinloss, and their brief was to find out how much was known of Essex's dealings and where Robert Cecil actually stood on the issue.[61]

For the time being their mission hung fire, because Mar purported to find his instructions inadequate, but in truth probably because he did not know quite what to say to a queen whose death was his real concern. Sir Robert wrote to George Nicholson, who was the English representative in Scotland, pointing out gently (for James's benefit) that this was no way to conduct business between princes. At the same time he endeavoured by roundabout means to convey to the king that there were some in Scotland who were already seeking his favour. They, at least, were expecting his influence to continue.

James, although no novice in the arts of government, was out of his depth diplomatically. He was, on the one hand, very sorry for the loss of one whom he had taken to be his main supporter in England, but at the same time relieved that he would have no major obligations to redeem. Towards Robert he was at first clumsy and misguided. When his revised instructions eventually reached Mar, they contained the clause 'Ye shall plainly declare to Mr. Secretary and his followers, that since now ... they will thus misknow me, when the chance shall turn, I shall cast a deaf ear to their requests ...'[62]

However, it is extremely unlikely that this threat was ever issued, because second thoughts followed hard upon. Mar was to sound out Robert and, if he found him responsive, to assure him of James's future favour. Towards the end of April 1601 they obtained a confidential interview, which was conducted in the duchy chambers in the Strand. Sir Robert was alone, and about to take one of the biggest political gambles of his career. He had first to disarm suspicion, because without mutual trust the whole exercise would have been not only fruitless, but impossibly dangerous. What transpired can only be conjectured, because no one recorded these sensitive exchanges. However, Sir Robert seems to have started by reserving his allegiance to the queen during her lifetime. Whatever might transpire thereafter, she had the first claim, and that was understood.[63] His second stipulation was that all communications between himself and James must be kept totally secret—which was another way of saying the same thing. These points being accepted, he undertook to bring James to the throne upon Elizabeth's death.

In one sense this was a great undertaking, and James certainly saw it as such. But at the same time, given the nature of the alternatives, it presented no great difficulty. James was so much the front runner in the race that, barring his sudden death or some similar catastrophe, success was assured. What it did mean, of course, was that Robert Cecil picked up that sense of obligation that Essex had been forced to drop—although he knew better than to hint at any such thing. Mar's

official mission to the queen for some assurance in respect of the succession made no progress. 'She loves neither importunity nor expostu-
lation', the earl was truthfully informed, and now, with Sir Robert's
assurance in his hand, James could afford to refrain from both—and
relations improved. Mar's report to his sovereign of the outcome of
these exchanges does not survive, and may even have been verbal.

James initiated the subsequent correspondence, carefully coding the
sensitive parts of his letter:

> I AM MOST *heartily glad that 10 [Robert Cecil] hath now at last
> made choice of two so fit and confident ministers [Mar and Bruce]
> whom with he hath been so honourably plain in the affairs of 30
> [James], assuring 10 that 30 puts more confidence in them than in any
> others that follow him ... When it shall please God that 30, he shall no
> surelier succeed to the place than he shall succeed in bestowing as great or
> greater favour upon 10 as his predecessor doth bestow upon him ...*[64]

It was not exactly Bletchley Park cryptography, but it was sufficient for
the purpose!

More letters were exchanged and a confidential relationship grew
up. Sir Robert made it clear that he would do nothing to assist James to
the throne before the cause of nature would dictate it, and he was brief
and discreet on the subject of the Earl of Essex. James, in return, was
friendly to the point of effusiveness. It was a situation that suited both
of them, because each had assured his own future, and it is a clear indication of the extent to which Sir Robert was perceived to be in control
of the political scene in England. Unlike Essex, the English Catholics
did not believe that Robert favoured the Infanta. They held him to be
'a professed enemy', and circulated rumours that he intended to make
himself king by marrying Arabella Stuart.[65] Apart from the fact that
Robert was a widower and Arabella at the time unmarried, there was
no plausibility, let alone truth, in these stories. Sir Robert showed no
disposition to remarry.

In his own words, Sir Robert continued to 'labour like a packhorse'
for the rest of Elizabeth's life, taking due care to bestow upon her the
flattery that had long since taken the place of real admiration.[66] By
1601 she was living on borrowed time—and she knew it. The parliament that opened on 27 October was fractious, and could only with
difficulty be persuaded to pass the subsidy bill, in spite of the fact that

the war continued with general support. Sir Robert crossed swords with Raleigh over the assessment of the subsidy, a distraction that he could have done without. This was also the parliament that worked up such a head of steam about monopolies, a policy with which the Cecils had had much to do — and from which they had both profited. From the session, Sir Robert learned a lesson. The House of Commons was poised to be an independent player on the political stage, and although at this stage it could still be cajoled, it would be a foolish councillor who attempted to bully it in the future. Nor was this all. He was maintaining his secret-service network, particularly in France, Spain and the Low Countries, and trying to cope with the ambition, greed and sheer factiousness of many of his colleagues. James was being pressed to assure toleration for English Catholics after his accession, a policy with which Cecil knew that the parliament would have nothing to do. Tyrone's revolt ground on in Ireland, although largely contained by the efficient Mountjoy.[67] The Spaniards landed a token force at Smerwick, in the Dingle peninsula, in his support, but it was quickly eliminated. Above all, the queen became increasingly petulant and irrational.

By 1602 Robert's health was giving way under the sheer strain — not in the obvious way in which his father had been invalided by gout, but rather the result of general debility. Meanwhile it seemed that Robert's great achievement, the unopposed succession of James, might unravel. How serious the threat was is hard to determine, but by the beginning of 1603 there was a crypto-Catholic party in the council, numbering some three or four members, who were minded to make their support for the Scottish king dependent upon his agreement to 'a toleration' — just the point that Robert had warned James against. Whether they would really have been prepared to back the Infanta if it came to an issue is a moot point — probably not, although there were those who thought differently. Robert Persons had a network in England, and the recusants, although mostly loyal to Elizabeth, might not transfer their allegiance to an unsympathetic successor. When Elizabeth fell ill at the beginning of March 1603, it looked as though the secretary might yet have a battle on his hands — and although his spirit might be willing, his flesh was undoubtedly weak.

# CHAPTER 10

# Salisbury and the New Regime

KING JAMES had been preparing to emerge from his Scottish chrysalis for a long time. As long ago as 1586, the Treaty of Berwick had given him a realistic hope—and a pension of £3000 a year.[1] Publicly, he had been much offended by the execution of his mother the following year, but he chose (as Elizabeth probably intended that he should) to blame Lord Burghley for that outcome rather than the queen herself. Although the Act for the Queen's Safety had carefully avoided placing any obstacle in the way of his succession, James had nevertheless become convinced that the Cecils, both father and son, were opposed to him, which was why he had fished rather tentatively in Madrid and rather less tentatively with the Earl of Essex. As we have seen, Essex's demise looked at first as though it was going to cause him a problem, but it eventually helped to clear the air.

From the summer of 1601 James's affairs in England were in the hands of Robert Cecil, who tactfully arranged for the Scottish king's pension from the cash-strapped exchequer to be raised from £3000 a year to £5000, which was quite a lot of money to a monarch of very limited means.[2] The real problem towards the end of Elizabeth's life had been the hints of Catholic toleration that James had been dropping in what he thought were appropriate places. As we have seen, there were those, even as high as the council, who were hinting that they might make their support conditional upon such an undertaking. Others, including the Earl of Northumberland, feared that if some sort of toleration were not conceded, James might be tempted to seize the throne by force, which would inevitably have provoked a civil war. Northumberland was unaware that Cecil was already in touch with James, and took pains to ensure that his correspondence with the Scottish king was known to the secretary, but the latter did not disclose his own contacts in return. It was rather like a game of blind man's buff.[3]

Meanwhile, the English Catholics were very far from united. There were those who were prepared to accept James without any formal declaration of toleration, on the grounds that he was sympathetic and some amelioration of their condition was to be expected. There were those who would support him if he made such a declaration, but not otherwise; and there were those who wanted the Infanta. The difficulty, from Robert's point of view, was that the Catholics were politically top-heavy. A small minority of the population as a whole, they were numerous among the gentry, particularly in the north, and proportionately even more numerous amongst the nobility.[4] As at the time of the Armada, no one could tell what sort of a force they could raise in support of a cause to which they were committed. Sir Robert set out to prevent any sort of consensus from forming and, by exercising political skills of no common order, he succeeded in detaching the Howards, including the lord admiral, from any possibility of support for the Infanta. Having got these important noblemen (more or less) behind James, he had left the remaining crypto-Catholics, such as Lord Buckhurst, with only a forlorn hope, for which they were not prepared to take any risks.

However, the one person that Sir Robert could not control was James himself. If he took it into his head to issue a toleration, no one could stop him, least of all now that Sir Robert had virtually removed the only alternative. The only thing that he could do was to eliminate the temptation by causing the Catholics to self-destruct—in other words, to discredit them. This he was able to do, not completely but sufficiently for his purpose, by taking advantage of the so-called 'Wisbech stirs'. These were disputes that arose originally between Jesuits and secular priests imprisoned together in Wisbech Castle. The former were so unpopular with their colleagues that certain seminarians, particularly Thomas Bluett and Chrisopher Bagshaw, offered their services to Archbishop Whitgift in order to expose what they called the *regnum Jesuiticum*, maintaining that it was the ethos of the Jesuit order that was justifying the harsh measures that the government was currently applying to all Catholics.[5] It was thus under the (secret) auspices of Robert Cecil and Richard Bancroft, the Bishop of London, that Bluett and some other seminarians set off for Rome in February 1602. They bore a petition against the political involvement of the Society of

Jesus and against the maladministration of George Blackwell, their own archpriest, who was (they alleged) in the pocket of Father Garnett, the Superior of the Jesuits. Robert Persons was, they alleged, the origin and cause of the fact that the Roman Church was 'under the cross' in England.[6] Garnett and Persons had plenty of support in Rome, and the petitioners made a mess of presenting their case. As a result they spent some time in the prisons of the Inquisition and the brief that eventually emerged reprimanded their action, although it did place some restraints upon Blackwell.[7]

Meanwhile, with government encouragement, a number of bitterly anti-Jesuit tracts were published in England, the work of William Watson, William Clarke and Anthony Copley. Anger at the papal rejection of their petition also fuelled this bitterness, and by November 1602 the Catholic camp was split right down the middle, those opposed to the Jesuits known as the Appellants. Sir Robert then took advantage of this situation by issuing a proclamation declaring that, 'Toleration of two religions within her realm is indeed far from the imagination of her Majesty, being a course that would not only disturb the peace of the church, but bring this her state into confusion ...'[8]

Priests who submitted to the queen's authority would be allowed to remain, but Jesuits and anyone else rejecting such a submission would have to leave the country by 1 January 1603. Watson and his colleagues submitted, thus confirming the split and effectively preventing the dissidents from raising their heads above the parapet when the queen died at the end of March. Sir Robert was thus able to assure the new king that 'most of them [the Catholics] do declare their affection absolutely to your title'.

At the time of James's accession, neither the Appellants nor their opponents made any kind of public appearance. By linking his actions against the Catholics to the promotion of the king's title, the secretary not only reinforced James's gratitude to him, but also made any granting of a general toleration completely redundant.

The queen died on 24 March 1603, and the first few days after her death were crucial. There was, for the time being, no lawful government, and the pessimists had stockpiled weapons and prepared for the worst. In fact, nothing untoward happened at all, 'no tumult, no contradiction, no disorder ... every man went about his business [as] readily, as peaceably, as securely, as though there had been no ... news

ever heard of competitors'.[9] Sir Robert had already drafted the proclamation announcing James's accession, and he was the first to read it at
Whitehall on the morning of 24 March. Thereafter it was read in the
City, and copies sent out to the counties, amid almost audible sighs of
relief. Quite apart from the peaceful nature of the succession (so different from the last such event 45 years earlier), it would be good to
have a king again. During her last years Elizabeth had become a very
difficult old lady, and always over her histrionics and procrastination
had been the unanswered question—what next? Now they knew.
James might be a foreigner, but he was of the right religion, spoke the
same language (more or less) and had two growing sons.

Meanwhile, the existing councillors and officers of state formed an
interim government and the tidings sped to Edinburgh. The news was
not, of course, unexpected, but James's first thoughts turned to the
man who had made it all possible—Robert Cecil. 'How happy I think
myself by the conquest of so wise a councillor,' he wrote, 'I reserve to
be expressed out of my own mouth unto you.'[10] The compliment was
well deserved, but the king's own wisdom had played a part. He had
not responded, or rather he had responded non-committally, to suggestions from Rome and Madrid that he might undertake to 'change
the state' of England, and above all he had refrained from promising
any toleration.

On 27 March, as soon as the news reached him, James wrote to Sir
Robert authorizing the interim government that had been put in
place; on the receipt of that letter three days later, the existing council
and officers were functioning in the name of King James I. The only
slight cloud on the immediate horizon was that the king's first communication to his government in London was a request for money, a
request that the state of the treasury made an embarrassment. Meanwhile, the faithful were flocking north, not only to present their dutiful greetings to their new prince, but also in the hope of picking up
some of the fruits of his already notorious generosity. Many of them
gained knighthoods for their pains, but the substantial rewards went
mostly to his fellow Scots, another somewhat ominous sign, although
not much commented upon at the time.

With the exception of Robert Cecil himself, the council were constrained by their various responsibilities to remain about London, but
the secretary, who was at the cutting edge of all business, had no

option but to go and seek responses to a variety of urgent matters and
to dissuade James (if he could) from meddling with the coinage,
which was reported to be his intention. The two men met at York on
18 April.[11] James had not yet recovered from the euphoria of his accession, and at first little business could be discussed apart from fixing a
date for his coronation—25 July. Robert dutifully tracked the party for
six days, managing to transact some (but not nearly enough) business,
until they reached his half-brother's house at Burghley where they
came to rest for a few days. Having satisfied himself that the king was
too preoccupied to do anything about the coinage, on 25 April Robert
returned to London. A few days later the royal party reached
Theobalds, where they stopped for a further four days, moving on to
London on 7 May.

Within a short space James's host, guide and general facilitator had
entered the peerage as Lord Cecil of Essendon. His days of managing
the House of Commons from within were over. Like Essex before
him, he provided to about 30 seats (and that conflicted with James's
somewhat idealistic notions of 'free election'), so he retained a vicari-
ous presence, but the days when he could sway the House with his
oratory were over.[12]

The title was well deserved, and if Elizabeth had not been so mean
with peerages she might have thought of it herself. Not that Robert's
services had been unrewarded. At a time of private affluence and public squalor, he had taken his chance with the best. Between 1593 and
1603 nearly two million pounds had been spent on warfare, a lot of it
in Ireland, and the treasury was, as we have seen, so empty that Lord
Buckhurst had to resort to expedients to meet the king's travelling
expenses. At the same time, Robert Cecil was spending some £4500
on estates in the west of England, including Cranborne in Dorset,
which he bought from Sir Ralph Horsey for £2000. In January 1602
he spent another £5000 on former crown properties, taking advantage of his 'insider knowledge' to get good bargains.[13] In case awkward
questions should be asked in high places, he also presented the queen
with a richly set ruby—the quickest way to Elizabeth's heart being
through her jewel box.

Robert Cecil was not exactly corrupt—certainly not by the standards of the time—but he was less scrupulous than his father and more
interested in money. Quite apart from his income from the Court of

Wards, which amounted to some £2900 between 1600 and 1603, he also used his office to award himself customs leases, which, when his son surrendered them in 1615, were valued at £3000 a year.[14] In 1602 his gross rental from lands alone has been estimated at about £6000 a year. This would have made him the fourth or fifth richest peer, and his income from offices and other perks doubled that so that, at the time of his elevation, Lord Cecil was probably the richest of James's subjects.[15] This is confirmed by the fact that between 1608 and his death in 1612, the Earl of Salisbury (as Robert had then become) spent the staggering sum of £49,014—averaging over £12,000 a year.

Much of this was spent on building.[16] Cranborne, for example, was totally rebuilt shortly after it had been purchased, to designs by William Arnold, the leading architect of the day. As Earl of Salisbury, Robert spent some £3500 a year on building at his various residences. His household expenditure had been exceeded only by the Duke of Somerset some 50 years before, although inflation in the interval had made that discrepancy greater than at first appears. Typical of his hard-nosed approach to estate management was the fact that he bought and enclosed Brigstock Park in Northamptonshire, an action that pro-voked riots among the tenants and an unfavourable reaction from the king. So Cecil met the king's objection by retaining a small hunting park, and ignored the more general protests.

It is perhaps not surprising that death threats were occasionally made against Cecil, or that his funeral was marred by discontented demonstrations from his tenants at Hatfield. The scale of his financial resources (as distinct from his actual income) can be judged by the fact that in the early 1590s he had 'bought out' the Earl of Essex's interest in a cochineal monopoly for £50,000. Not even a very rich man could afford that sort of sum without favoured access to the credit facilities of the City.[17] Whichever way you look at it, Robert Cecil's financial pos-ition at the time of James's accession was extremely strong.

Rescuing the finances of the crown, however, was another matter, and for that peace was absolutely essential. The Earl of Tyrone had finally submitted in the last weeks of Elizabeth's life, and there was every prospect of scaling down the expensive military presence in Ire-land. Discussions with Spain and the Netherlands had been going on for some time, so far without success, but having negotiated the rapids of the royal handover, the secretary, now confirmed in the post by the new king, was in the mood to try again. Congratulatory embassies from all over Europe could be expected, and Lord Cecil decided to take advantage of this fact to seek a new opening.

Unfortunately he soon found himself at odds with James. His own policy was quite clear—peace meant peace, not the excuse to build a new European alliance. The French envoy de Rosny, who was the first to arrive, had other ideas.[18] To de Rosny's mind the occasion was not so much one for an Anglo-Spanish peace as a chance to rebuild the Anglo-French alliance, which had collapsed with the Treaty of Vervins five years earlier. Lord Cecil carefully disabused him of this expectation, only to discover to his horror that it had been taken up by the king. James was literally uncounselled in making this response. He had disclosed his thinking to no one and, although he was perfectly entitled to take whatever initiatives he chose in foreign policy, in practical terms he was acting irresponsibly.

Lord Cecil reined him in by exploiting a series of apparently unrelated events. When, in response to overwhelming demand, James had enlarged his council shortly after arriving in London, the Howards, Thomas and Henry, had been included, but Walter Raleigh and Lord Cobham had not. As a result both Raleigh and the Brookes became disaffected, and George Brooke, Lord Cobham's younger brother, became involved in a plot. Such substance as there was to this was provided by the Appellants Watson and Clarke, who were fed a story by Brooke about a powerful revival of Jesuit influence in England in the new reign.[19] This was supposed to be Lord Cecil's fault and, swallowing the story whole, the conspirators planned an early strike. Some plausibility was given to the conspiracy by Sir Griffin Markham, a disillusioned courtier who claimed to have more than 500 men at his command. The plan was to kidnap the king and Prince Henry at Greenwich on midsummer night and force the king to dismiss Lord Cecil, but James changed his plans at the last moment and nothing happened. Meanwhile, the unrelated John Cecil had been rashly approached to join the conspiracy, and had promptly told Robert all about it. Markham also seems to have been a double agent.[20] By early July, the promoters of this non-existent *putsch* were being rounded up.

The whole thing would have been farcical had it not been for the precedent set by the Earl of Essex and for the fall-out that resulted. As soon as the interrogations of the plotters started on 12 July, George

Brooke began to make desperate attempts to save himself. His confession implicated both Lord Cobham (his brother) and Walter Raleigh —not in this plot, which became known as the Bye Plot, but in another conspiracy altogether, the so-called Main Plot, to replace James with Arabella Stuart.[21] The smooth transition of April had, apparently, been deceptive. Raleigh and Cobham proceeded to incriminate each other and both ended up in the Tower, where Cobham was to remain until shortly before his death in 1619.

So tortuous is the politics of these events that it is tempting to see Lord Cecil as the inventor of the whole show, because it played so completely into his hands. James was badly shaken by the revelations, and as a result the prestige of the secretary who had saved him rose to even greater heights. By this means, Lord Cecil was able to derail the king's independent initiative in foreign policy and bring him back on side. There was to be no question of continuing the war, with or without France. Peace was unequivocally at the top of the agenda.

Now that James was concentrating, his cooperation could be taken for granted. Not only had he received a sharp lesson in the realities of English domestic politics, he had also had time to assess the state of his treasury. Negotiations did not actually begin until the following June, but by that time James was wondering whatever could have possessed him to stray from the path that his secretary had laid down, professing that without him, 'if he wanted to, he would not know what to do'.[22] By March 1604 the commissions had been issued on both sides, and Lord Cecil was optimistic. 'There is now nothing so certain as a treaty', he wrote.

The bargaining, when it came, was hard because Spain, like France, was looking for an offensive and defensive alliance, which the secretary was determined not to concede. He recognized that by ceasing to be a belligerent, England would also have to withdraw help from the Dutch, but did not want to find himself on the other side. The Dutch were perfectly capable of looking after themselves, but they wanted to retain freedom of trade, and Robert Cecil wanted to retain the four Dutch 'cautionary towns' given over to English authority—not for belligerent purposes, but because they represented a security for the large sums of money that Elizabeth had loaned and had spent there when it was most needed. Eventually he was successful on both points, the Spaniards having to be satisfied with a formula of 'friendship and amity'.[23] In return, the English conceded over a demand for unrestricted trade to the Spanish colonies. The treaty was signed on 19 August 1604, thus bringing to an end one of the longest conflicts of the period (19 years).

The investigations into the plots that had so contributed to this favourable outcome had been conducted during the previous autumn. The case against George Brooke and the Appellants was fairly straightforward. Whatever had led them into such a far-fetched scheme, they were guilty as charged. They had accused each other and there was corroboratory evidence. On 15 November they were tried and found guilty.[24] Raleigh and Cobham, however, were in a different position. They ultimately refused to testify against each other, and so in each case the prosecution could muster only one witness, where two were required by the existing treason laws.

The real situation seems to have been that Raleigh was so anti-Spanish that he was determined at all costs to sabotage the peace negotiations, and had taken part in various underhand schemes for that purpose. Whether he had really been prepared to go as far as to replace James on the throne was, and remains, unproven. What is perfectly clear is that Lord Cecil, his one-time friend, was now determined to destroy him. As Raleigh himself said, 'I have been strangely practised against, and ... others have their lives promised to accuse me', and Sir John Harrington observed, 'Cecil doth bear no love to Raleigh'.[25] A precedent was found to enable him to be tried by a single witness, and he was duly convicted, but he did not face the executioner for many years, and then it was for a different offence. In fact he outlived Cecil, although it is doubtful whether that was any consolation to him.

The manner in which Robert Cecil manipulated the case against Raleigh, which involved chicanery and betrayal, forms one of the least creditable episodes in his long and generally honourable record of service. Why he should have pursued his victim with such determination is something of a mystery. Once the king had been convinced of the need for peace, Sir Walter is unlikely to have been able to change his mind—and indeed, he would have been in no position to have done so. Perhaps he really had conspired James's deposition, and Cecil knew it, although the nature of the evidence was such that it could not be produced in court. Given the flexible rules of evidence in use at the time, this seems unlikely.

Perhaps the real reason for his animus was more personal. Robert's son, William, had spent part of his youth in Raleigh's household and had formed a close bond with this surrogate father, who was a warm-hearted, passionate, outgoing man. Robert was none of those things; indeed, he was something of an emotional cripple, particularly after the deaths of his father and his wife. He seems to have been simply unable to relate to the growing boy, who was left to find affection where he could. He found it with Raleigh, and it is entirely likely that Robert Cecil resented this bitterly. William was barely 14 when his mentor was struck down in this fashion, and we have no idea of his reaction, but it is reasonable to suppose that it would have been one from which his father would have drawn small comfort.

James celebrated his peace by conferring more knighthoods, bringing to over 900 the total for the first year and a half of his reign, and by promoting Lord Cecil to be Viscount Cranborne.[26] Apart from the exchequer, the biggest gainers from the treaty were the merchants, whose routes to Iberia were reopened after nearly 20 years, and who now found access to the Mediterranean and to the New World a good deal easier.

The losers, paradoxically, were the English Catholics. The pope was not, of course, a party to the treaty, but that was not the real point. The spin-off from the two plots of the summer of 1603 somewhat irrationally reduced James's threshold of tolerance. The Main Plot, involving Raleigh, had been aimed against the king and had not involved the Catholics, but the Bye Plot, aimed against Robert Cecil, had been the work of the Appellants. There was, as Raleigh pointed out at his trial, no connection between the two sets of allegations, but nevertheless James made it.[27] No new measures were decreed against recusants, but instead of the slack enforcement that had generally been expected, there was a rigorous tightening of the existing laws. In the spring of 1605 some 5000 offenders were convicted and fined. This was a blow to all Catholics, moderate or extreme, but the latter also suffered directly from the treaty in a different way.

For years they had buoyed themselves up with the hope that, one day, Spain would succeed in forcing a regime change on England and they would be the beneficiaries. Now that hope was gone, and Spain was no longer interested in them. Left to their own devices, some of them decided that direct action was called for, and planned to blow up

king, lords and Commons all together at the opening of parliament on
5 November 1605. The plotters were the veriest amateurs and their
network was penetrated by Cecil's agents early in the proceedings.
Securely convinced that he knew exactly what was supposed to happen, the secretary held back, hoping to catch some of the conspirators
in the act—and that is what happened.[28] A sudden search of the cellars
of the palace of Westminster on the night of 4 November famously
revealed 'two hogsheads and 32 small barrels' of gunpowder presided
over by one Guido Fawkes (plate 27), a minor plotter who had the
dangerous task of lighting the fuse. The names of the other plotters
were already known, but none had been taken into custody in case the
others should be warned that their plans were known. On 7 November a proclamation was issued for the arrest of eight gentlemen, headed
by Thomas Percy and Robert Catesby, for having 'contrived the most
horrible treason that ever entered into the hearts of men, against our
Person, our Children, the whole Nobility, Clergy and Commons in
parliament assembled, which howsoever cloaked with zeal of Super-
stitious Religion, aimed indeed at the subversion of the state.'[29]

Those named were all members of a family network and, although
they were undoubtedly Catholics, had also been marginally involved
in the Essex rebellion five years earlier. Indeed, they have been characterized as 'the old Essexians, the idiot fringe of the indebted gentry'.

It was the most famous plot in English history, but it was also the
most transparent. The French king had got wind of it months before,
and had warned James against 'violent attempts', although he had no
details. The plotters had also been insufficiently secretive. Lord Monteagle, a Catholic peer with no appetite for blowing up his colleagues,
disclosed more particulars (plate 28) to an agent of the secretary, and
Lord Cecil took the well-known counter measures.[30] It was probably
one of his easier victories, as well as being the most spectacular.

While the business of rounding up the fugitives went on, his main
concern was to protect the Spanish ambassador from any suspicion of
involvement, because the first thoughts of Londoners ran on their old
enemy, and the mayor was ordered to provide him with special protection. It seems, however, to have been an entirely home-grown affair,
and the recently established peace was not disturbed. The effects of the
plot were two-fold, and both positive from Cecil's point of view. In
the first place parliament, on the rebound from its 'narrow escape',

enacted new sanctions against those recusants with any amount of property, requiring occasional conformists to receive communion at Easter, under penalties ranging from £20 to £60 a year.[31] This not only increased their lawful burdens but also made them even more vulnerable to blackmail from unscrupulous informers. A further statute required an oath from all Catholics denying the pope's claim to depose kings, which, in the resulting polemical exchanges, James justified on the grounds of political self-defence.[32] This was to prove a significant step in the development of his divine right theory, because it emphasized his own direct dependence upon God. The second effect was a perceptible rallying of the political nation behind its Protestant prince.

This was important because in other respects, things were not going so well. In spite of ending the war, the royal debt had nearly doubled since Elizabeth's death. This was partly caused by the fact that paying off soldiers and decommissioning ships was in the short term an expensive business; but it was also partly due to the king's extravagance. Rewards were dealt with a lavish hand, not only to the Scots who had followed James to England, but also to existing office holders. Sometimes these were for tangible services. Lord Monteagle got £500 for betraying the Gunpowder Plot. Sometimes they were in compensation for the surrender of a patent when the king wished to make a change. The Earl of Nottingham, for example, was awarded £1000 for surrendering his office as lord admiral in 1619, when James wished to appoint his favourite, George Villiers, to the position.[33] James also had a family to provide for and a consort and two princes did not come cheap. Moreover, there was still much resentment about monopolies. In other words, there was plenty of raw material around for the Commons to get their teeth into, and to have made themselves very difficult. But that did not happen, and the king was provided with over £450,000 in direct taxation. This was almost unprecedented in peacetime and a great tribute to the euphoria of the moment, as well as to Robert Cecil's skilful exploitation of the situation.

Robert Cecil, Viscount Cranborne, by this time could no longer attend the House of Commons in person. He was promoted to the earldom of Salisbury on 4 May 1605, for no particular reason other than that the king was feeling generally grateful to him. Unusually for a man of such status, Salisbury continued to be secretary, as well as lord privy seal and master of the wards. However, he had to operate through agents in the Commons, and his principal representatives were Sir Robert Wroth and Sir John Herbert, the second secretary. The problem of funding the crown was a perpetual headache, and it really could not be left to the mercies of an unpredictable 'feel-good factor' in the House.

In 1606 another issue rumbling on was the question of a constitutional union between England and Scotland. This was James's idea and had much to commend it, but the problems were substantial. James had been accompanied south by a numerous retinue, and Scots came to dominate the 'bedchamber', the successor to the old privy chamber. However, there had been no 'flood of Scots' as such into England and only two or three were added to the privy council in spite of the large number of new appointments. What tended to happen was that Scottish lairds and nobles took financial rewards and returned to the north. Nevertheless there had been real hostility for a while, especially in London, where street gangs known as 'swaggerers' had gone on the rampage, beating up any Scots they could find.[34] Such casual violence was shortlived, but a more considered antipathy remained. The issue had dominated the debates of the first session of parliament in 1604, but Robert Cecil had skilfully steered the discussions, and secured the appointment of a parliamentary committee to report back at the next session. As far as we can tell, he had no very strong feelings himself on the issues raised, but was doing his job for the king, and wanted the matter to be properly investigated.

When the committee reported back in November 1605, Sir Edwin Sandys stuck a spanner in the works by declaring that such a union would be very welcome — provided the Scots abandoned their distinctive legal system and submitted to the common law.[35] This somewhat mischievous suggestion was paralleled by the reaction in the north. The Scots parliament not only insisted that its own rights be continued, but issued a solemn warning against any interference with the kirk. Robert Cecil seems to have been working along with the Earl of Mar and Lord Balmerino to overcome this hostility, but little progress was made. A joint commission did succeed in sorting out the border administration and agreeing mutual freedom of trade, but on the more important points there was deadlock. The king had styled himself King of Great Britain, France and Ireland as early as October 1604, but there the matter stuck.[36] The Venetian ambassador was speculating as early as October 1605 that the union would be dropped, but for the time being James persisted. The joint commission reported its limited achievement in November 1606, but the wrangles went on and the king, who seems to have hoped to base his new monarchy upon mutual consent, finally abandoned his efforts in disgust in May 1607.

On the positive side (although Robert Cecil probably did not view it in that light) the anti-Catholic panic of the previous year had subsided. Parliament was prorogued on 4 July, and by the end of the year the slackness of early 1605 had returned to administration of the recusancy laws. Meanwhile, a still grateful king had caused the new Earl of Salisbury to be elected to the Order of the Garter in April 1606.

## THE INVESTITURE OF THE GARTER

A FEW DAYS AGO *the Earl of Salisbury and the other new knight [Viscount Bindon] went to Windsor for the solemn reception of the investiture of the Garter. The pomp was such that the like is not in the memory of man; indeed all confess that it surpassed the ceremony of the very King's coronation; so great is the power of this minister. All envy of him is now dead; no one seeks ought but to win his favour; it is thought that his power will last, for it is based not so much on the grace of his Majesty as on an excellent practice and ability which secures for him the universal opinion that he is worthy of his great authority and good fortune.*

[Zorzi Giustiniani, the Venetian ambassador in England, to the Doge and Senate, 31 May 1606. Taken from the *Calendar of State Papers, Venetian, 1603–1607*, p. 354.]

On 19 April 1608 the lord treasurer, since 1604 the Earl of Dorset, died, and on 4 May the Earl of Salisbury was appointed to the role once occupied by his father.[37] On 22 May the new lord treasurer gave the king his magnificent house at Theobalds, where James had often stayed and which he greatly admired. There was probably no direct connection between these events, although the timing is suspicious. Robert Cecil was in every way the obvious person for the appointment, as he not only had the king's full confidence, but many years of experience in dealing with the problems of royal finance. In return for Theobalds, he received Hatfield, an historic but obsolescent royal palace, which he immediately set out to rebuild.[38] The old house was allowed to remain, but beside it a new 'prodigy house' sprang up, the cost of which was to cripple even his enormous resources. In the last few years of his life, Cecil borrowed £61,000 from various merchants in London, and by 1612 his debts amounted to £37,867. 'I beseech your Lordship', wrote John Daccombe, his man of affairs at the end of 1611, 'to forbear building.'[39] The plea fell on deaf ears. Hatfield remained unfinished at Robert's death, but he had had laid out the magnificent gardens (recently restored) and the house remains privately owned by the Cecil family to this day (plates 29 and 30).

Unlike his father, Robert was apparently not uneasy with the position of a grandee. He was no less a service nobleman than the first Lord Burghley, but quite uninhibited by his lack of a grand pedigree or martial accomplishments. William Cecil had painfully fabricated a descent from the Welsh princes to enhance his status, but Robert never bothered with such fictions. With only a few exceptions, such as the earls of Pembroke and Northumberland, he was surrounded by other peers of James's creation. It was a new world of new men, and status depended only upon the king's favour and the wealth that that favour brought. The war was over, and soldiers were no longer in credit. Conspicuous consumption, on the other hand, mattered a great deal. The first Lord Burghley, as we have seen, spent more generously while he was building up his position than he did once he was established. His son did not enjoy that luxury, as he lived only for seven years after his promotion, and he seems to have spent lavishly throughout that time. Appearances had to be maintained.

Like his father, Robert supported mineral prospectors, in his case in partnership with the Earl of Shrewsbury. He was conscious of the fact that the Talbots had a much longer (or at least more authentic) pedigree than the Cecils, but in his case it is much more likely that he had profit in mind. The evidence suggests that Robert was a shrewd man of business. He bought up nine acres of land along what is now St Martin's Lane, London, in 1608 for £500, and developed it into 31 building plots, which he then leased out for the creation of shops and other businesses. When the leases expired in 1642, the 2nd Earl was able to charge £750 each for their renewal.[40]

What proportion of Robert's income came from such speculation is difficult to assess. It is possible that at its peak his annual revenue from all sources may have been as much as £24,000 a year. This was at a time when the mean gross income for a peer was under £4000 per annum. However, since his recorded expenditure came to no more than £12,000 a year, and his debts continued to mount, it is likely that his real income was substantially less.[41]

One of the reasons why Robert Cecil decided to surrender Theobalds may have been the fact that his relations with his son, William, were almost as bad as those between Lord Burghley and Thomas Cecil nearly 50 years before, and he probably did not mind very much if his heir inherited a building site. The young William had virtually abandoned his studies at Cambridge to go off hunting with the king at Newmarket and Royston—not in any spirit of politcal ambition (the king hardly noticed him), but out of sheer physical exuberance. 'He cannot speak six words of Latin', his exasperated father declared, rebuking his allegedly negligent tutors. It seems that there was little that they could do.[42] As with his Uncle Thomas earlier, William had no aptitude for study, nor any particular promise as a statesman, but he did become a personal friend of Prince Henry. Henry was three years his junior, but he was nobody's fool, and if he had lived William's subsequent career might have been much more distinguished.

As it was, when William reached the age of 17 in 1608, he was packed off to the Continent on an early version of the Grand Tour. He went first to France, and was backwards and forwards for about three years. His father first brought him home at the end of November 1608, because he had arranged a marriage for him with Frances, the daughter of Thomas Howard, Earl of Suffolk. This was a prestigious (and expensive) match, but what William thought of the young lady we do not know. Later they seem to have got along pretty well.[43] In 1610 Frances Cecil, Robert's daughter, was also married, to Lord Henry Clifford, later the 5th Earl of Cumberland, a union (unfortunately childless) that cost her father over £2000 in entertainment costs, marriage portion and allowances.

Once William's marriage rituals were over, the young man was unceremoniously returned to his tour, remaining in France until he was recalled again to play a part in the creation of his friend Prince Henry as Prince of Wales on 4 June 1610. This was an opportunity that Robert would not have wanted to miss, and they both played parts in the ceremony. When it was over, William again returned to France, and then on to Italy, where he fell ill in Padua towards the end of the year.[44] Unlike his father's experience in similar circumstance (or his uncle's), we know relatively little about this tour, except its interruptions and the fact that he was accompanied and well cared for. Even his illness provoked little comment, but he returned to England in February 1611, and for just over a year was Lord Cranborne, living with his wife in one of his father's minor residences and carrying out the normal duties of a man of his station.

For the time being, however, Robert as the new lord treasurer faced more important challenges than his son's dislike of study. The king's debts stood at £280,000, with an annual deficit of some £50,000 on the ordinary revenue.[45] Retrenchment was an urgent priority (as it had been for several years). Robert had managed to increase the customs rates in 1604, but it was a lawsuit arising out of that action that promised the real fiscal breakthrough. He had acted on the king's behalf, using the prerogative to increase the rates rather than negotiating either with parliament or the City. This was something that Elizabeth had always refrained from doing, partly because it caused so much bad feeling in London and partly because she had no desire to see any definition of her prerogative powers. James was less sensitive. The rates had not been increased since 1558, and there had been an inflation of about 100 per cent since then, so an increase was long overdue. Also the customs formed one of the pillars of his revenue. Technically they were not ordinary income, because they were voted by parliament. However, it was customary for the levy to be voted for life to each monarch on his (or her) accession, and that custom had been observed in 1604.

In 1605 a dispute arose between merchants of the Levant Company over the import of currants, and in the course of the wrangling one John Bate refused to pay the assessed rate on the grounds that it had not been approved by parliament.[46] This resulted in a case in the court of the exchequer, which had ruled (quite correctly) that such rates were a royal prerogative matter and could not be challenged—not, at least, on those grounds. This decision was delivered in 1606, and in 1608 the new lord treasurer used the same prerogative to place 'impositions', or new tariffs, on just about all imports except basic foodstuffs. The additional revenue was about £70,000 a year, and it appeared that a loophole had been found in the traditional control of parliament over all extraordinary revenue. As the chancellor of the exchequer, Sir

Julius Caesar, observed, the decision in Bates's case would prove 'the most gainfull to the King and his posterity as any one day's work'.[47] Bad as it might be for the crown's public relations, the existing deficit and James's extravagance towards his friends meant that there was no option but to exploit the loophole provided by the customs for all that it was worth.

Apart from anything else, such a situation imposed a stranglehold on foreign policy. James was not inclined to war, but the assassination of Henry IV of France in 1610 and the stirrings of new religious strife within the Holy Roman Empire might leave him with no option. Unlike Elizabeth in 1585, he had no reserves, and if the country were attacked he literally did not have the resources to defend himself. It was all very well to say that in such circumstances parliament would have provided. No doubt it would, but taxes took time to vote, and even longer to collect, and invaders would not wait upon the convenience of their victims. Something had to be done. It was against this background that the Great Contract was conceived. Basically, this was no more than a return to his abortive proposal of 1604 whereby the king would, among other measures, surrender wardship, purveyance and the right to make impositions without parliamentary consent in return for a lifelong parliamentary grant of £200,000 a year.[48]

By the time that parliament was prorogued in July 1610, it looked as though some hard bargaining had resulted in a deal. However, the members were told to go away and consult their constituencies during the recess, because the constitutional as well as the fiscal implications of such a deal were considerable. In practice, the parliament had long since provided extraordinary revenue in peace time, but always with some semi-military pretext, such as provision for the defence of the realm. In strict theory, extraordinary taxation should only have been provided to meet an extraordinary need, of which war was by far the most common, so in entering into an agreement of this kind, a new legal precedent was being set.[49] There was also the consideration that if taxation became ordinary in this sense, there would be less need of parliament in the future. As the lawyer James Whitelock warned the Commons, 'Considering the greatest use they [kings] make of assembling of parliaments, which is the supply of money ... if that need were taken away, there might be little future for their assemblies.'[50]

This was, perhaps, unnecessarily alarmist. Given James's notorious capacity to get through money, there is no reason to suppose that the Great Contract would have solved all his problems. However, when parliament came back on 16 October, its mood was uncooperative. The potential fate of parliament may have been in their minds, but the issue that they chose to raise was an old grievance against the Scots. For some obscure reason the members had convinced themselves that this contract was not a device to pay the king's debts, but to enable him to be still more lavish to his favourites. It was alleged that James's court cost four times as much as its French or Spanish equivalents—a fiction, the origin of which is obscure, but its impact was considerable.[51] Salisbury and his assistants laboured against this tide of prejudice in vain. Nor were they helped by the more realistic objection that whereas the feudal dues that were being abrogated had fallen only on the gentry and other rich men, the taxes that would replace them would fall on everyone.

By the beginning of November the tide of opposition was flowing strongly. James then made this situation worse by demanding the immediate payment of his existing debt, to the tune of £600,000, as part of the bargain. Deadlock ensued, and the parliament was dissolved on 6 December with nothing accomplished. In a sense the whole idea had been unrealistic: few of the abuses that so exercised the men of property would have been removed, while the king would have surrendered a flexible income for an inflexible one that would diminish in real value. Any future monarch, no matter how frugal, would have been unable to fight a war, or even conduct a significant police operation, without the assistance of further taxation. Robert Cecil's contract seems to have been a carefully weighted attempt to ameliorate an immediate problem, without necessarily solving it, or letting either James or his successors off the parliamentary hook.

Whatever the finer nuances of motivation, the Great Contract failed.[52] However, it failed eventually by mutual consent, and consequently there was no sharp deterioration in relations between king and Commons, and the idea that they were constantly at loggerheads is a myth. Between 1604 and 1610 about 150 statutes were processed, compared with less that 100 in the last three parliaments of Elizabeth.[53] There was a good deal of shadow boxing as the king discovered that his ideas of monarchy were at odds with the political realities of his new kingdom, but (except over money) James was canny and pragmatic.

Most notably his Calvinist theology, strict insistence on episcopacy and sensible handling of the Hampton Court conference in 1604, called in response to the puritan Millenary Petition, managed to keep Protestant dissent off the political agenda for about 20 years.[54]

The loser by the failure of the Great Contract was the Earl of Salisbury. Perhaps he had invested too much political capital in the deal, or perhaps James was merely tired of his effortless superiority. In December 1610 he wrote his minister a fierce rebuke, implying that he had some doubts over his sanity: 'in the perturbation of your mind you have broken forth in more passionate and strange discourses these last two sessions of parliament than ever ye were wont to do.'[55]

However, too much should not be made of this hostile language, because at the same time the king made it clear that he had no intention of dismissing him. 'It is now time', his letter went on, 'for you to cast your care upon the next best means to help my state.'

Failure had made James impatient of his dependence, but it had not removed it. On 10 December he renewed Salisbury's silk farm monopoly, which was worth £7000 a year to him and was crucial to his financial survival.[56] Nevertheless, the political map was changing. The king's new favourite, Robert Carr, was created Viscount Rochester in March 1611, which signalled the fact that James had found another diversion apart from hunting.

The king's decision to tackle some of his financial problems by the sale of honours was a part of that reorientation, although there is no reason to suppose that the lord treasurer opposed it. The rank of baronet was created specifically for that purpose, but it also had the advantage of being open to Catholic recusants, which enabled the richer among them to demonstrate their support for the regime. Although James had been so generous with the ordinary variety, this idea of an hereditary knighthood had an immediate appeal, and the asking price of £1095 produced an immediate queue of customers. Eighty-six were taken up almost at once, of whom twenty-four were Catholics, and within three years some £90,000 had been raised.[57]

Carr was not the only courtier to benefit from this change of climate. Henry Howard, Earl of Northampton, and his kinsmen the earls of Nottingham and Suffolk began to set up a family network that was soon to bring the court to one of its lowest points.

By 1611 Robert Cecil was a physical wreck. He had never been robust, and the ceaseless effort of trying to keep on good terms with two very different but equally difficult monarchs had undermined him further. Early in that year he wrote to James implying that he felt that he had little further to offer. 'I am not able to recover your estate out of the hands of those great wants to which your parliament hath now abandoned you.'[58] However, he was far too professional to despair. The king must continue to demand his traditional rights, but on the other hand he must 'restrain his bounty'. Above all, he must not give up on negotiating with parliament, because ultimately the estates 'hath ever been the only foundation of supply to those princes whose necessities have been beyond the cures and endeavours of private men'— however those necessities had arisen.[59]

In spite of his ailments and the changes that Carr and Northampton had wrought at court, in February 1611 all council business was still being channelled through the secretary. He appeared to be as indispensable as ever, and suitors continued to queue at his door. However, appearances were in a sense deceptive, and by the beginning of 1612, his career was at a low point in terms of the specific problems which still confronted him.

A general debility seems to have possessed Cecil. He was still a very powerful man, both secretary and lord treasurer, and he played his proper part in such negotiations as those for the marriages of Princess Elizabeth to the Elector Palatine and Prince Henry to the Infanta, as well as in foreign policy transactions in general. Yet much of his old enthusiasm and application had deserted him. He played (as far as we know) no part in the imprisonment of Arabella Stuart for her unauthorized marriage to the Earl of Hertford, although it was a matter that concerned him as secretary.[60] The bond of mutual confidence and respect that had bound him to the king and underpinned all his work since 1603 appears to have dissolved in the last months of his life. When he died in May 1612, he was unmourned at court. His secretaryship was conferred within days on Viscount Rochester, and the treasurership put into commission with the Earl of Northampton as first lord. Having once declared that he did not know how he could manage without him, in the event James seems scarcely to have noticed his passing. Sir Walter Cope felt constrained soon after to remind James that 'He [Salisbury] lost the love of your people only for your sake, and for your service'.[61] It was a point that needed to be made.

As a statesman and politician at national level, the 1st Earl of Salisbury had no heir. He had, we are told, 'a passion for power that never dimmed, and would tolerate only subordinates whose independence was governed by personal loyalty.'[62] Whether he realized just how far he had fallen out of favour in the last months of his life is an open question. His health was so poor that he would have been unable to attend to most of his normal duties in any case by the beginning of 1612. He had been out of action before, sometimes for weeks at a time, so it may not have struck him that anything had changed, but that in due course he would be able to resume his position at court as though nothing had happened. It is only with the benefit of hindsight that we can appreciate that was unlikely to have happened. At the start of May he had travelled painfully and slowly to Bath, to seek what relief he could from the waters—as his father had done many years before. While returning to London he stopped at Marlborough, and there, on the 21st of the month, he died. An eyewitness reported that 'he repeated the principal [prayers] with affection, then lying with his head on two pillows and his body in a sling [he] called for Dr. Poe's hand, which he gripped hard ... and sank down without a groan or a struggle'.[63]

His son William, in spite of having been forbidden to come, was with him when he died, a situation that suggests that the young man may have felt an affection that was not reciprocated. Robert left a vast amount of paper behind, that being typical of his way of doing business, as it had been of his father, but he kept no diary, and many things about him remain shadowy. He loved his parents, his sisters and his wife, and was deeply grieved by their deaths, but of his relations with his half-brother we know nothing, and his affection for his own children remains problematic. He had many acquaintances, clients and dependants, but of real friends hardly any, and one of those, Sir Walter Raleigh, he turned against him. Salisbury visited Sir Walter in the Tower not long before he died, and the prisoner found his visit painful, not only because of what had passed between them, but also because he recognized a man upon whom death had laid his hand.

Robert's Protestant faith seems to have been strong and genuine, although there is evidence that he embraced a high-church position in the last years of his life, and his chapel at Hatfield was lavishly redecorated not long before his death. His tomb in Hatfield parish church, by Maximilian Colt, is similarly ornate.[64] His relations with the City of

London were ambiguous, because although he recognized the importance of trade and the need to promote it, he nevertheless raised the
customs rates twice in a few years, and invested only the paltry sum of
£17 in Virginia Company shares. The first colony in the New World
was established in 1607, when he was at the height of his power, but we
know nothing of his attitude to the venture, although others did realize something of its importance.

For 20 years, between 1590 and 1610, Robert Cecil was ceaselessly
busy with public affairs, with accumulating and spending his private
resources on an enormous scale. Apart from the heroic proportions of
both his resources and his debts, his great achievement was probably
the smooth handover of power from Elizabeth to James. It was for that
transition that he earned his titles, and an unchallenged position in the
state, which lasted for about eight years.

Much of Robert Cecil's activity is beyond the scope of this narrative. But the extent to which he was his father's heir, and the degree to
which the England of Elizabeth and James I can (or should) be called a
*regnum Cecilianum,* should be clearer. Above all, perhaps, it should be
emphasized that in an age in which politics were supposedly dominated by the court and by the personality of the monarch, neither
William nor Robert were courtiers. Neither held any important court
office, or played a leading part in entertainments — except by acting as
hosts to the court on progress. Both were public servants and civilians,
of a kind more familiar to later generations. William maintained his
position largely by disagreeing with Elizabeth, and then carrying out
her instructions; Robert by agreeing with James, and then persuading
him to change his mind. They were remarkable individuals with the
abililty to survive and influence some of their age's most important
events. Between them, they were a phenomenon of government, and
without them Elizabeth possibly, and James almost certainly, would
have self-destructed.

# Afterword

WILLIAM CECIL'S SONS founded two noble families, the earls of Exeter (Thomas and his successors) and the earls of Salisbury (Robert and his successors). Both earldoms were raised to marquisates, Salisbury in 1789 and Exeter in 1801, and both survive today.

Over the intervening years, the Exeter line has kept a generally low profile. During the 17th century probably the most conspicuous member of the family was Sir Edward Cecil, Viscount Wimbledon, the 1st earl's third son. He was a professional soldier who spent many years in Dutch service; his performance in the ill-fated expedition to the Ile de Rhé in 1627 has been described, unfortunately, as 'ineffably feeble'. The 4th earl, John, served as lord lieutenant of Northamptonshire after the Restoration, living until 1678. After that the family settled into the social and political duties appropriate to its status. They regularly became MPs, prior to acceding to their titles, either for Rutland or Northamptonshire seats, and performed ceremonial duties at successive coronations.

This placid life was to some extent disrupted by the 5th earl, John, who refused any oath to William III. However, he never became an active 'Non-Juror' and neither his title nor his estates were forfeited. David Cecil, later the 6th Marquis of Exeter,was to become an Olympic athlete in the 1920s; he succeeded to the title in 1956 and remained an energetic patron of athletics. The present marquis, William, is his grandson; he succeeded to the title in 1988, and has sons to succeed him in due course.

Of the Salisbury line, the 3rd earl, James, succeeded his grandfather in 1668, as his own father, Viscount Cranborne, died relatively young in 1660. In his youth the 3rd earl served in the navy against the Dutch, and became a privy councillor in 1678. However, he quarrelled with

Charles II over the attempted exclusion of the future James II from the succession. Salisbury resigned his position in 1679.

The family developed its Tory credentials in the 18th century, but it was not until James, the 2nd marquis, married Frances Gascoyne in 1820 that the fortunes of the family began to revive. In 1821 he adopted the surname of Gascoyne-Cecil by royal warrant. He became a knight of the garter in 1842, and lord privy seal in 1852, serving briefly as lord president of the council in 1858–9. His son Robert, the 3rd marquis, became a politician and statesman of distinction. He has been described as a 'Victorian Titan' and served as prime minister four times between 1885 and 1902.

The 3rd marquis was succeeded on his death in 1903 by his son James, but it was James's younger brother, Edgar (rather misleadingly known as Lord Robert Cecil) who caught the public attention. He trained as a lawyer, taking silk in 1900, and entered the House of Commons in 1906. During the First World War, to old for active service, he worked with the Red Cross in France, and what he saw there turned him into a passionate peace crusader. Edgar wrote vigorously in support of his views, and was awarded the Nobel Peace Prize in 1937. He lived the last decade of his long life in retirement, and died in 1958.

Meanwhile James, the 4th marquis, had died in 1947 and had been succeeded by his eldest son, another Robert. This Robert, as Viscount Cranborne, had served as dominion secretary in Churchill's first government (1940) and as colonial secretary and Conservative Party leader in the House of Lords from 1942. His younger brother Lord David Cecil (1902–86) was a notable literary scholar and biographer. The 5th marquis died in 1972, and his son, the 6th marquis, in 1994. The present incumbent has revived the political traditions of the family to some extent, serving as lord privy seal under Margaret Thatcher and as Conservative Opposition leader in the House of Lords in 1997–8.

Over centuries of political change both Cecil families have demonstrated a genius for survival. Two of their great houses have also endured. Theobalds is gone, but both Hatfield House and Burghley House still stand as a vivid reminder of the days when England was (in a sense) a *regnum Cecilianum*.

# Notes on the text

Full author names and publication
dates are given for the first citation of
a book or article; thereafter, short
references are used.

ABBREVIATIONS USED IN
THESE NOTES

| | |
|---|---|
| *APC* | *Acts of the Privy Council* |
| BL | British Library |
| *Cal. Pat* | *Calendar of the Patent Rolls* |
| *Cal. For.* | *Calendar of State Papers, Foreign* |
| *Cal. Span.* | *Calendar of State Papers, Spanish* |
| *Cal. Scot.* | *Calendar of State Papers, Scottish* |
| HANDOVER | P.M. HANDOVER, *The Second Cecil* (1959) |
| HMC | Historical Manuscripts Commission |
| *L&P* | *Letters & Papers* |
| READ | Conyers READ, *Mr Secretary Cecil and Queen Elizabeth* (1965) |
| RSTC | Revised Short Title Catalogue |

# 1

## FROM DAVID SITSYLT TO WILLIAM CECIL

1 D. REES, *The Son of Prophecy* (1985), p. 41.

2 Ibid., p. 59.

3 G. WILLIAMS, 'Prophecy, Politics and Poetry in Medieval and Tudor Wales', in H. HEARDER and H.L LOYN (eds) *British Government and Administration* (1974).

4 R.A. GRIFFITHS, *Sir Rhys ap Thomas and His Family* (1993), pp. 41–2.

5 M.K. JONES and M.G. USHERWOOD, *The King's Mother* (1992), p. 281.

6 *Cal. Pat. 1494–1509*, p. 29.

7 Ibid., p. 80. He received this appointment jointly with Mathew Baker. A terminal date may be guessed from the fact that accounts for the Isle of Jersey from 1504 to 1506 survive among the Salisbury MSS. HMC, Salisbury MSS, I, p. 3.

8 Ibid., p. 514.

9 S.T. BINDOFF, *The House of Commons 1509–1558* (1982), *sub.* Cecil, David.

10 Richard BUTCHER, *The Survey and Antiquity of the Town of Stamford* (1717), p. 56. BINDOFF, *House of Commons*.

11 READ, p. 19.

12 *Cal. Pat. 1494–1509*, p. 515, 12 November 1506. The subsidy assessment appears in *L&P*, Addenda, 2.

13 BINDOFF.

14 Ibid. David seems to have died on 14 September 1540. A summary of his will is given in F. PECK, *Desiderata Curiosa* (1779), p. 80.

15 Records of attendance at court were not systematically kept. Richard appears sporadically in the accounts of the Wardrobe, receiving payments and signing warrants. He was fee'd at the rate of 31s a month.

16 BINDOFF. Sir William Compton was groom of the stool.

17 Ibid.

18 READ, p. 21.

19 Unlike his father, Richard made no provision for posthumous prayers or masses, and in 1552, when he was staying at Bourne, the Duke of Northumberland planned to visit him. *Calendar of State Papers, Domestic, Edward VI* (1992), 664.

20 READ, pp. 22–3.

21 K. CHARLTON and M. SPUFFORD, 'Literacy, Society and Education', in D. LOWENSTEIN and J. MUELLER, *The Cambridge History of Early Modern English Literature* (2002), p. 44. Stamford School was re-endowed in 1532 when Alderman William Ratcliff left

provision in his will for an additional
chaplain to pray for his soul and to
teach grammar. G.A.J. HODGETT,
*Tudor Lincolnshire* (1975), p. 143.

22 READ, pp. 24–5.

23 The fellows were paid a stipend of £6
a year, and the scholars received an
allowance of £3. As a commoner,
Cecil would have paid a tutorial fee of
about 40 shillings a year. Ibid.

24 T. BAKER, *History of St. Johns*, ed.
J.E.B. MAYOR (1869).

25 READ, p. 26.

26 READ, p. 27.

27 For a discussion of Richard Cecil's
attitude to his son's marriage, see ibid.,
pp. 27–9.

28 Very little is known about Mary Cecil,
but see the contemporary life of Lord
Burghley, published by Francis Peck in
*Desiderata Curiosa* (1779) from a lost
original.

29 Ibid., p. 5. He is alleged to have 'played
the ghost' through a hole in the wall.

30 HMC, Salisbury MSS, 140, p. 13.
BINDOFF, *sub.* William Cecil

31 The anonymous biographer attributes
Richard's hostile will to the time when
he went to Boulogne, but that was in
1544, by which time Mary was already
dead.

32 BL Lansdowne MS CIII, no.94.

# 2

## OPPORTUNITY
## AND DANGER

1 D. HOAK, *The King's Council in the
Reign of Edward VI* (1976), pp. 115–16.

2 Printed in A.F. POLLARD, *Tudor Tracts*
(1903), pp. 53–158.

3 Ibid., p. 155.

4 Patten's reference to him in that capacity dates from January 1548. A letter
of Sir Anthony St Leger dated 13 July
1548 confirms the appointment, but
not the date. TNA SP 10/4, no. 27.

The grant to Calverley is recorded in
*Cal. Pat., Eliz., 1572–75*, no. 2854.

5 Reproduced in the *Harleian Miscellany*,
I (1808), pp. 286–313.

6 Ibid.

7 Cecil's diary. BL Lansdowne MS
CXVIII, f. 81b. READ, p. 42 and note.

8 Sir Anthony Cooke's son was elected
at Stamford in his place, and at his
suggestion. HAYNES, *State Papers*,
pp. 201–2.

9 READ, pp. 83–4.

10 G. REDWORTH, *In Defence of the
Church Catholic* (1990), p. 245.

11 READ, p. 46, citing a MS at Longleat.

12 D. LOADES, *John Dudley, Duke of
Northumberland* (1996), p. 129, citing
BL Add. MS 48126, f. 6.

13 See 'The Letters of William, Lord
Paget of Beaudesert', ed. B.L. BEER and
S. JACK, *Camden Miscellany* 25 (1974).

14 LOADES, *John Dudley*, pp. 130–1.

15 For a detailed narrative of events, see
particularly W.K. JORDAN, *Edward VI*
(1968), pp. 506–23.

16 Salisbury MSS, cxl, 13. *HMC
Salisbury*, V, p. 69.

17 LOADES, *John Dudley*, p. 140 and n.

18 *Acts of the Privy Council*, II, p. 372. 25th
January 1550.

19 T. RYMER, *Foedera, Conventiones etc.*
(1704–35), xv, pp. 205–7.

20 TNA SP10/10, no.2.

21 TNA SP10/10, no.9.

22 REDWORTH, p. 287. It seems clear
from this letter, as well as from his
earlier actions over the 'test sermon',
that Cecil was hostile to Gardiner,
a hostility that was probably repaid
when the bishop was in power.

23 READ, p. 63.

24 *APC*, II, p. 342.

25 TNA SP10/10, no. 12.

26 He missed only two meetings between
the beginning of September 1550 and
the end of February 1551, a time at
which the council was meeting several
times a week. *APC.*

27 TNA SP10/10, no. 39.

28 READ, p. 70.

29 To the value of £152 3s 3d, for which he paid £50 into Augmentations. *Cal. Pat., Edward VI*, IV, p. 197.

30 W.K. JORDAN (ed.), *The Chronicle and Political Papers of Edward VI* (1966), pp. 86–7.

31 J.G. NICHOLS, *Literary Remains of Edward VI*, Roxburgh Club (1857), II, p. 354.

32 He was convicted under the statute 3 & 4 Edward VI, cap. 5, for having assembled his followers without authority and in excess of a certain number.

33 READ, p. 78.

34 J. STRYPE, *Ecclesiastical Memorials* (3 vols, 1820–40), II, ii, 505.

35 LOADES, *John Dudley*, pp. 231–3.

36 Ibid., p. 241.

37 READ, pp. 98–9.

38 Ambassadors to the Emperor, 9 July 1553. *Cal. Span.*, IX, p. 74.

39 TNA SP11/1, no. 4.

40 *Desiderata Curiosa*, p. 8.

41 BL Cotton MS Julius F. VI, f. 166. John CLAPHAM, *Elizabeth of England*, ed. E.P. and C. READ (1951), p. 74.

42 READ, pp. 104–5.

43 D. LOADES, *The Reign of Mary Tudor* (1991), pp. 181–2. This ambition, which was known in England, was immensely controversial.

44 J. LOACH, *Parliament and the Crown in the Reign of Mary Tudor* (1986), pp. 140–1.

45 *Desiderata Curiosa*, p. 9.

46 Ibid.

47 BL Lansdowne MS, III, f. 130. J. STRYPE, *The Life of the Learned Sir John Cheke* (1821), p. 99.

48 D. LOADES, *Mary Tudor: A Life* (1989), p. 287.

49 HAYNES, *State Papers*, p. 203.

50 Ibid., p. 205

51 BL Lansdowne MS, CXVIII. READ, p. 113.

52 READ, p. 115.

53 LOADES, *Mary Tudor*, pp. 301–2.

54 Ibid., pp. 307–9. Philip was ten years younger than Mary, and had only one son (by his first marriage). A barren wife was no use to him.

55 'The Count of Feria's Despatch to Philip II of 14 November 1558', ed. M.-J. RODRIGUEZ SALGADO and S. ADAMS, *Camden Miscellany* 28 (1984), p. 336.

56 Ibid., p. 332.

# 3

## SECRETARY TO THE QUEEN

1 For a full discussion of this aspect of Mary's regime, see Loades, *The Reign of Mary Tudor*, pp. 57–95, 157–93, 262–303. Sir Nicholas Throgmorton advised Elizabeth 'to call Master Cecil to exercise the room of secretary about your person', but the decision appears to have been made before his advice arrived. S. ALFORD, *The Early Elizabethan Polity* (1998), p. 7.

2 TNA SP12/1, no. 7.

3 For Heath's speech against the Supremacy Bill, see T.E. HARTLEY (ed.), *Proceedings in the Parliaments of Elizabeth I*, I, *1558–1581* (1981), pp. 12–17.

4 Robert CECIL, *The State of a Secretary's Place and Peril*, cited by READ, p. 120.

5 *See* ALFORD.

6 Sir Edward Hastings, Sir Henry Bedingfield, the Earl of Oxford, Sir John Mason, the Earl of Arundel, Sir Thomas Cheney. Cheney died before the end of the year and was replaced with Sir Thomas Parry.

7 BL Lansdowne MS III, f. 193.

8 LOADES, *Reign of Mary Tudor*, p. 200.

9 John FOXE, *Acts and Monuments* (1583), pp. 2081–7.

10 C.E. CHALLIS, *The Tudor Coinage* (1978), pp. 248–74.

11 D. WILSON, *Sweet Robin: A Biography of Robert Dudley* (1981), pp. 32–3.

12 'The Count of Feria's Despatch ...', *op. cit*, p. 332. Henry MACHYN, *The Diary of Henry Machyn*, edited by J.G. Nicholls (1848), p. 180.

13 *Cal. Span. 1558–67*, pp. 57–8.

14 BL Stowe MS, f. 180b.

15 WILSON, pp. 118–133.

16 HAYNES, *State Papers*, pp. 161–2.

17 Sir Nicholas Throgmorton (in France) was a particularly assiduous recounter of such stories.

18 *Cal. Span. 1558–67*, p. 178. READ, pp. 203–4.

19 Ibid., pp. 206–8.

20 *Cal. Span. 1558–67*, p. 194.

21 TNA SP12/70, no. 26.

22 Ibid. READ, pp. 212–14.

23 S. DORAN, *Monarchy and Matrimony* (1996), pp. 73–98.

24 Henry Hastings, who succeeded to the title in June 1560, was the son of Catherine, daughter of Henry, Lord Montague, who was the son of Margaret, Countess of Salisbury, daughter of George, Duke of Clarence, Edward IV's brother. His claim thus came through the female line twice. Henry, Lord Stafford and Henry, Lord Darnley also had remote claims, but neither was considered at this juncture.

25 For de Quadra's analysis of the situation, see *Cal. Span. 1558–67*, pp. 262 ff.

26 W. MACCAFFREY, *The Shaping of the Elizabethan Regime* (1969), pp. 108–9.

27 READ, pp. 278–9.

28 Ibid., p. 280.

29 DORAN, pp. 93–4.

30 TNA SP12/40, no. 68.

31 HARTLEY, *Proceedings in Parliament*, pp. 160–61.

32 Ibid., pp. 171–2.

33 READ, p. 359.

34 *Cal. Span. 1558–67*, p. 609.

35 H. KELSEY, *Sir John Hawkins* (2003), p. 51.

36 Ibid., p. 100. C. READ, 'Queen Elizabeth's Seizure of Alba's Pay Ships', *Journal of Modern History*, 5 (1933), pp. 443–64.

37 Ibid.

38 READ, pp. 432–3.

39 Ibid., p. 433.

40 TNA SP63/27, no. 35.

41 *Cal. Span. 1568–79*, p. 107. For the fortunes of the Queen of Scots, see below.

42 *A Short Memorial* is printed in HAYNES, *State Papers*, pp. 579 ff.

43 From an English translation of the Latin original, 1635. READ, p. 441.

44 CLAPHAM, pp. 75–6.

45 B. de S. DE LA MOTHE-FENELON, *Correspondance diplomatique* (1838–40), I, pp. 233 ff.

46 BL Lansdowne MSS CII, f. 78.

47 HAYNES, *State Papers*, p. 522.

48 *Cal. Scot. 1563–69*, p. 684.

49 *Calendar of State Papers, Domestic, Addenda, 1566–79*, p. 89.

50 READ, p. 464. MACCAFFREY, *Shaping*, p. 232.

51 Sir C. SHARP, *The Rising in the North* (1840/1975). Foreword by Robert Wood.

52 Ibid., p. 132.

53 *The State Papers and Letters of Sir Ralph Sadler*, ed. Arthur CLIFFORD (1809), II, p. 343.

54 P. HUGHES, *The Reformation in England,* III (1954), p. 272 and note.

# 4

## RECONCILING CHURCH AND STATE

1 TNA SP12/1, no.2.

2 MACHYN, p. 178

3 The bishops who died were Holyman of Bristol and Christopherson of Chichester. The other vacant sees

were Canterbury, Hereford, Norwich, Oxford, Rochester, Salisbury, and Sodor and Man (which was constantly unfilled).

4 READ, pp. 127–8.

5 TNA SP70/28, July 1561.

6 HARTLEY, pp. 3–6.

7 READ, p. 131. N.L Jones, *Faith by Statute* (1982).

8 Ibid.

9 An account of this conference was published by authority, and it is reproduced in Holinshed's *Chronicle* (1587 edition), III, p. 1182.

10 *Cal. Span. 1558–67*, pp. 50, 62.

11 TNA SP12/3, no. 9.

12 *Zurich Letters ... during the Reign of Queen Elizabeth*, ed. Hastings ROBINSON (1842–5), I, p. 55.

13 TNA SP12/4, nos 38, 39. B. USHER, *William Cecil and Episcopacy, 1559–77* (2003), p. 7.

14 HUGHES, pp. 36–9.

15 1 Elizabeth I, c. 24. About £2000 of the income came from the Abbey of Westminster.

16 USHER, *Episcopacy*, pp. 19–23.

17 Ibid., pp. 30–31.

18 F.E. BRIGHTMAN, *The English Rite* (1921), p. 1014. K. CARLETON, *Bishops and Reform in the English Church, 1520–1559* (2001), p. 186.

19 USHER, *Episcopacy*, p. 118, note 51.

20 BL Lansdowne MS 396, f.16r.

21 *Parker's Correspondence*, pp. 269–70.

22 27 August 1566. *Zurich Letters*, I, p. 168.

23 For a full discussion of Cecil's attitude towards Mary at this time, see READ, pp. 390–415.

24 ALFORD, p. 40. P. COLLINSON, *Archbishop Grindal, 1519–1583* (1979), pp. 187–9.

25 Ibid.

26 Neither Sandes's letter nor Cecil's original rebuke survive, so we are dependent upon the bishop's letter of apology. BL Lansdowne MS XII, f. 179r.

27 T. RYMER, *Foedera*, XV, pp. 681–84.

28 B. USHER, 'The Deanery of Bocking and the Demise of the Vestiarian Controversy', *Journal of Ecclesiastical History*, 52 (2001), pp. 434–55.

29 USHER, *Episcopacy*, pp. 115–6.

30 Elizabeth's supposed objection to married clergy is largely based on a letter from Cecil to Parker of 12 August 1561, in which he says 'Her majesty continueth very ill affected to the state of matrimony in the clergy ....' That may well have been what she said, but her actions were not entirely consistent with such a view. *Parker's Correspondence*, pp. 148–9.

31 BL Lansdowne MS XXIV, f. 36r.

32 USHER, *Episcopacy*, p. 122.

33 Richard GAWTON, *A Parte of a Register* (1593), p. 395.

34 USHER, *Episcopacy*, p. 123.

35 *Cal. Pat. 1569–72*, no. 1070.

36 USHER, *Episcopacy*, Appendix I, no. 30.

37 TNA SP70/26, 8 May 1561.

38 V.J.K. BROOK, *A Life of Archbishop Parker* (1962).

39 *Parker's Correspondence*, pp. 472–3.

# 5

## FRENCH SUITORS AND THE QUEEN OF SCOTS

1 READ, p. 125.

2 TNA SP52/3.

3 ALFORD, p. 6.

4 Ibid., p. 7.

5 M. MERRIMAN, *The Rough Wooing* (2000).

6 A. RYRIE, *The Origins of the Scottish Reformation* (2006), pp. 95–116.

7 Ibid., p. 157.

8 BL Harley MS 7004. Printed in D. LAING (ed.), *The Works of John Knox* (6 vols, 1846–64), V. p. 15.

9 RYRIE, pp. 178–80.

10 *Cal. Scot. 1547–63*, p. 223.

11 J.E.A. DAWSON, *The Politics of Religion in the Age of Mary, Queen of Scots* (2002), pp. 96–103.

12 Ibid., p. 99. On the Marquis's general attitude of conservative opposition, see D. LOADES, *William Paulet* (forthcoming 2008).

13 BL Cotton MS Caligula B.9, f. 34. J.E.A. DAWSON, 'Two Kingdoms or Three? Ireland in Anglo-Scottish Relations in the Middle of the Sixteenth Century', in R. MASON (ed.), *Scotland and England 1286–1815* (1987), pp. 113–38. DAWSON, 'William Cecil and the British Dimension of Early Elizabethan Foreign Policy', *History*, 74, 1989, pp. 196–216.

14 HAYNES, *State Papers*, p. 318.

15 *Cal. For. 1559–60*, p. 104.

16 P. FORBES, *A Full View of the Public Transactions in the Reign of Elizabeth* (1740–41), I, p. 494. READ, pp. 175–6.

17 The treaty is printed in R. KEITH, *History of the Affairs of Church and State in Scotland from the Beginning of the Reformation to the Year 1568* (1844), I, pp. 296–306.

18 For the options open to Mary at this point, see particularly J. WORMALD, *Mary Queen of Scots* (1988).

19 *Cal. Scot. 1547–63*, p. 520.

20 READ, p. 223.

21 *Cal. Scot. 1563–69*, p. 19.

22 Ibid., p. 80.

23 Dawson, *The Politics of Religion*, pp. 116–7 and notes.

24 Ibid., pp. 126–36.

25 Ibid., pp. 137–42.

26 *Cal. Scot. 1563–69*, p. 125. Randolf to Cecil, 12 February 1565.

27 Ibid. p. 150.

28 BL Cotton MS Caligula B.X, f. 298.

29 READ, p. 339.

30 *Cal. Scot. 1563–69*, p. 292. Letter written jointly with Randolf, then at Berwick.

31 READ, p. 349.

32 TNA SP63/20, no. 3.

33 MACCAFFREY, *Shaping*, pp. 149–50.

34 *Cal. Scot. 1563–69*, p. 324.

35 Ibid., pp. 378–80.

36 *Cal. Span. 1558–67*, 35–6.

37 Ibid.

38 For a detailed discussion see READ, pp. 431–54.

39 BL Cotton MS Caligula C.I, f. 456r.

40 DORAN, pp. 76–7.

41 V. VON KLARWILL, *Queen Elizabeth and Some Foreigners* (1928), pp. 208–9.

42 HAYNES, *State Papers*, p. 444.

43 VON KLARWILL, pp. 241–4. DORAN, pp. 80–82.

44 VON KLARWILL, pp. 279–82. BL Cotton MS Julius F.VI, f. 61.

45 DORAN, pp. 92–3.

46 ALFORD, p. 7.

47 *Cal. For. 1560–61*, p. 143.

48 For a fuller account of these struggles within France, see N.M. SUTHERLAND, *The Huguenot Struggle for Recognition* (1980).

49 *Cal. For. 1562*, p. 125.

50 FORBES, II, p. 1.

51 *Cal. For. 1562*, p. 192. It was some time before Sir Nicholas could actually extract himself.

52 FORBES, II, p. 2. Full text also in READ, pp. 248–9.

53 *Cal. For. 1562*, p. 268.

54 R. BONNEY, *The European Dynastic States 1494–1660* (1991), pp. 168–9.

55 BL Lansdowne MS CII, f. 15.

56 For a discussion of these complicated negotiations, see READ, pp. 285–8.

57 J. ISRAEL, *The Dutch Republic … 1477–1806* (1995), pp. 101–5, 119–23. For a full discussion, see P. Geyl, *The Revolt of the Netherlands 1555–1609* (1932).

58 N.A.M. RODGER, *The Safeguard of the Sea* (1997), p. 199–203.

59 D.R. BISSON, *The Merchant Adventures of England* (1993), pp. 95–101.

60 READ, p. 294.

61 TNA SP12/35, no. 33. Printed in Tawney and Power, *Tudor Economic Documents*, II, pp. 45–7.

62 READ, p. 422.

63 Ibid., pp. 424–5.

64 ALFORD, p. 40.

# 6

## LORD BURGHLEY, THE LORD TREASURER

1 TNA SP12/77, no.1 7.

2 Parry had died on 15 December 1560, and Cecil was appointed master on 10 January 1561. J. HURSTFIELD, *The Queen's Wards* (1958), p. 246.

3 L. STONE, *The Crisis of the Aristocracy* (1965), pp. 368–70.

4 DORAN, p. 99.

5 BL Cotton MS Caligula C. II, ff. 88, 92.

6 C. READ, *Lord Burghley and Queen Elizabeth* (1960), pp. 38–50.

7 The agent was William Herle. Cobham's role was a major embarrassment to Burghley, who wrote, 'My Lord of Cobham is in my house a prisoner, who should otherwise have been in the Tower.' They were close friends and Robert Cecil was later to marry Cobham's daughter. E. LODGE, *Illustrations of British History* (1838), I, p. 526

8 An account of the plot, entitled *Salutem in Christo*, which was probably inspired officially, appeared at the same time, RSTC 11504.

9 READ, *Lord Burghley*, pp. 40–1.

10 HAYNES, *State Papers*, p. 185. Elizabeth's letter to Alba announcing de Spes's expulsion.

11 Ibid., p. 57.

12 MACCAFFREY, *Shaping*, pp. 277–8.

13 Sir Dudley DIGGES, *The Compleat Ambassador* (1635), p. 164.

14 READ, *Lord Burghley*, p. 41.

15 *Cal. Span. 1568–79*, p. 364.

16 HAYNES, *State Papers*, p. 772.. Herle's letter is preserved among Robert Beale's papers in BL Add. MS 48023.

17 *Cal .Span. 1568–79*, p. 295.

18 READ, *Lord Burghley*, p. 49.

19 DIGGES, p. 219.

20 Two copies of this account survive, both (apparently) written by William Penson, Lancaster Herald. TNA SP12/88, no. 20. BL Sloane MS 1786, f. 92b.

21 BL Cotton MS Vespasian F. VI, f. 131.

22 TNA SP70/98, f. 245. DORAN, pp. 99–100.

23 'Egerton Papers', *Camden Society* XII (1840), p. 58.

24 DIGGES, *Compleat Ambassador*, p. 67.

25 DORAN, pp. 99–129.

26 LA MOTHE FENELON, V, p. 121.

27 READ, *Lord Burghley*, p. 87.

28 LODGE, I, p. 547.

29 TNA SP70/122, f. 43.

30 DORAN, p. 143.

31 Bodleian Library, Carte MSS 55/130–1.

32 BL Harleian MSS 6991, f. 216.

33 TNA SP12/103, no. 48.

34 DORAN, p. 143.

35 Ibid., p. 145.

36 READ, *Lord Burghley*, pp. 159–60.

37 ISRAEL, pp. 185–88.

38 Most of these documents are printed in J.M.B.C. KERVYN DE LETTENHOVE, *Documents inedits relatifs a l'histoire du xvi siècle* (1883).

39 W.J. TIGHE, 'The Counsel of Thomas Radcliffe, Earl of Sussex, Concerning the Revolt of the Netherlands, September 1578', *Sixteenth Century Journal,* 18 (1987), pp. 327–9.

40 ISRAEL, pp. 189–91.

41 READ, *Lord Burghley*, pp. 183–4. COLLINSON, *Archbishop Grindal,* pp. 233–53.

42 BL Lansdowne MS CIII, no. 8.

43 HAYNES, *State Papers*, pp. 230–34.

44 BL Harleian MS 215, f. 62. The patent is TNA C66/1130, m. 31.

45 READ, *Lord Burghley*, pp. 193–9.

46 STOW, *Survey of London* (1980 edition), p. 399.

47 READ, *Lord Burghley*, pp. 121–2.

48 Ibid., p. 122.
49 *Desiderata Curiosa*, p. 34.
50 John GERARD, *The Herbal, or Generall Historie of Plantes* (1597)

# 7
## THE ELDER STATESMAN

1 There has never been any satisfactory explanation of Elizabeth's sudden revival of a marriage plan that had been abandoned months before. The account of her behaviour is in Camden, *Annals*, III, p. 12. For a discussion, see Doran, pp. 186–7.
2 READ, *Lord Burghley*, pp. 207–8.
3 Hatfield. Cecil Papers, 148/23.
4 He concluded that the queen's 'censure and liking shall be the best rule to warrant all other men's judgements'. Ibid., 148/25.
5 BL Harleian MS 285, f. 77.
6 READ, *Lord Burghley*, pp. 212–15.
7 RSTC 23400.
8 DORAN, pp. 168–70
9 W. MacCAFFREY, *Queen Elizabeth and the Making of Policy* (1981), p. 148 etc.
10 BL Cotton MS Galba E.VI, f. 47.
11 CAMDEN, *Annals*, III, p. 12. *Cal. Span. 1568–79*, p. 277.
12 READ, *Lord Burghley*, p. 262.
13 ISRAEL, p. 213. The Act of Abjuration of 1581 had formally repudiated Philip's authority in the rebel-held lands. Ibid., p. 210.
14 Cecil Papers 163/50, 52, 54. BL Cotton MS Caligula C.IX, ff. 64.
15 Ibid. CAMDEN, *Annals* (1635 edition), p. 282.
16 BL Harleian MS 168, f. 102.
17 R.B. WERNHAM, 'English Policy and the Revolt of the Netherlands', in *Britain and the Netherlands* (1960), pp. 29–40.
18 READ, *Lord Burghley*, pp. 318–19.

19 Ibid., pp. 327–8.
20 J. BRUCE (ed.), *The Correspondence of Robert Dudley, Earl of Leicester*, Camden Society 27 (1844), pp. 237–9.
21 *Cal. For. 1585–6*, p. 370.
22 *Elizabeth I: Collected Works*, ed. L.S. MARCUS et al. (2000), pp. 273–4.
23 He left Scotland at the very end of 1582, as a result of English pressure, and died in France the following year MacCAFFREY, *Making of Policy*, pp. 415–7.
24 Ibid., p. 479.
25 P. COLLINSON, 'The Elizabethan Exclusion Crisis and the Elizabethan Polity', *Proceedings of the British Academy*, 84 (1994), pp. 51–92.
26 MacCAFFREY, *Making of Policy*, pp. 463–99.
27 Statute 27 Elizabeth I, cap. 1. *Statutes of the Realm*, IV, pp. 704–5.
28 On the mysterious Parry and his doings, see READ, *Lord Burghley*, pp. 300–1.
29 J.H. POLLEN, *Mary Queen of Scots and the Babington Plot* (1922). C. READ, *Mr Secretary Walsingham and the Policy of Queen Elizabeth* (1925), II, p. 44.
30 POLLEN, p. 41.
31 READ, *Lord Burghley*, p. 347.
32 BL. Cotton MSS Caligula B.IX, f. 448.
33 READ, *Lord Burghley*, p. 349.
34 *Cal. Scot. 1586–88*, p. 54.
35 [Hardwicke State Papers] *Miscellaneous State Papers from 1501 to 1726* (1778), I, p. 224.
36 Huntington Library, Ellesmere MS 1191.
37 N.H. NICOLAS, *The Life of William Davison* (1823), pp. 221 et seq. The sentence had been proclaimed on 4 December. Hughes and Larkin, *Tudor Royal Proclamations*, II, no. 685.
38 READ, *Lord Burghley*, p. 371.
39 Ibid., p. 375.
40 *Cal. Span. 1587–1603*, pp. 166, 184.
41 *Cal. For. 1587*, p. 472.

42 *An Admonition to the Nobility and to the People of England.* TNA SP12/211, no. 15.

43 TNA SP12/209, no. 83.

44 For a discussion of the Book of Sea Causes and its implication, see D. LOADES, *The Tudor Navy* (1992), pp. 178–82.

45 H. KELSEY, *Sir John Hawkins* (2003), pp. 143–182.

46 J. BRUCE, *Report on the Arrangements which were made for the Internal Defence of these Kingdoms ...* (1798), p. cxiii.

47 READ, *Lord Burghley*, pp. 413–14.

48 Ibid., p. 417. *The Acts of Privy Council* puts the figures at 18,000 foot and 2000 horse, *APC,* XVI, p. 222.

49 TNA SP12/168, no. 3.

50 READ, *Lord Burghley*, p. 425.

51 RSTC 15412; 23011.

52 C. READ, 'Lord Burghley's Household Accounts', *Economic History Review* (1956), p. 346.

53 TNA SP12/219, no. 37.

54 BL Lansdowne MS CIII, f. 117.

55 READ, *Lord Burghley*, p. 444.

56 W. MACCAFFREY, *Elizabeth I: War and Politics* (1992), p. 257.

57 S.G. ELLIS, *Tudor Ireland* (1985), pp. 298–312.

58 HANDOVER, pp. 22–4. It is not known which constituency he represented.

59 *APC,* XXI, p. 358.

60 READ, *Lord Burghley*, p. 467.

61 MACCAFFREY, *War and Politics,* pp. 485–7.

62 *Tudor Royal Proclamations,* III, no. 738.

63 Statute 35 Elizabeth I, cap. 1. *Statutes of the Realm,* IV, pp. 841–3.

64 TNA SP12/255, no. 84.

65 CLAPHAM, pp. 77 *et seq.*

# 8
# PRODIGALS AND PRODIGIES

1 BL Lansdowne MS CXVIII. The household book.

2 See his entry in the *Oxford Dictionary of National Biography.* Mildred is not known to have expressed an opinion about her stepson.

3 TNA SP70/26.

4 READ, p. 213.

5 BL Harleian MS 3638.

6 TNA SP12/20, no. 20.

7 READ, p. 215.

8 BL Add MS 35831, f. 36. Throgmorton to Windebank, 2 June 1562.

9 READ, p. 216. Throgmorton to Cecil.

10 TNA SP12/22, no. 49.

11 Knollys to Cecil, 14 December 1562. TNA SP70/41.

12 Ibid., SP12/27, no. 13.

13 Percy to Cecil, January 1562. TNA SP12/21, no. 26. Dorothy was 15 when this encomium was written, and 17 when she married Thomas.

14 *Cal. Pat. Elizabeth, 1569–72,* no.1020.

15 Ibid., no. 1871, no. 1943.

16 *Cal. For. 1585–86,* p. 133.

17 HANDOVER, pp. 222–3.

18 As we have seen, William's father, Richard was very opposed to the marriage at the time, and William never spoke or wrote of the circumstances later. It is highly likely that they had slept together, and he felt that he had no option.

19 Recorded in a memorandum by Robert to the churchwardens of St Clements Danes, 1601. Hatfield, Cecil MSS, XI, f. 321.

20 Subsequently Bishop of Durham and Winchester, and Archbishop of York. Died 1640.

21 HANDOVER, p. 13.

22 This information is taken from a schedule prepared for the education

of the Earl of Oxford, and printed by B.M. WARD, *The Seventeenth Earl of Oxford 1550–1604* (1928), p. 20.

23 This is nowhere stated, but 14 would have been an appropriate age for a bright boy to matriculate, and there is otherwise no record of his where-abouts.

24 BL Lansdowne MS XXXVII, no. 5.

25 In 1593 he declared that he had sat in five parliaments, which would take his membership back to 1581. There is no other trace of his sitting, and P. W. HASLER, in *The House of Commons 1558–1603* (1981), does not accept it.

26 Robert seems to have had a sense of humour, which his father conspicu-ously lacked.

27 BL Stowe MS, CXLIII.

28 HANDOVER, pp. 29–37.

29 Ibid., p. 34.

30 Sir Edward Stafford to Burghley, 21 October. *Cal. For. 1583–4*, p. 158.

31 Stafford to Burghley, 12 December 1583. Hatfield, Cecil MSS, III, no. 19.

32 HANDOVER, p. 40.

33 Robert Cecil to Michael Hickes, 28 September 1584. BL Lansdowne MS CVII, no. 76.

34 TNA SP12/177, no. 1.

35 READ, *Lord Burghley*, pp. 340–70.

36 TNA PS12/195, no. 22.

37 RSTC 6052, where the attribution to Richard Crompton is corrected.

38 LOADES, *Elizabeth I*, pp. 259–60.

39 HANDOVER, pp. 52–3.

40 Anthony Bagot to his father, May 1587. HMC, 4th Report, xiv, p. 39. Bagot MSS.

41 READ, *Lord Burghley*, pp. 399–400.

42 Cited by HASLER, *sub.* Robert Cecil.

43 BL Lansdowne MS CIII, f. 68.

44 Sir Philip Hoby to Sir William Cecil, 30 November 1557. P.F. Tytler, *The Reigns of Edward VI and Mary* (1839), II, pp. 494–5.

45 READ, pp. 436–7.

46 Ward, *The Seventeenth Earl of Oxford,* p. 20.

47 Hatfield Cecil MSS, ix, f. 92.

48 READ, *Lord Burghley*, p. 126.

49 HMC, *12th Report*, Rutland MSS, I, p. 95.

50 Ibid.

51 READ, *Lord Burghley*, pp. 128–9.

52 LODGE, II, p. 16.

53 READ, *Lord Burghley*, p. 132.

54 WARD, p. 110.

55 Ibid., p. 115.

56 READ, *Lord Burghley*, pp. 136–7.

57 Ibid.

58 READ, pp. 308–9.

59 LODGE, II, p. 52.

60 TNA SP12/149, no. 35.

61 READ, *Lord Burghley*, p. 272.

62 Ibid.

63 BL Lansdowne MS XXXI, no. 71.

# 9

## ROBERT CECIL, SECRETARY AND HEIR

1 'Conference ... before the Queen ... by John Davies, 16th May 1591'. John Nichols, *Progresses of Queen Elizabeth* (4 vols, 1828), IV, p. 76.

2 *APC*, XXI, p. 358. 2 August 1591.

3 It was, however, the queen who vetoed Bacon's appointment. READ, *Lord Burghley*, p. 496.

4 T. BIRCH, *Memoirs of the Reign of Queen Elizabeth* (1754), I, p. 150. Two letters relating to the plot are at Lambeth, MS 650/66–7.

5 M.A.S. Hume, *Treason and Plot* (1901), pp. 115 *et seq.*

6 A draft, corrected in Burghley's hand, is in TNA SP12/250, no. 10.

7 BIRCH, *Memoirs*, I, pp. 114–16.

8 READ, *Lord Burghley*, p. 496.

9 HULME, *Treason and Plot*, p. 131.

10 'The Taking of the *Madre de Dios*' ed. C.L. KINGSFORD in the *Navel Miscellany*, II (1912), pp. 116–18. BL

Lansdowne MS LXX art. 81. Hatfield MS IV, p. 127. TNA SP12/243 no. 16.

11 Ibid., SP12/246, nos 40–1. HANDOVER, pp. 85–90.

12 READ, *Lord Burghley*, pp. 487–90. Puritanism was not a party issue in that sense.

13 RSTC 19398.

14 HANDOVER, *Second Cecil,* p. 200.

15 On the Dutch position at this time, see ISRAEL, pp. 24–50.

16 HANDOVER, p. 134.

17 See, for example, Lord Charles Howard to Robert Cecil. Hatfield MS VI, p. 144.

18 Ed Reynolds to Essex, 18 May 1596. BIRCH, II, p. 5.

19 Dr Hawkins to Anthony Bacon, 30 July 1596. BIRCH, II, p. 86.

20 BIRCH, II, p. 61.

21 Hatfield MS VI, f. 321. Sir Fernando Gorges to Robert Cecil, 7 August 1596.

22 HANDOVER, pp. 139–40.

23 'Their earl, though he was continually baited, like bear of Paris Garden ... yet shook them [the dogs] off lustily, and would tire them all.' Anthony Bacon to Dr Hawkins, 11 September 1596. BIRCH, *Memoirs,* II, p. 137

24 Essex's name was being scandalously linked with that of a married woman of high rank, a rumour that the earl strenuously denied. Ibid., pp. 218–20.

25 HANDOVER, pp. 147–8. Birch, II, p. 241.

26 William was being educated at Sherbourne School, but spent much of his time with the Raleighs, who seem to have been better equipped to satisfy his emotional needs. Hatfield MS, X, f. 459.

27 BIRCH, II, p. 289.

28 MACCAFFREY, *War and Politics,* pp. 126–36. For an account of the Islands Voyage, see S. PURCHAS, *Hakluytus Posthumus* (1907), XX, pp. 24–33.

29 This office had been vacant since the death of the Earl of Shrewsbury in 1590. The marshall's only function was to preside over the trial of peers. His alleged authority to arrest the monarch for misconduct was never tested.

30 J.A. GUY, *The Reign of Elizabeth I* (1995), p. 5.

31 BL Cotton MS Caligula E IX, f. 145.

32 HANDOVER, p. 171.

33 S.G. ELLIS, *Tudor Ireland* (1985), pp 301–3.

34 Francis BACON, *Apothegms,* cited in James SPEDDING, *The Life and Letters of Francis Bacon* (1857), II, p, 91.

35 HANDOVER, pp. 179–80.

36 Joel HURSTFIELD, *The Queen's Wards* (1958), pp. 297–325.

37 HMC, Salisbury MSS, XI, p. 251.

38 GUY, *Reign of Elizabeth,* p. 6.

39 Hatfield MS IX, p. 41. 25 January 1599.

40 ELLIS, pp. 305–6.

41 BIRCH, II, p. 415. MACCAFFREY, *Elizabeth I,* pp. 420–1.

42 Ibid., pp. 424–5.

43 Hatfield MS IX, p. 357.

44 TNA SP12/267, p. 277.

45 HANDOVER, pp. 196–7.

46 Ibid.

47 J. Petit to Peter Halins, 6 October 1599. TNA SP12/267, p. 422.

48 Same to same. 7 December 1599. TNA SP12/267, p. 356.

49 Narrative, perhaps by one of Francis Bacon's servants. SPEDDING, *Life and Letters of Francis Bacon,* II, p. 175.

50 TNA SP12/267, p. 442.

51 MACCAFFREY, *Elizabeth I,* p. 529.

52 William CAMDEN, *The History of the Most Renowned Princess Elizabeth* (1635), pp. 602–3.

53 HANDOVER, pp. 204–6.

54 SP12/267, pp. 549–51.

55 HANDOVER, p. 222.

56 Hatfield MS XI, p. 37.

57 TNA SP12/267, p. 590. 24 February 1601.

58 HANDOVER, p. 226.

59 W. COBBETT et al. (eds), *A Complete Collection of State Trials* (1816–1898), I, p. 1351.

60 Essex's connections with James went back at least to 1596 and had always been in the vein of cultivating his favour. Hatfield MS VII, p. 10.

61 Robert Cecil to George Nicholson (in Scotland), 21 March 1601. Hatfield MS XI, p. 137.

62 James's instructions to the ambassadors, 8 April 1601. Sir David DALRYMPLE (Lord Hailes), *The Secret Correspondence of Sir Robert Cecil with James VI* (1766), nos 9 and 6.

63 Francis BACON, *Apology*, in SPEDDING, III, p. 148. See also C[ambridge] U[niversity] L[ibrary] MS ee 3.56.85.

64 James to Robert Cecil (undated, Spring 1601). John BRUCE, *The Correspondence of King James VI of Scotland with Sir Robert Cecil and Others,* Camden Society 78 (1861), pp. 1–3.

65 TNA SP12/268, p. 37.

66 LOADES, *Elizabeth I*, pp. 282–302.

67 The defeat of the Spanish incursion at Kinsale in September 1601 effectively broke the back of the rebellion, although it was to be another eighteen months before Tyrone finally surrendered. ELLIS, pp. 309–11.

# 10

## SALISBURY AND THE NEW REGIME

1 P. CROFT, *Robert Cecil and the Stuart Monarchy* (2005), p. 3.

2 Ibid.

3 James to Northumberland, 1602. *Correspondence of King James VI*, p. 61

4 J. BOSSY, *The English Catholic Community 1570–1850* (1975), pp. 77–108.

5 Hatfield MS IX, f. 203.

6 HANDOVER, pp. 288–90.

7 D. LOADES, 'Relations between the Anglican and Roman Catholic Churches in the Sixteenth and Seventeeth Centuries', in J.C.H. AVELING (ed.), *Rome and the Anglicans* (1982), pp. 31–2.

8 Proclamation banishing all Jesuits and seminary priests, 5 November 1602. *Tudor Royal Proclamations,* III, p. 250.

9 D. HIRST, *Authority and Conflict* (1986), p. 96.

10 James to Robert Cecil, 27 March 1603. Hatfield MS, XV, f. 10.

11 Cecil to the Council, 18 April 1603. Ibid., f. 52.

12 A. HAYNES, *Robert Cecil, Earl of Salisbury* (1989), p. 136.

13 Ibid., p. 76.

14 Ibid., p. 80.

15 STONE, *Crisis of the Aristocracy*, Appendix XXIII.

16 Ibid.

17 N. MEARS, 'Regnum Cecilianum?' in GUY, p. 46 et seq.

18 HANDOVER, p. 305.

19 William Watson's confession 18 August 1603. Hatfield MS XV, f. 238.

20 Bancroft to Cecil, 9 August 1603. Ibid., f. 237.

21 HANDOVER, p. 309.

22 Hatfield MS XV, f. 379.

23 Ralph WINWOOD, *Memorials of the Affairs of State in the Reigns of Queen Elizabeth and King James the First* (1725), II, p. 22.

24 HANDOVER, p. 311.

25 Sir John HARRINGTON, *Nugae Antiquae* (1792), II, p. 150.

26 HIRST, p. 100.

27 Raleigh's trial is recorded in BL Harleian MS XXIX, and printed in D. JARDINE, *Criminal Trials* (1832), which also includes George Brooke's examination, I, p. 249.

28 HAYNES, *Robert Cecil*, p. 154. There are numerous discussions of the Gunpowder Plot. For sources, see TNA SP14/216, no. 6.

29 HUGHES and LARKIN, *Stuart Royal Proclamations* (1973), I, no. 58.

30 TNA SP14/216, no. 6.

31 Statutes 5 James I, cc. 4 & 5. *Statutes of the Realm*, IV, p. 1074. Cecil had also extracted political advantage from the situation by publishing *An Answer to Certain Scandalous Papers Scattered Abroad* (1606), RSTC 4895.

32 James MONTAGUE (ed.), *The Works of the Most High and Mighty Prince James* (1616).

33 STONE, *Crisis of the Aristocracy*, p. 420, citing TNA SP14/78, no. 6.

34 HAYNES, *Robert Cecil*, p. 129.

35 HIRST, p. 107.

36 HUGHES and LARKIN, I, no. 45. 20 October 1604.

37 HIRST, p. 109.

38 HAYNES, *Robert Cecil*, p. 170. For general extravagance of this kind, see STONE, *Crisis of the Aristocracy*, pp. 459–55.

39 L. STONE, *Family and Fortune* (1973), p. 32.

40 STONE, *Crisis of the Aristocracy*, p. 359.

41 Ibid., p. 135 and Appendix XXIII.

42 HAYNES, *Robert Cecil*, p. 161. He had matriculated as a fellow commoner at St John's in 1602, but he never proceeded to a degree.

43 *Oxford Dictionary of National Biography*, *sub.* William Cecil, 2nd Earl of Salisbury.

44 Ibid.

45 HAYNES, *Robert Cecil*, p. 189.

46 W. COBBETT and T.B. HOWELL (eds), *State Trials* (1809–26), II, pp. 287–94.

47 HIRST, p. 110.

48 F.C. DIETZ, *English Public Finance* (1964), II, 134–40.

49 J.D. ALSOP, 'Innovation in Tudor Taxation', *English Historical Review*, 99 (1984), pp. 83–93.

50 COBBETT and HOWELL, II, 481–3.

51 HIRST, p. 111.

52 DIETZ, pp. 141–2.

53 HIRST, p. 111.

54 J.P. KENYON, *The Stuart Constitution* (1966), pp. 125–34.

55 G.P.V. AKRIGG (ed.), *The Letters of James VI and I* (1984), pp. 316–7.

56 Croft in *Oxford Dictionary of National Biography*.

57 HIRST, p. 113.

58 P. CROFT (ed.), *A Collection of Several Speeches and Treatises of the Late Lord Treasurer Cecil, Camden Miscellany* 29 (1987), p. 313.

59 Ibid., p. 315.

60 P.M. HANDOVER, *Arabella Stuart, Royal Lady of Hardwick* (1957).

61 MONTAGUE (ed.), *Works*, 121,133. Sir Walter Cope to James. See also P. CROFT, 'The Reputation of Robert Cecil', *Transactions of the Royal Historical Society*, 6th series, I (1991), pp. 43–69.

62 HAYNES, *Robert Cecil*, p. 187.

63 CROFT, 'The Religion of Robert Cecil', *Historical Journal*, 34 (1991), pp. 773–96.

64 CROFT, *Oxford Dictionary of National Biography*.

# Further Reading

S. ALFORD, *The Early Elizabethan Polity* (1998)

S. ADAMS and M.-J. RODRIGUEZ SALGADO, 'The Count of Feria's Despatch ... of 14th November 1558', *Camden Miscellany* 28 (1984)

B.W. BECKINGSALE, *Burghley: Tudor Statesman 1520–1598* (1967)

G.W. BERNARD, 'The Downfall of Sir Thomas Seymour' in his (ed.) *The Tudor Nobility* (1992)

S.T. BINDOFF, *The House of Commons 1509–1558* (1982)

V.J.K. BROOK, *A Life of Archbishop Parker* (1962)

W. CAMDEN, *The History of the Most Renowned Princess Elizabeth* (1635)

C.E. CHALLIS, *The Tudor Coinage* (1978)

J. CLAPHAM, *Elizabeth of England,* ed. E.P. and Conyers Read (1951)

P. COLLINSON, *Archbishop Grindal 1519–1583* (1979)

P. CROFT, 'The Reputation of Robert Cecil', *Transactions of the Royal Historical Society,* 6th series, I (1991)

— 'The Religion of Robert Cecil', *Historical Journal,* 34, 1991

SIR S. D'EWES, *The Journals of All the Parliaments during the Reign of Queen Elizabeth* (1693)

SIR D. DIGGES, *The Compleat Ambassador* (1635)

S. DORAN, *Monarchy and Matrimony: The Courtships of Elizabeth* (1996)

R.A. GRIFFITHS, *Sir Rhys ap Thomas and His Family* (1993)

P.M. HANDOVER, *The Second Cecil* (1959)

SIR J. HARRINGTON, *Nugae Antiquae* (1792)

P.W. HASLER, *The House of Commons 1558–1603* (1981)

A. HAYNES, *Robert Cecil, Earl of Salisbury* (1989)

D. HOAK, *The King's Council in the Reign of Edward VI* (1976)

J. HURSTFIELD, *The Queen's Wards* (1958)

D. JARDINE, *Criminal Trials* (1832)

N.L. JONES, *Faith by Statute* (1982)

W.K. JORDAN, *Edward VI: The Young King* (1968)

— *Edward VI: The Threshold of Power* (1970)

J. LOACH, *Parliament and the Crown in the Reign of Mary Tudor* (1986)

D. LOADES, *John Dudley, Duke of Northumberland* (1996)

— *Elizabeth I* (2003)

W. MACCAFFREY, *The Shaping of the Elizabethan Regime* (1969)

— *Queen Elizabeth and the Making of Policy, 1572–1588* (1981)

— *Elizabeth I: War and Politics 1588–1603* (1992)

L.S. MARCUS et al. (eds), *Elizabeth I: Collected Works* (2000)

F. PECK, *Desiderata Curiosa* (1779)

J.H. POLLEN, *Mary Queen of Scots and the Babington Plot* (1922)

C. READ, 'Lord Burghley's Household Accounts', *Economic History Review,* 1956

— *Lord Burghley and Queen Elizabeth* (1960)

— *Mr Secretary Cecil and Queen Elizabeth* (1965)

A.L. ROWSE, 'Alltyrynys and the Cecils', *English Historical Review,* 75 (1960)

JAMES SPEDDING, *The Life and Letters of Francis Bacon* (1857)

L. STONE, *The Crisis of the Aristocracy 1558–1641* (1965)

— *Family and Fortune: Studies in Aristocratic Finance* (1973)

J. STOW, *Survey of London* (1980 edition)

J. STRYPE, *The Life ... of Sir John Cheke* (1821 edition)

B. USHER, *William Cecil and Episcopacy 1559–1577* (2003)

B.M. WARD, *The Seventeenth Earl of Oxford 1550–1604* (1928)

J. WORMALD, *Mary Queen of Scots: A Study in Failure* (1988)

# Index

Numbers in *italic* denote a plate number.
WC denotes William Cecil.
RC denotes Robert Cecil.
TC denotes Thomas Cecil.

## Picture Credits
(by plate number)

1 Burghley House Collection   2 Parham Park, Mark Fiennes / Bridgeman Art Library   3 © 2007 The British Library   4 Courtesy of the Warden and Scholars of New College, Oxford / Bridgeman Art Library   5 Trustees of Weston Park Foundation / Bridgeman Art Library   6 The Royal Collection © Her Majesty Queen Elizabeth II   7 Walker Art Gallery / Bridgeman Art Library   8 Yale Center for British Art, Paul Mellon Collection / Bridgeman Art Library   9 Private Collection / Bridgeman Art Library   10 Courtesy of the Marquess of Salisbury / Hatfield House   11 © Jason Hawkes / Corbis   12 Burghley House Collection   13 Burghley House Collection / Bridgeman Art Library   14 Private Collection © Richard Philp / Bridgeman Art Library   15 © 2007 The British Library   16 © 2007 The British Library   17 The National Archives, Kew [TNA SP12 / 1, no.7]   18 Courtesy of the Marquess of Salisbury / Hatfield House   19 Burghley House Collection   20 Woburn Abbey, Bedfordshire / Bridgeman Art Library   21 Burghley House Collection   22 National Portrait Gallery of Ireland / Bridgeman Art Library   23 Courtesy of the Warden and Scholars of New College, Oxford / Bridgeman Art Library   24 Burghley House Collection   25 Burghley House Collection   26 akg images   27 The National Archives, Kew [TNA SP14 / 216 f.112v]   28 The National Archives, Kew [TNA SP14 / 216 f.11a]   29 © 2007 The British Library   30 The National Archives, Kew [TNA SP14 / 67]   31 Private Collection, photo © Bonhams / Bridgeman Art Library

## Author's and Publisher's Acknowledgements

I am grateful to Catherine Bradley and Mark Hawkins-Dady of the National Archives for the opportunity to undertake *The Cecils*, and to generations of students and colleagues who have helped to shape my perceptions of Tudor England.

The publishers would like to thank the following for their assistance in creating this book: Jon Culverhouse, of Burghley House; the archival staff at Hatfield House; Gwen Campbell (*picture researcher*); Sarah Hoggett (*copy editor*), Sarah Chatwin (*proofreader*), Patricia Hymans (*indexer*), and for his usual patient professionalism Ken Wilson (*designer*).